MOTEL NIRVANA

MOTEL NIRVANA

Dreaming of the New Age in
the American Desert

Melanie McGrath

Picador USA
New York

Picador® is a U.S. registered trademark and is used by St. Martin's Press under license from Pan Books Limited.

Library of Congress Cataloging-in-Publication Data

McGrath, Melanie
Motel Nirvana : dreaming of the New Age in the American desert / by Melanie McGrath.
    p.   cm.
ISBN 0-312-14372-9
1. New Age movement.   2. Spiritual biography.
    3. McGrath, Melanie.   I. Title.
    BP605.N48M377   1996
299'.93—dc20   96-63   CIP

First published in Great Britain by
HarperCollins*Publishers*

First Picador USA Edition: May 1996

10   9   8   7   6   5   4   3   2   1

For Paul and my mother, Margaret

ACKNOWLEDGEMENTS

I would like to thank Stuart Proffitt and
Philip Gwyn Jones for taking a chance on me,
and Philip in particular for his patience
and enthusiasm.

'What do I know of life?
What of myself?
I know not even my own
work past or present;
Dim ever-shifting guesses
of it spread before me,
Of newer better worlds,
their mighty parturition
Mocking, perplexing me.'

WALT WHITMAN,
'On the Last Thoughts
of Columbus'

Prophets

DAY ONE

One afternoon in late April last year, sitting on a bed in the second cheapest motel in Santa Fe, New Mexico, staring at the TV and waiting for something important to happen. A welcome-pamphlet lies open on the floor, turned to the page on altitude sickness and a small gold box with its wrapper printed 'The Ark Bookstore, Romero St,' squats by the remote control and digs into a toenail. Outside the high, empty air of a north New Mexico spring loiters in the parking lot and, beyond the lot, an idle slipstream of traffic waits for the lights on Cerillos Road before heading south into a thousand thousand square miles of New Mexico desert.

On one of the network channels Geraldo Rivera is quizzing a panel of prepubescent urban terrorists, closing for the commercial break with a hook: 'What kind of society are we living in today? We'll be right back with the answer.' A web of contradictory signals baffles the screen, then surrenders to a Lexus ad. In among the static lies the insubstantial reflection of a woman with hair cut short as Irish moss. The inconstant lines about the mouth and the restive expression of the lips are set in, but the eyes, same dirty blue as the screen, appear unsettled, no more than holes. Those eyes I followed in the rear-view mirror half the way across the state of Texas. They seemed to me more solid then. Perhaps it was just that the light was different.

The border between Texas and New Mexico happens to be where the American West truly begins. All but the southern tip of western Texas belongs to the great plain lands, in geography as well as in spirit. The region still seems raw and new, without past or future, defined only by its current usage. For hundreds of miles across the Texas Panhandle only the monstrous panorama of derricks pumping crude disturbs the tepid sky. Beneath them lies the rich green Texan turf, metaphor for Texan style – brash, resilient, thrusting. In western Texas the air bears the odours of cattle shit and oil and the distant horizon appears as a glittering mineral line levitating just above the highway.

By contrast, all but the most northerly region of New Mexico is old and frail, a jumble of crepey rock and thinning, age-stained soil. Heading west, beyond Amarillo, TX, brittled turf gives out to bunch grass and yucca. The first blue mesas bubble the plain at Clovis, on the New Mexico border. All across eastern New Mexico the range stretches out vast and undulant to the curve of the earth, still open in places and the soil baked dun with red swatches between, like shortbread fingers laid out on a plate of ripened beef. This is where the magical palette of the southwest begins. Further west still the rivers dry up into arroyos, sagebrush replaces bunch grass and the tarry, fecund aroma of creosote bush competes with the smell of sage.

New Mexico towns are less ambitious than Texan towns; poorer too, by and large. Many consist in nothing more than a few mobile homes, a gas station and a single, neglected store selling liquor and animal feed. Maybe there will be a small poly-mall, laid out in horseshoe shape around a parking lot, with a Philips 76, a Bashas, a frozen yoghurt kiosk and a Radio Shack. Unlike the Panhandle, though, New Mexico is well-travelled. Along every main highway plantations of fast food joints and rest areas and cheap motels have sprung up. Every so often you drive by a WalMart or some other hyperstore strapped to the plain like a torah.

The southwest, and more specifically New Mexico state, is the place all America goes to find itself, just as it found itself in California thirty years before. Empty, yet historically rich, materially poor (forty-seventh poorest state in the Union) and thus apparently spiritually uncompromised, New Mexico has found itself become the baptismal font of secular and humanist America. Santa Fe, the City of the Holy Faith, is its focal point. Visitors and settlers congregate in Santa Fe to indulge in that peculiarly American pastime – working on the self. The deeper America's spiritual crisis gets, the more spiritual self-improvement is deemed necessary and the more money and visitors fetch up in Santa Fe.

A greater number of American people believe in extra-sensory perception than believe in the existence of hell. Rolfing, rebirthing and psychic surgery are now more widely practised than rhinoplasty or liposuction. And even though most Americans would like to think of themselves as Christians, there are more alien abductions reported every year than sightings of Jesus or the Virgin Mary. I read as much in an article, and found it easy to believe. In fact, on the strength of the article's two assertions – more people believe in esp than in hell, and more Americans are abducted by aliens than are visited by the Virgin Mary – I took a plane to Texas and bought a wretched car and drove seven hundred miles to Santa Fe. There was something about the New Age that fitted into the American story, somewhere, or so I thought. And that, in brief, is why I am sitting watching TV in a cheap motel and waiting for something important to happen. I have with me a copy of *The Aquarian Conspiracy*, as yet unread, a gold card box, a guidebook to New Mexico and a hunch that whatever I find will tell me something about what is happening at the end of the century in which America finally became too big for itself.

Inside the gold box is a collection of cards and an instruction booklet. The booklet invites its reader to pick a card at random from the God Insight Box and connect to the eternal unity through the principle of synchronicity. Baking soda brings teeth up whiter than any ordinary toothpaste, adds a woman on the network channel. I close my eyes and pick a card:

> As Above, So Below.
> As Within, So Without.
> Everything I see
> is a Reflection of Me.

A rose bush taps on the window outside, sending an iridescent hummingbird spinning briefly above it before disappearing from view. Already the sluggish heat of the afternoon has passed, and in its place breathes an easy wind. The sky's so cataracted with dust-filled clouds I can no longer see the sun. Maybe there will be some rain, but most likely it will not rain again until late July or August, when the late summer thunderstorms begin. I am considering naming the tin-can Chevy 'Caboose' from part of a line in a country song. Sums up a distant kind of affection, that word, and I don't like to get too sentimental about cars. Sentimentality is something I avoid.

In the bathroom swigging Pepto-Bismol from the bottle it occurs to me that the insight card has got it wrong. It's just not true that everything I see is a reflection of me, only the *way* I see it. The ghoul-face with its inconstant mouth grins modestly back from the bathroom tiles in cubist manner.

Back on the network Geraldo is being shown how to kick box by a Crips girl. I lean over for the remote, sending the gold box sliding off the bed and ejecting a 'Don't worry, Be Happy' card with a smiley face printed around the text. The moment I see that smiley face I *know* I want my money back.

'Hello, this is The Ark bookstore?' says a man's voice in uncertain tone.

'I'm calling from a pay phone,' I reply. I don't know why I say this, but I often do, even when I'm not. 'I came in earlier and bought a God Insight Box?'

'Uh, huh,' acknowledges the voice.

'I'd like to change it.'

No answer.

'I don't know, it's something about the insights. They don't feel very deep to me. I thought they'd be deeper.'

'Oh,' says the voice. 'Okey doke. No problem. Just swing by.'

A thin young woman sits cross-legged at the entrance of The Ark flicking through a picture postcard book of celestial beings. Next to her stands a man, about twenty, turning a gold loop around in his ear.

4

'Angels?' I ask as an opening gambit, pointing towards the book.

The man nods.

'Uh-huh, I did a thesis. Healing studies,' replies the young woman, returning to her pictures. The man reads my confusion and says 'Cool,' as both a confirmation and an expression of general amiability.

'The thing about healing', I volunteer, responding to the signal, 'is it never seems to end. I mean, I never met anyone who was actually healed.'

'Yeah, right,' replies the woman, 'I think I read a book about that.' She tips her head to one side and gazes at me with an arch little smile.

'English?'

I nod.

'I went to Avebury once . . .'

The man with the gold hoop, who is oscillating awkwardly in and out of this conversation, introduces his friend as Nancy and himself as Walker, 'ex-pro-surfer, ex-Angelino, currently member of Mobillus Trip'.

'That a band?' I ask. Walker, who does not seem at first acquaintance to be a man of great intellectual fluidity, glances down at his friend for reassurance, but, seeing she has already returned to her picture book, he takes stock and thinks for a few seconds, twirling the loop in its tunnel.

'Hard-core funk rap psychedelic, with some West Coast hip-hop influences, uh, but we're kinda dropping those.'

The skinny woman shakes her hair, looks up, ignoring the conversational diversion; 'I had this dissertation to do on crop circles? I went to Avebury? And it was cool? I saw these things, like black butterflies hovering above the stones? And, like, I just knew that they were in touch with my higher self? It was like through the third eye?' She taps her forehead.

I recall a newspaper article I had read some time before which had speculated that some of the stones would be removed to make way for a new road and relaid on a green site outside the town.

'Wow.' She wrinkles her brow. 'You know, the Goddess is real strong there, I don't think they would be allowed to do that. In Avebury, the Goddess is all over the place.'

'Perhaps I was mistaken.' I begin a retreat towards the centre of the store.

'Hey,' says the woman, tearing a corner from the book and scribbling something on it, 'Here's our number. Call.'

In a large aviary opposite the astrology section are stationed a dozen half-bald canary birds perched mute on dowelling rods. A series of Tibetan wind chimes moves in draughts, and behind a blonde wood counter at the back a woman wearing unbleached drawstring pants fiddles with a volume knob to adjust the level of whale song in the background. Another woman with a birthmark sits cross-legged on the floor behind the counter polishing a didgeridoo with a can of Pledge, but there is no sign of the man I might have spoken to on the telephone. A spirit of unease prowls around The Ark, due in part to its interior décor – an emulation of a home improvement catalogue circa 1972, with softly padded armchairs and cushions reeking of patchouli grouped around an Afghan rug – and in part to some ambience more mysterious. The customers, wary as beaten dogs, cling to the sides of the room, making occasional nervous sorties out from palmistry to crystals across a no man's land of bean-bags. I make for the woman with the unbleached pants, and am attempting a precise explanation as to why the insights in the gold box are a little short of satisfactory, when my stomach gives an unexpected, vertiginous heave and sends a fragment of taco chip topspinning out onto the stripped wood floor.

'Altitude sickness,' I shrug.

The cashier shakes her head.

'I don't think we can change that Insight Box, now, ma'am,' she says, as if the taco chip had automatically divested me of all consumer rights, 'because you've already benefited from the Insights. You wouldn't take a bottle of Tylenol back after your headache was all gone,' she smiles indulgently, 'I can recommend a few things for the altitude sickness, though.' Altitude sickness is pronounced "Altitude sickness" and finished off with a small cough.

Ten minutes later I've agreed to purchase an African fetish (vegetarian camel tail-hair), two shards of crystal quartz in different good karma colours, four sticks of Bophuthatswana sandalwood incense, a Hopi dream-catcher, a subliminal Higher Consciousness tape and a book promising to reveal what my personal task will be 'in the glorious New Age, as we rapidly approach the "End Times" and the start of a new awakening for all of humankind'.

'Where are you headed?' asks the cashier, counting up the value of my purchases.

'Los Angeles?' I have no idea.

'Oh, I went once,' leaning forward and curling her hand around her mouth, 'The entire city smelt of faeces.'

'Yeah, well, it's a long drive anyway,' I reply, disheartened.

'They're having some real bad drainage problems.'

'I probably won't make it.'

'Well, anyways, come back just before you set off and I'll recommend some things for your psychic protection.'

'Oh?'

'Sure. Bad karma in LA. Whoopsi, here's your credit card. Enjoy your purchases. And you think yourself into wellness, you hear?'

At the southern end of Romero Street, uphill from The Ark bookstore, is a flat, rusty griddle of iron tracks, switches, sidings and signalling from the old Santa Fe railroad. Some workmen are renovating a clapboard barn by Guadalupe St, which was once, perhaps, the station warehouse. It's now still possible to drive across the old track to get from Romero into Guadalupe, but sometime in the near future the whole station will no doubt be cordoned off, polished up and converted into a museum of one kind or another, for Santa Fe is a tourist town, and said by those who think in superlatives to be one of the most beautiful spots in the USA. Downtown, towards the plaza and the Palace of Governors, where the Spanish and Mexicans administered most of what are now the states of New Mexico and Arizona from 1599 until the land was ceded to the USA in 1846, Santa Fe settles into a parody of its tour-guide hagiography – all narrow streets and landscaped verges, chocolate brown and pink adobe architecture, spicy historical air. The City Different, the chamber of commerce calls it. I've read somewhere that movie stars own more property per square foot of the city than anywhere else on the continent; more than in Aspen, Colorado, more than in Jackson Hole, Wyoming, more than in Los Angeles or Martha's Vineyard.

In any case, Santa Fe may well fall by its own success. Marketed as a little pearl set on a desert sea, the town is beginning to sprawl. Cerillos Road, where the King's Rest and most of the city's cheap motels are situated, has become a long strip of fast-food palaces, sorry-looking lube joints and shopping plazas just like those in any other desert town. The strip even has its own rush hour as commuters from as far away as Albuquerque, sixty miles to the south, drive in to service the tourist business. Over the last ten years the price of real estate has risen so high that many of the hispanic families whose roots are in Santa Fe have already been pushed out to cheaper towns nearby, like Española and La Cienega. And so the town empties of the folk who both (in stereotype) attract and (in actuality) service tourism and fills up with folk who were once tourists returning as settlers and retirees – movie stars, 'artists', hangers-on, and, of course, people working on themselves.

After packing the crystals and Bophuthatswana incense sticks in my suitcase, I take two sleeping pills and a long draft of Pepto Bismol, set the Higher Consciousness tape running, open up the book and crawl into bed with the rest of the motel wildlife. 'Thousands are here now to help the unenlightened endure the spiritual and physical transformation of our world, which is soon to be swept into a higher level of consciousness,' reads the book blurb. The author's face smiles up from the inside cover, next to a tributary poem. In the preface she promises to share her glories, before returning to the octaves of home.

DAY TWO

Seven in the morning. The Higher Consciousness tape has run
the tape machine dry and is silent. I get up and take a long
look at myself in the mirror, but can't make out anything much
different. Yesterday's nausea has almost gone although I still feel
a little light-headed. The altitude has subtly altered the tone of
my muscles, which are firmer now than yesterday. I cannot say
that I feel more conscious though. The instructions on the tape
box fail to explain how long the tape takes to work, or, for that
matter, exactly what it does. Does it expand conscious awareness
of the conscious or expand conscious awareness of the unconscious, or increase higher consciousness or raise higher consciousness of consciousness or something entirely different? I should
have asked in the store.

KIOT radio runs an early morning interview with Kenny
Kingston, psychic to the stars, who claims 'Harry Truman was
the most psychic president the US ever had.' Was that because
of the Little Boy? Kenny K. doesn't say.

Up on the dresser sits the God Insight Box waiting to be
consulted. The insight for the day, printed on orange card, in
soy-based ink, is 'I can change any thought that hurts.'

The full weight of this piece of wisdom hits me in the shower.
An end to personal failure and social guilt. I emerge feeling like
a new person.

At ten Gita comes in to dust. Gita is the Indian wife of the
Indian proprietor of the King's Rest.

'No work?' she asks. I smile and shrug.

'Alone?' She considers this before adding,

'Always alone,' giggling at her own presumption. 'Wasting
time,' she concludes as though witness to the sad but inevitable
path of an anti-social life.

I make a decision to call Nancy and Walker.

'Is that Walker?'

'Yes,' says Walker.

'I'm in a payphone, Walker. What I wanted to know . . . what
I wondered if you knew is why Santa Fe's become, you know,

9

a place where people, uh . . .' – searching for an acceptable phrase – '. . . uh, work on themselves.'

'Sure,' says Walker, unfazed. 'Ask just about anyone on the street. We're all working on ourselves. It's like, Santa Monica is full of surfers, and Santa Fe is full of seekers.'

'But why *is* that?'

'Well, the ocean's there I guess.' Walker pauses to give me time to get the joke. 'Oh, you mean . . . I guess it's, like, the energies and the desert, man.'

'Desert energies?'

'Uh, yeah.'

I am about to bring the conversation to a close when Walker adds: 'You could go to a therapist, or an empath or a psychic or something.' Some woman in Walker's room starts mantra chanting.

'Do you know anyone?' 'Om' throbs over the phone like a distant headache.

'There are, like, *thousands* of 'em in this city. You should check the Yellow Pages.'

To me, psychics have always been the lament of evangelical Christians in suburban neighbourhoods, character parts in police dramas and a counsel-of-last-resort for the desperate. I suppose it had just never occurred to me that anyone could pick a psychic from the Yellow Pages and fix an appointment. My mother saw a clairvoyant after my father died. The clairvoyant told her that my father came out of the spirit world with this message: 'Don't drive so fast.' It's true, she does drive too fast. And then the psychic apparently said 'Plus, you have a daughter who's selfish to the core.' But I don't know if mum got the psychic's name from the Yellow Pages or from somewhere else.

Much though I'd like to believe – I mean I really would – in psychic phenomena, and however comforting it would be to know that my father was up in the ether somewhere supervising my driving, I find it difficult to believe in anything without first understanding it. For example, as a child in a Catholic school, I found the Catholic notion of transubstantiation particularly tricky. I would worry about the finer details: how come Jesus' body wasn't all eaten up? Wouldn't it be rotten after two thousand years? Even now, knowing that belief is based not on literal truths, but on metaphorical ones, I remain confused. Although I don't believe in them, if a psychic told me I was going to die the next day, I'd probably still be worried.

'I'm not going to any psychic from the Yellow Pages. You don't know what you're getting.' This for my own benefit as much as Walker's.

'Sure,' replies Walker, good-humouredly, 'You could go see Chris Griscom. She's got this school called the Nizhoni School for Global Consciousness and this, like, *place*, the Light Institute? They deal with the Earth Mother and the Goddess and all? Uh, it's not psychic though, it's more like consciousness and the healing energies. I kinda learned a lot from her. She converted Shirley Maclaine.'

With hindsight, I see that it was at this point I came to the realization that I was dealing not just with an unfamiliar set of behaviours but with an entirely foreign inner architecture. It was like being propelled back into that period in adolescence when even though everyone listened to the same music, you still felt that you were the only one who really understood the lyrics or that you were the only one who didn't understand the lyrics, but that in any case you were alone. It occurred to me then that I was suffering from the kind of numb insensibility brought on by navigating through an emotional and intellectual territory that might be labelled 'here monsters lie' on the map of experience. This realization was to bring with it a solitude more complete than my habitual isolation. The longer I considered it, the more it gripped me. How long would it be before I scuttled back empty-handed to my familiar world or capitulated to the demands of the new one and assumed its principles and unconscious ideologies – in short, became one of *them*?

Mid-morning I order a cup of coffee and a donut at Galisteo News, a New Age-y dive which carries papers from outside the state and is popular with tourists and transplants. One of the local freesheets leads with the headline 'Whole Life Special',

previewing some sort of New Age-fest to be held in Santa Fe
the following week. It continues with the sub-header 'Connect
with the transformational energy of your "real" self.' On the
inside back is a picture of a thin woman with big hair and mas-
cara, and underneath her the legend 'Chris Griscom shows you
how to expand your perception to include the multi-dimensional
perspectives of global consciousness,' with the address of the
Light Institute of Galisteo and a phone number.

I have a friend, called Fergus, who lives in New York and is
very dear to me. I cannot remember how we met, or where, so
there can't be much of a story to it. In any case, Fergus is one
of four people I know who are currently living in the USA. Two
have disappeared completely and the third always says he can't
talk whenever I call him. Fergus, on the other hand has promised
to fly over and spend a weekend with me while I am in the
southwest, but I don't think he will. In some ways he's reliable,
but in others, he's just another SOB.

'Ferg, it's me.'

'You still in Texas?'

'Santa Fe.'

Fergus, I know, does not approve of Higher Consciousness
tapes and God Insight Boxes and psychics and angels, but I
mention them anyway in the hope that I am wrong. I am not
wrong.

'Kooks.'

'That's easy to say,' I reply, 'but if enough people believe it,
you can't just write it off.'

A bitter laugh.

'That's the democratic principle, isn't it?' I'm wounded, 'Anyway, how come you're such a cynic?'

'Don't call me that,' Fergus is wounded. 'This is America,
remember.'

'OK, muddafukka.'

'Much better.'

'Fergus, I can change any thought that hurts.' At that moment
a voice comes on the line and asks for another $2.75. Then the
phone begins ringing without my having hung up. 'Hello?'

The voice replies 'You owe $2.75.'

'Yeah, I know, I'm just trying to find it.'

'You owe $2.75,' says the voice for the third time.

'Look,' I counter, needled, 'I never asked for credit.'

The voice persists: '$2.75.'

I hang up. It rings, I pick up, a voice says 'You owe $2.75.' It's still ringing ten minutes later, by which time I'm sitting in room 12 with the TV tuned into Oprah and a collection of compulsive eaters.

This is the start of my lost week.

Five days anyway. Five mornings at The Ark, five afternoons and evenings at the public library on East Macy Street. In between only Gita's morning dirges – 'Work?', 'Alone?', muffins, coffee, Camels and a couple of unisom at bedtime. By the end of the week, I have conquered the astrological texts, esp and the paranormal, read interminable accounts of alien abductions, absorbed Tibetan reincarnation prayers, books on angels and Ascended Masters, followed recipes to make the body invisible, interpreted chanting records, xeroxed a chart indicating in diagrammatic form how best to hug a tree, taken advice on organising your own rebirth, skimmed guides to the millennium, noted apocalyptic predictions of the earth changes and begun the long preparation for a course in miracles.

At the end of the fifth day I compile a list:

PATHS TO SPIRITUAL FULFILMENT (NEW AGE)

1. *Intuitive development*
   Chakras, auras, astrology, channelling, oracles, tarot
2. *Creating your own reality*
   Transformational journeys, meditation, dreamwork, astral projection, brain machines, drugs
3. *Transitions*
   Birth, death, reincarnation, past lives
4. *Spirituality*
   Mysticism, Native American spiritualism, nature worship, the Goddess, the Crone, miracles

5. *Consumption*
   Shopping

and resolve to make this my agenda.

DAY EIGHT

Awake at six, feeling elated. It's sunny outside, but cool still. A rust-coloured hummingbird motors around the agave outside my room. In the shower I am overtaken by the uncomfortable but undeniable possibility that the longer I spend alone the lonelier I may become.

My God-Box insight for the day is:

It's never too late to have a happy childhood

printed in soy-based ink with a picture of an ancient swinging in a child's playground.

A woman at the juice bar in Wild Oats on Cordova Street recommends wheatgrass juice on account of its positive impact on prana. She doesn't say whether it takes prana away or gives it to you, but at $3 a pop you'd have a right to expect it to do one or the other, surely. She directs me to the seating area, where, pinned up on the corkboard is a notice advertising a drum birthing workshop: 'The second day of the workshop is spent in birthing teams ritually birthing both your drum and yourself. You will be guided in how to co-ordinate sound, breath, your body and the team's energy in order to give your drum the best life possible. A properly birthed drum will pull tremendous amounts of energy from you in order to begin its life, just as a baby does.'

'You here for Whole Life or just doing some work on yourself?' asks the juice-bar attendant, with the dilute resignation of a person who finds that life in the periods between trips tends towards the crushingly predictable.

'Bit of both, I guess,' I reply in non-committal tone. She waves away an insect, suppressing a yawn with a flailing hand.

'Have you been out to the desert yet?'

I shake my head.

She opens her eyes in mild surprise, as if offended by my unconventional behaviour.

'You *must* go! The life force there! I mean, the whole desert energy thing roots you into this amazing consciousness of your interconnectedness with all beings.'

'What,' I suggest, recalling the texts of the lost week, 'transformative at the soul level?'

'We're talking *molecular*.'

'So you're saying it acts as a kind of metaphor for the holographic universe?' I persist.

'Right.'

'Biocosmic resonation?'

She smiles a smile a highway wide. 'Hey, you're into that too.' Then leaning in close enough for me to be able to smell the tang of grease in her hair. 'Tell me, did we meet in a past life?'

'Uh huh,' I reply, returning the smile.

'I *knew* I'd seen your face before.'

I'm driving to Chris Griscom's Light Institute in Galisteo, about twenty miles south of Santa Fe, for a 'Knowings' in which people gather 'knowing' from themselves and 'apply it from a place of enlightenment'. I had always imagined wisdom to be an accumulated quality, only now I am told it can be taught in Knowings workshops.

South of Santa Fe, the sky unfurls to an artificial blue, scribbled over with cirrus. Last night's roadkill still lies moist and filleted on the highway, as yet undiscovered by the ravens sunning themselves in the squawbush on either side of the road. It is the first day of summer heat. The sun is yellow now; by noon it will shine as whitely as magnesium flare.

The highway passes right through Galisteo then out onto the other side, across the Galisteo basin. At speed, you might pass

the village of Galisteo altogether before your eyes had even registered it. The main street is little more than a strip of dry clay
messed up into troughs by the winter rains. A black mongrel
dog tied to a loop set into an adobe wall pulls at its chain and
howls. Caboose draws up and slides into the verge, too early
for the 'Knowings'. On the pavement lies an old fake swiss army
knife, handle picked at by ants, blade sound enough. Near to
the place where the dog is tied, two hispanic women and a man
in a straw hat sit in the shade of a mesquite tree still covered in
the papery casings of its lost blossom. Across the road towards
the Spanish church, the plastic honeycomb from a six-pack drifts
in the breeze. A car runs over it, slows momentarily then flows
south leaving its image slipping into the heat shine.

The *patrona* of the local store is stationed on a wooden chair
outside brushing away the dust with a Spanish fan. A radio tuned
into a Santa Fe station spits out part of the signal. She follows
me into the store, lined along one side with Uncle Ben's; she
smoothes her hair, lifts the plastic cover from a plate of danish
pastries, wipes off a fly and moves along the counter. Taking
my five-dollar bill and making a little show of it, she opens a
wooden drawer where there are five-dollar bills and one-dollar
bills, fixed together with an iron bulldog clip and passes back
some coins. I sit up against a wall hard from the sun, sip from
a bottle of warm, sweet soda and watch the black dog shivering
on its chain. A boy with worn down shoes comes by carrying
a bunch of mint with the leaves dragging in the dust.

Over the wall in someone's garden two cockerels are doing
violence to each other, throwing pieces of flinty stone up into
the air and a chestnut horse with a paper fringe over its head to
keep away the flies rubs its neck against a little bothy built into
the wall. The chickens don't bother it, the dog doesn't bother
it. A man passes in a tow truck, makes a wide turn at the end
of the road and cuts the engine. He sits and waits for something
to happen, but nothing does. Around the town in each direction
lies almost silent a fauvist bowl of bluegreen laterite edged in
navy where the sky scrolls down onto its beginning.

The world headquarters of the Griscom global enlightenment

enterprise is a collection of modest little buildings surrounded by cottonwood bosque up a remote and self-effacing dirt track to the east of Galisteo. By six-thirty, fifty people or so have gathered in a prefabricated building on one side of the main administrative building, behind an adobe barn. To the front of this building a line of cars waits to park: Mercedes estates, Mitsubishi four-wheel-drives, GM minivans, the odd station wagon. A waspish woman in linen tells me she makes the round trip (seven hundred miles or so) from Denver each week. It costs her $50 in gas, *plus* the $15 Light Institute fee. Chris Griscom is a very fine person, and a very famous person she says. It occurs to me that since my last visit to America celebrity has become a moral value as well as informing the predominant popular ideology.

We sit and wait in silence. Every now and then Wasp's stomach chirps. An Institute assistant, also dressed in linen, begins setting up tape machines and microphones by the door, and after a wait of a few minutes Griscom herself hovers in, head-to-toe white silk robes with white silk hair and golden tan, smiling an abstracted, internalized kind of smile, and stands with arms outstretched for the assistant to wire her up. Fully wired, she processes to a chair at the front of the room, lowers herself into it and does something Hindu with her hands.

'Enlightenment is really the recognition . . .' Griscom pauses, regarding with indulgent modesty the microphone clipped to her breast. The chic assistant grapples with the connection, the tape rolls, the microphone picks up and Griscom begins again. 'Enlightenment is really the recognition and acceptance of all energies and the capacity to be where they intersect, where those spin points are, where the negative pushes itself into the light, or is drawn into the light, so that there is a correspondent intersection between the doing and the being.'

Her audience shifts, then settles. The wasp leans forward and starts to take notes.

'Enlightenment', continues Griscom, voice creamy, sweeping long silver hair languorously from her face, 'has to do with freedom of choice. When you are looking at the incarnations that you're looking at this week you're having an opportunity to be the killer and the lover at the same time.'

A man behind kicks the back of my chair, causing a cold rill of sweat to leave its source between my legs and begin a journey across the thigh. Others fan themselves with their hands and purses. In my row about three along, someone struggles against sleep.

'So, once we realize that even if you are there in the place of wrong there's still a spark in there, there's still something that, if you can look at it from a witnessing position which is what you're sort of doing here, you can see that you did what you could with the consciousness you had, and that being didn't understand wrong the way you might now, and so through that experience they gained some recognition.'

'Does that mean we can go away and do anything we like, and still get enlightened?' I whisper across to my neighbour.

'Shh,' she replies.

'One of the lessons that has stopped human evolution at this point is the incapacity to see the purpose of all experience and therefore to embrace and comprehend what we would call the meditative. Everything is there exactly as it needs to be in order to allow the motion to continue because evolution is a part of the pulse, it is the pulse, of the universe. So, if we can sit in that space, letting even a flicker of the master that we have been, that we can recognize, that comes from our recognition from our incarnations, just a flicker of that to sit with us . . .'

A toddler runs over to the Griscom throne and attempts to mount. Griscom smiles and pushes it off.

'. . . then we can perceive in a totally different way. The difficulty with linear is that it's always out in front or behind instead of here, right here now. And with that, the scope to see its purpose, because it either hasn't come yet, or it's already shut off, then we can't recognise purpose. Purpose is a living thing, it's life itself, that ecstasy, when it needs no more explanation, it just is.'

I turn to my neighbour who is trying her best to balance the demands of note-taking and staring intently ahead.

'I'm completely lost. What was that about linear?'

'After.'

My eyelids begin an inexorable downward progress. Half an hour or so later I'm woken by the voice of the woman next to me, who is explaining to the assembly how she was psychically attacked in a dream the previous night and woke up to discover red welts all over her body, and Chris Griscom is congratulating her on fending off the psychic invader and mentioning the undeniable increase in the number of aliens feeding on human energies in the region and pointing out that this is happening to test our strength and make us more whole. I wonder vaguely if the hungry alien argument was part of the reason for Shirley Maclaine's conversion to the New Age. I think I'm beginning to grasp Griscom's vision thing. It goes like this: we are all here for a purpose, we're entitled to constant bliss, we don't need to feel pain, we are in the inevitable process of evolution, we can be free of our bodies and inhabit the universe. That's about it, simply put.

And all those hungry souls, with their unsatisfying, slipaway lives, the souls of the ones who are *not* Shirley Maclaine and never will be, all the ordinary ones, can rest reassured by a simple weekly payment of $15 to the Light Institute of Galisteo that there is a higher reason for it all. Whereas, of course, there may well not be.

The way I see it, a pile of money goes round in circles in the little community of Santa Fe, and every time it comes round to the Light Institute of Galisteo, a bit more drops off.

DAY TEN

A queue winds down from the ticket booth at the Whole Life Expo in the town centre, across West Marcy Street towards the public library. From up ahead comes the sound of drumming. A printed programme available at the door details the lectures and workshops for the day:

* 'Is there an Alien-Multinational Connection?'
* 'Learn how bone-headed misinformants are placed in
  UFO conferences as speakers to baffle and confuse you'
* 'The Vampire and the Psychic Gatekeeper,' talk given
  by Helaine Harris, creator of Psychoshamanism™
* 'The Virtual Reality of MetaNeurological Genesis'
* 'The Properties of Extraterrestrial Science and
  Tibetan-Andromedan Intervention in World Affairs
  during 1993'
* 'Soul Triggering of the Brain's Joy Center – Super
  Conscious Self-Technics to Save Us From Extinction',
  by Orayna Orr, empath

The list continues: workshops on angels, astral projection, colonic irrigation, past lives, auric massage and discovering the wild woman within. It's going to be a busy day.

From among the vendors of extremely low-frequency head-sets, magic wands, colonic irrigation suppositories, copper pyramids and high energy gloves I select the Kirilian photography booth. A Kirilian photograph can produce an image of the aura. Now the existence of auras seems pretty plausible to me. How else could a person sense when another enters the room, without seeing or hearing them? What other explanation can there be for the ability to detect a mood or tension in the air? It doesn't matter to me whether the aura is electromagnetic energy, sixth sense, sophisticated heat detector, lifeforce, or anything else, only that it exists. To be able to have physical evidence of it would be an assurance that some things are beyond the reaches of science. It would be a sign that mysteries still exist. I have a hunch that, once I know all there is to know about my aura, I'll feel more attuned to the New Age altogether.

While we're standing in line, a woman in an outsized orange beret solicits my opinion of the Mississippi floods. Pictures of broken levees and devastated homes are being shown on every news programme on the TV, and occupy the front pages of much of the printed press too. I say I think they're terrible.

'No they're not,' replies the orange beret.

'Really?'

'Of course not, they're all part of the earth changes.'

Haven't I heard? The planet is on the brink of an apocalyptic phase, during which storms and floods and earthquakes and all kinds of natural disasters will kill most of the world's population – especially the unspiritual ones – leading those remaining to a new era of peace and higher consciousness.

'The Age of Aquarius,' she says, 'you *must* have heard.'

'Is that the same thing as the New Age?'

'Aquarius,' repeats the orange beret, sounding confused.

A Kirilian photograph looks very much like a regular polaroid, as it turns out, but at $15 a shot it has to be different. In any case, Kirilian photographs are taken by a highly complex Kirilian mechanism, requiring the subject to place his or her palm on a metal plate and visualize the auric field while the booth assistant shouts instructions from beneath a piece of black cloth. There then follows a soft popping preceded by an intense white light, and the aura photograph spools from a flap in the side of the machine. Mine is a chemical green, with two livid haloes floating above it like aerial ringworm sores.

'Oh my,' says the booth assistant, 'this is *interesting*. See that green? That's healing. And the red is passion.' Passion and healing, I'm thinking, not bad.

'You have a young soul, not too many lifetimes here, full of energy, adventuresomeness, you're highly active physically, probably travel a good deal, veerrry creative. I'd guess you make your living by your wits. You're *fascinated* by what goes on in the world, are you in the news? Something like that, I'm only guessing.'

And she's on to the next in line, orange beret. I indulge my ego in a small self-congratulatory moment. Young soul, fascinated, adventuresome. Hotdamn! My aura is telling me I'm the person I always wanted to be.

'Oh my.' The booth assistant is speaking to orange beret now, holding the beret's aura image, 'this is *interesting*. See that green? A young soul. Veery creative.'

I call Fergus collect to let him know first that my aura is green for healing, red for passion and second that the earth is about to implode. He seems unimpressed, but then he is a New Yorker. As I'm leaving the phone booth someone presses a flyer into my hands and invites me to a lecture at 4pm given by a Princess Sharula Dux who will be demonstrating the tools and format to bring the planet into the Aquarian Age as prescribed by the Melchizedek Temple of Telos. Topics covered will include passing through the astrological doorway of 12:12, and the restructuring of the Melchizedek Priesthood, the spiritual warriors and world leaders of the Golden Age. Pretty comprehensive.

At some point in my lost week I read about Princess Sharula and her theories. The Princess Dux I read about is a 267 year-old Ambassador from a subterranean city called Telos which is in turn part of the ancient underground kingdom of Lemuria, sister civilization to Atlantis and Mu.

At four sharp she arrives at lecture theatre number three, blinking at the crowd, an immensity in a marine-theme catsuit, and makes her way to the front of the room with that rolling gait peculiar to the corpulent, closely followed by a young outdoors type with long hair tied back in a ponytail, who introduces himself as Shield Dux and asks us to give a big hand to Her Excellency the Princess Sharula Dux, his beloved wife and distinguished Ambassador from the court of Telos.

Sharula wants her public to understand that the world is in disarray, convulsed by greed, natural disasters, cancer, urban violence, tax evasion and cruelty to animals. She wants us to know that we are standing at a crossroads in the 1990s. A crossroads, every generation needs to hear it. In the 1890s our great-grandparents were standing at a crossroads. We were standing at a crossroads when Martin Luther King took the fatal bullet, when Reaganomics was in vogue. We have always, I fear, been standing at a crossroads.

In Princess Dux's opinion the New Age is coming pretty soon now, about as soon as it takes for the gargantuan crystal matrix computers of the universe to receive a cosmic refurbishment. There's good news for Americans, says Dux; the United States of America is programmed to become the world's first crystal matrix paradise because it is in America that the current global cauldron of ills is bubbling away the hardest.

Eventually, question time comes round, and no-one seems to have much to say so I stand and venture:

'One thing I've always wanted to know is whether it gets a little smoggy down underground, you know, without the benefit of the wind?'

The princess smoothes her pearl-grey hair and winds a thread around one of the anchor buttons of her catsuit.

'You must have learned such a lot in your 267 years.'

'I have had the occasional enlightenment, it's true. Actually, all our power comes from an electromagnetic injection into the crystal matrix that harnesses the ethereal power and provides energy for a million years. It is completely clean and entirely without ecological consequences. So, you see, we have no smog at all. You have yet to learn such technologies. Earth people are remarkably backward in some respects.'

'You know, your majesty or whatever,' I continue, emboldened. 'I sometimes feel confused and barely human.' There's a rustle of recognition in the audience. 'I do have this weird little birthmark on my back. Suppose I'm Lemurian, like you. I mean, how could I tell?'

She looks at me darkly, smile faded away to a little flicker about the nostrils.

'I don't think that's likely, you're probably just an extra-terrestrial.'

Sometimes I can be so cheap it gets me down.

In the coffee bar, a Californian called Talon invites me to a free demonstration of his Tachyon energy bodysuits. Now, in different circumstances nothing would have kept me from Talon's Tachyon energy bodysuit, but I am committed to the Brad and Sherry Steiger lecture at 5.30. No matter, says Talon, why doesn't he swing by after the lecture, and he'll give me an individual session 'with no obligations', so we fix a vague time and Talon wanders off back to his Tachyon energy booth and I never do discover exactly what Tachyon energy is.

Brad Steiger and Sherry Hansen Steiger are New Age celebs,

which is to say, they have made appearances on *The Joan Rivers Show* and can afford a half-page ad in the Whole Life Expo catalogue. Their books include *Hollywood and the Supernatural* and *Mysteries of Time and Space*. The most recent, *Strange Powers of Pets*, was a Literary Guild selection. In addition Sherry Hansen Steiger is a licensed publicist while Brad once won the Film Advisory Board's Award of Excellence. The *Milwaukee Sentinel* apparently says they have 'a wonderful understanding of the forthcoming changes.'

After a 267 year-old Princess, can anything surprise?

By their own account, Brad and Sherry Steiger stumbled across intimations of an answer to the question: 'Who made us what we are?', quite by accident. After years of painstaking research they discovered, almost as a by-product of their work into alien intelligence, that the great human tribe, far from being mere cosmic incidentals, had in fact been shaped many thousand years ago by collectives of advanced entities from other planets, and in particular from Venus. Suddenly, everything else made sense to them. The giant fossilized footprints they had come across in Peru (was it Peru? I forget) were obviously those of an advanced reptilian being which had evolved on earth and migrated to another part of the solar system; and the well-documented Mayan practice of elongating infant skulls by squashing them between boards was doubtless intended to be a sign of deference to the Indians' oval-headed alien masters. Why, rock pictures show that the aliens even knew about photosynthesis and were employing it for their own ends, not least of which was to splice up some human genes and cross-breed them with other useful things – plants and spaceships. They'd even got the technology to manufacture human beings from the Madagascan common ring-tailed lemur.

And to think that without the Steigers the world would have remained ignorant of these things.

So the tenth day ends, without satisfaction, in room 12 at the King's Rest. Gita has been in to clean and left a few nominal swirls in the dirt on the dresser. Outside the air is still as sleep and pearly with dusk. Roseanne Barr's disembodied voice oozes through the wall from the room next door. For some days now I have felt a strange longing which is neither a longing for contact nor a longing for conversation, but rather, a need to be on familiar ground. Had I been travelling in the Solomon Islands I should have faced my isolation with greater equanimity, but every westerner expects at least to comprehend America, if not to feel in some measure at ease there. Here I find so many hints of common ground give out quite suddenly, like false byways. Someone you can rely upon to have an opinion about soap opera or McDonald's turns out to have seen angels in her backyard and the man who sells you a cup of coffee thinks himself a reincarnation of Nefertiti. Even among the seemingly familiar there can turn out to be almost nothing recognizable.

Day Eleven

I wake with a start from some instantly forgotten dream as the sun begins to burn blue holes into the earliest light. Some overnight rain has stripped the rose outside of its petals leaving a few trembling stamens held fast in the arms of the calyx. A raven lifts itself from the roof and banks into the sky. The one other guest is packing his car and heading back home, to Colorado by the looks of it. There are no clouds now, just a wondrous filmic sheet flung about the earth and moving lightly in the void, as if pegged out to dry.

Remembering the despondent mood of the previous night, I unpack my African fetish, Hopi dream catcher and quartz crystals and arrange them about the room in an attempt to brighten up the place and construct the kind of homeliness which is at present missing. I light a Camel, drink the remains of last night's root beer, now flat, switch on the TV and wonder why it is that all American anchorwomen have the same hairdo.

At around nine Gita knocks and, without waiting for a response, lets herself in. Looking down at me sitting on the bed she says, to no-one in particular, 'Alone watching TV,' with the satisfaction of one delivering a biographical summation for the purposes of an obituary.

Breakfast of sour *frijoles* and *huevos a la plancha* in a cafe in Española, a small, hispanic town about thirty miles north of Santa Fe. Black water runs out from the beans, leaving strange Rorschach blots on a stack of flour tortillas heaped beside.

These I point out to the waitress when she returns to fill my coffee cup.

'What do they suggest to you?'

'UFO? I dunno.'

'Pick an insight card.' She looks down for a moment at the little gold box, pincers a card between brilliant red nails, studies it a moment, throws it back on the table and pours the coffee.

The card reads 'Slow down, you're going too fast; You gotta make the moment last . . .' with Paul Simon credited on the bottom in psychedelic letters enclosed by double quotation marks. "Paul Simon."

'What's that for, anyhow?' Before I leave she asks for it back to show to her boss, but he's too busy loading a delivery of icecream into the freezer.

Sixties, sixties, sixties. Sometimes it seems as though the sixties generation unplugged en masse after Woodstock. Do they suppose that nothing's happened since? Like, the end of the Cold War, like the digital revolution, like AIDS, like democratic elections in South Africa, like crack, like the rise and rise of the kind of people who still remember who Paul Simon was, or is, or who give a damn in any case.

Every time I hum the tune I get the line 'you *move* too fast' repeating in my head. 'You're going too fast' doesn't even scan.

During the drive back to Santa Fe it occurs to me that, despite having been in New Mexico for nearly two weeks, I have taken almost no account of the landscape outside the city limits, which is at least as great a draw to spiritual tourists as the New Age cafes and bookstores downtown. So I swing off the freeway at the next turning, signposted to Chimayo, and head up a single-track paved road onto a desert plateau lined in the far distance with naked mountains whose peaks, despite the sun, remain ice-powdered, giving them the appearance of cut salami sausages. A warm, desiccated wind exposes the matt grey underside of the sage and fragments the plain into a subtle mosaic of drab green and grey. Fifteen minutes of walking through the brush and my position feels unchanged, the mountains ahead as remote as Elysium. A deep cloud, dark as bomb dust, hangs over the horizon fifty or sixty miles away, tailing rain. I realize that it is not so much isolation that is at the heart of my dispiritedness, but claustrophobia.

Santa Fe is quiet today. Down in the plaza some Indian women are laying out jewellery on blankets under the shaded boardwalk of the Palace of the Governors. The afternoon wind has brought humidity, and the possibility of a thunderstorm; art stores and restaurants and parking lots are empty. Although the city is reputed to be at ease with itself, you only have to walk around the plaza before the tourists have arrived or after they have gone to sense the air of restlessness and disquiet. The chamber of commerce sells the city as a place of such antiquity and harmony that its three cultures – Hispanic, Native American and Anglo – coexist in steadfast and separate juxtaposition, and extrapolates from this the myth that the City Different is a place of relaxed permissiveness. In fact, New Mexico has a history sufficiently long to have blurred the distinctions between Hispanic and Native American into a complex and pleasing slurry, without annihilating either. It is the newcomers who, unable or unwilling to grasp the subtleties of the place, have saddled it with the label 'tricultural' and, with that simple tag, rewritten history. A colonial census of 1790 recognized seven ethnic groups in Santa Fe: White Spanish; Coyote, or Spanish and New Mexican Indian; Mulatto, or half-Afro-American; Genizaro, who were Indians captured by Plains Indians and sold back to Spanish colonists as slaves; Indio or Indian; Mestizo, or a mixture of Spanish and Mexican Indian; and Color Quebrado, which pretty much summed up anyone left over. They were in part united by the conservative lifestyles most suited to harsh terrain and in part by trading alliances. Anglo-saxon culture, in particular liberal anglo-saxon culture, came late to New Mexico, and laid itself like skin on the soup beneath. Since the influx of wealthy, liberal, overwhelmingly white vacationers and retirees in the 1980s and 1990s, land prices have soared in Santa Fe. Every day a letter or an op-ed piece in the Santa Fe *New Mexican* mourns the conversion of the city from living place to outdoor museum.

I'm going to tell you about Pete. Pete makes his living as a New Age technoshaman. A technoshaman is a shaman with a computer, apparently. It's a profession with a scientific bent. In fact, much that goes on among New Agers is of a scientific bent, for science can be harnessed in support of more or less any kind of ideology and, by being thus appropriated, spoiled for any other. Afterall, what does it matter if computers powered by crystal matrices and extra-low frequency psychic protector lenses and human beings grown from lemur babies sound improbable? Gene splicing and nanotechnology and virtual reality are pretty crazy too.

Pete the Technoshaman has been developing his technoshamanistic software for eleven years and has chosen to base his code on the Mayan calendar on the grounds that the mathematics of the Mayan grid is the same mathematics as the mathematics of life, a numerically reciprocal permutation table. Pete's mission has something to do with the rising level of chaos, which, according to Pete, will lead inexorably to the world being in flames and bridges burning behind us.

'There's no going back to the Garden of Eden,' he says, 'which didn't even really exist anyway.'

In his living room he has an AppleMac fixed to a number of electronic gizmos with flashing LED displays and impressive monitors. From here he carries on his practice, assisted by his wife, Beth, who is also and incidentally a shaman herself, although not of the technological variety.

Beth fetches some coffee.

'It all looks, uh, amazingly complex, but how is this Mayan grid business actually going to make a difference?' I ask.

Pete the Technoshaman gathers himself, sweeps his hair back, double-clicks on his mouse, and says with casual authority, 'Hey, I'm doing my bit.'

The coffee arrives, and we sit at Pete's Mac staring idly at a notice flashing on the screen which reads 'You may activate the program at any time.'

'You know,' says Pete with palpable sadness, sucking on his coffee cup, 'I don't have answers as to what can happen to the teeming billions, man, but at least I don't have to wonder what I'm doing here anymore.'

His friend Carl, stationed on the sofabed reading a copy of *National Geographic*, looks up and interjects:'Yeah, it sounds so cold-hearted to say that not a lot can be done, but you know, maybe that's not so bad. I mean, we're spiritual beings, right?'

'You know,' says Pete, bringing up a graphic of the solar system on the Mac, 'we're in a wrenching transitional period. Some people would say that because you're not handing out sandwiches in Somalia you're not doing anything. But McKenna's right. The world's salvation is in pushing the imagination.'

Carl throws down his *National Geographic* and shakes his head. McKenna, I happen to know, is a West Coast writer who thinks that magic mushrooms provide an insight into alien worlds. He's become somewhat of a cult figure among men of a certain age.

'The whole world's on LSD,' says Carl, randomly.

'Information's the thing, man,' continues Pete, 'The future of consciousness and the future of medicine.' He clicks on his mouse and brings up a flowchart marked in Greek lettering. Then, taking up a phial he walks over to Carl, yanks out a lock of hair with a quick flip of his wrist, puts the hair into the phial, and inserts it into a larger tube connected with electrodes to a piece of metal, and also by some mysterious means, to the computer.

'This, for example, is kinesiology.'

'Wow,' says Carl, evidently impressed.

'I just place my finger, thus,' placing his right index finger on the piece of metal, 'on the electro-kinesiological reaction plate and there's an electromagnetic disturbance created by the hair that my finger picks up, as it were, intuitively. Understand?'

I nod; Carl simpers.

'It's the same as if I touched you. Any live cell will do, you know, because they all react in unison. I don't need a liver cell to know what's going on in the liver.'

I mention in passing that I had always imagined hair cells to be dead.

Pete's wife returns from putting the baby to bed and proceeds to settle down to some other domestic chore.

'I am a biological scientist,' replies Pete definitively. In the corner of the room his wife bites her lip.

'So you know, I rub my finger on the plate and intuitively click the mouse on this list, so.'

He removes the hair phial and replaces it with a bottle of colourless fluid.

'All the restitutive elements – crystals, colours, food, so forth – are stored in the memory banks of the machine as holographic references, each item is associated with thirteen Mayan numbers, which store enough information on each substance not to have to bother having the real things.

'Take this bottle of water here. We simply . . .' Clicks on the mouse, two doubles.

'And the numbers are transferred into an electromagnetic pulse so the geometry of the water changes. Or the same information can be transferred to a lamp, or coded as a fractal type for psychoemotional problems or a sound with the information subliminally tagged onto it.'

'You mean, you don't need to see your patients?'

'Uh-uh. They just phone right up, and we send them a tape with the sound on it, whatever . . .' He's picking out the bottle of water and putting back Carl's hair. From another room the baby begins to howl.

'Oh Lordie.'

'What?' asks Carl, looking a little worried.

'Just checked the energy levels. Seems like your digestive problem is somewhat better already.'

'Yeah?' says Carl.

'See,' Pete points to a chart on the screen, which has changed from blue to yellow. 'If this technology developed you could just grow body parts. Incidentally . . .' He double-clicks, the screen shifts, blackens and the message 'You may activate the program at any time' blinks back. 'Tim Leary is speaking at the Sweeny Center today. Do you know who Tim Leary is?'

I smile.

'Only one of the most important minds of the twentieth century.' He rises from his chair and lifts a paperback from a pile under the coffee table. 'This is an original signed copy,' he says, holding the book out to me, then thinking better of it, he replaces the volume under the table, lining up the spine against a magazine beneath.

'You get many clients?' I ask, changing the subject.

Pete considers the question, which has taken him a little by surprise. Finally he says 'The thing with clients is that a lot of the work is just caring for them, which, you know, doesn't appeal to me. But I have to fund my research so we . . .,' gesturing towards his wife, 'take on a few clients. There *are* funding sources for fringe technology like this, of course, but they all want something for it. Nothing, for free, man.'

'Pow pow pow,' says Carl, knocking out the funding sources with his finger.

'This thing, you know, called my reality, is based purely on my own experience.' Pete clicks on the mouse and brings up a screen with a pattern of stars upon it. 'Expand my experience, and, man, you really turn me on.'

There is a bookstall in the foyer of the Sweeny Center selling guides to enlightenment, with a list of all the great teachers who have ever attained nirvana, and how they did it. Gautama sat under a Bodhi tree and waited, and, after seven days without food and water, he saw the morning star and was enlightened into formless bliss. Ming travelled for years looking for enlightenment and eventually found nirvana when Hui-neng asked him 'What is your original face, which you had even before your birth?' Neither of them had access to a computer. The process of their enlightenments was tortuous and thoroughly unscientific. We leave it to science, these days, to reveal the mystery of the everyday. Perhaps Gautama and Ming would have done better with Pete the Technoshaman's Mayan program.

Science, they say, is the Moses of the twentieth century and heaven knows, we need one.

There are, incidentally, no enlightened women on the list. There are books on women who run with wolves, women who love too much, women who love men who love other women, universal mother-women, crone-women, angels, goddesses, all sorts of women doing all sorts of things, in fact, but no *enlightened* ones. Why is that? The sales assistant suggests I listen to Joni Mitchell, whom she regards as highly advanced. I promise to think it over and buy a little beginner's guide to Zen containing this fragment, by Tung-shan:

> The man of wood sings,
> The woman of stone
> Gets up and dances,
> This cannot be done
> By passion or learning,
> It cannot be done
> By reasoning.

A man with a beard the colour of baked beans walks across my field of vision carrying a child in a turban, smiles at someone ahead and is devoured by the crowd. Here they all are, the success stories of late twentieth-century capitalism – sophisticated consumers, moneyed but not dangerously moneyed, educated, but not threateningly so – passing the hours irrigating their colons, birthing their drums and squeezing their higher consciousnesses. Fergus once remarked 'there's the work ethic and the self ethic and those two together made America what it is. If you have any criticisms I suggest you take them elsewhere. We're very protective of our ethics.'

Five minutes before Timothy Leary is due to come on stage the man with the beard the colour of baked beans sits down next to me and produces a yellowing copy of *Life* magazine with Leary's signature on it. Seeing me trying to catch the full inscription he leans over and whispers:

'Grew up with Tim.'

'Really?'

'*Man*, he's like, my *hero*. He's like taken the principle of questioning authority and moved with that in a positive way. Like, I don't even read the newspapers anymore on account of all the negativity. I've learned the hard way that everything you do has a purpose, it's there to teach you something and it's all OK . . . But we couldn't have evolved this far without people like Tim.'

'I missed the sixties.'

'The sixties was really all about, personal growth, being anything you want to be, the power of positive thinking. I mean, I get some negative thoughts, and I think, hey, these don't belong to me. That's what the sixties *was* so . . . by the way, what's your ascendant?'

In my mind's eye there are petals back on the rose outside my room and there is a hummingbird feeding on the waxy spike of the agave flower.

Baked Bean spends the remaining hour of Leary's talk in a state of intolerable suspense awaiting exactly the right moment to produce his faded copy of *Life* and ask Leary for an autograph. Meanwhile one of the most influential minds of the twentieth century fumbles around unrehearsed, contradicts himself, pauses, begins again, delivers a few lost eulogies to technology and digitalia, finally succumbs to his own boredom and produces a rave tape. A series of psychedelic images spirals round the room to a techno backbeat. During each lull, and there are many, Baked Bean puts his hand up, and then retreats rapidly, like a polyp feeling for its prey. Poor Baked Bean, I'm sure he's not so bad, it's just that I've had enough of him.

'The only way it's gonna happen is through science, right?' he whispers. A strobe hits the copy of *Life*. The music, techno, bam da da boom. 'I was at Woodstock, right?'

'Oh.'

'Yeah. And what did that do, right?'

'Well, it *was* only a rock concert.' The music stops.

'People working on themselves,' he nods his head in the direction of the crowd now filing out of the door.

'Uh huh.'

He says; 'From a scientific perspective you can't do anything for anyone without healing the inner person. Start with yourself.'

'Is that so?'

'In my experience,' he says, and leaves without the autograph. Ten minutes later he appears around a corner and hands me a leaflet about the spiritual implications of digitalizing dolphin song.

Here is the inconsistency of my position. I am envious of New Age certainties, but jealous of my own, which in general contradict them. Yet, if I am to make anything of the New Age I shall have to file those little prejudices away, for they will ensure that I fail in my attempt to comprehend the world I have chosen, temporarily, to inhabit. I admit to a tendency within myself to maintain a rather dismal inflexibility as shield against the clamour of contradiction. But at the same time I can see that the belief that there are no extra-terrestrials and the belief that there are coexist and have equal authority. It's insoluble.

I fall asleep with the TV tinting blue the web of nerves behind my eyes, like moonlight on some electronic planet, and I wake up sometime before dawn, chilled to the soul. Above the parking lot of the King's Rest Motel the sky is black and still as a dark-room, trapping in its invisible fibres the blossoms of a million stars.

Heading West

'Where the earth is dry the soul is wisest and best.'

HERACLITUS

Memorial Day, driving into afternoon sun on what was once Route 66. On the opposite side of the highway two lanes bumper-to-bumper trudge towards the Continental Divide like a train of metal mules. Bowling beside me is a line of Recreational Vehicles also heading west. Now and then the aluminium pod of an old-style trailer passes by, cutting the air with reflections.

To an American, and more particularly to a westerner, the Recreational Vehicle must be an almost invisible part of the mobile landscape, but a European can only stare as the hulking trucks, passing themselves off as miniature moving idylls, lumber gracelessly along the freeway. We don't have sufficient wide roads to accommodate them, our cities are too close together, the gas they require is too expensive, we are not rich enough to buy them, we go abroad for our holidays, and, most of all – although this is changing – we do not recreate. Recreating is an all-American invention. Americans are compelled to possess their leisure as they are compelled to possess most anything, and to be fully the owner of their leisure, they must accumulate experience. This is why the American recreator will happily schedule in a dozen European capitals in a week, but still won't hang around in the Sistine Chapel if the paper in the toilets runs out. For the American recreator it is the quantity of experience that matters, not its quality.

After two hours on the road I pull into a rest area, find a spot under a mesquite tree and doze a while with the air conditioning high. I wake up to a woman knocking on the window for two quarters to put in the soda machine. Quite a crowd has gathered in the parking lot, a line of RVs competes for space directly in front of the restrooms, map and vending machines. The woman returns, wanting to introduce me to her dogs. Jeez, dog-lovers.

'You know,' she says, 'this place is full of Mexicans and Indians. Mexicans and Indians. Folks like us are outnumbered. At least it feels that way.' We finish the soda in the '65 Scottie trailer she bought six months ago with the redundancy payoff from a marketing job in Pennsylvania. 'Came out here, followed the myth,' she says, 'and I liked it.' She doesn't know how much longer it will be before she settles down somewhere and builds another life.

'This dog here's too old to be on the road,' she says, 'he needs a place where he can feel comfortable enough to go ahead and die.'

Pinned up in the Scottie is a portrait of Ross Perot taken during his presidential campaign, still looking like a VE-Day vet after all these years.

The rest area feels as though an RV convention pulled in; RVs piled high inside with kids and bulk-buy Kool Aid alongside modest little trailers with chromium trim and lines of rivets, looking like some by-product of rocket science. A couple descend from an ancient Winnebago with Illinois plates and sit under the shade of a cottonwood sucking Diet Cokes in silent contemplation.

Homelessness is a profound anxiety in the American psyche, a cyst buried in the deeper, more feral places of the mind. At the wheel of an RV you can travel a thousand miles and never leave home; there it is in miniature, rolling along behind. For American recreators the RV acts as a kind of mediator between the fear of homelessness and the fascination with freedom. Think of that couple eating up the miles in their mechanical homestead, raw with anticipation, drinking in the road, surveying with pride the empire unfolding before them – their empire. And think of that couple sitting watching TV or flipping cards or making out in a desert trailer park at the side of an indistinct highway on a blackened plain, pulled up alongside a line of other RVs bigger and newer and more expensive than their own.

Getting Off

'Beneath him with new wonder now he views
To all delight of human sense exposed
In narrow room nature's whole wealth, yeah more,
A heav'n on earth . . .'

JOHN MILTON

The road north up through Tucson towards Oracle is known as
the Magic Mile, although quite why it's difficult to say. The
kind of stores and services littered along it suggest a highway
favoured only by truck drivers en route to somewhere else. Just
where the mile begins there is a series of blacked-out bars with
billboards made up of women's torsos, announcing '24-hour
show girls'. From the slow lane on the Interstate all you can see
of the Magic Mile is a row of gargantuan cardboard legs in spike
heels and garter belts the colour of cotton candy.

It's a busy road, though, not because it runs up to Oracle,
which is a sclerotic little nowhere of a place, but because a few
miles beyond that town lies an oracle of another kind, as much
of a draw to apostates and New Age types as Lourdes is to
Catholics.

What drew me to this oracle was a set of circumstances sufficiently strange to warrant explanation. It began quite by accident in western Belize some years ago, in a ramshackle town
called San Ignacio, near the border with Guatemala. I had become
entangled in a brief and unhappy love affair from which I made
a cowardly escape very early one morning by stealing away and
boarding a bus heading to Dangriga, a swamp town on the Carib-
bean coast. There I found a boarding house and resolved to lie
low. Creosote tar sweated from the stilted shacks gathered
around the little harbour and the air was so sullen that it was
difficult not to be lowered by it. At night liverish land crabs

37

scuttled from their holes and took over the streets, like an army
of dismembered hands. Every structure in Dangriga not actually
made from mud was covered in it. A few lugubrious rastafarians
hung about what passed for the centre of the town, which was
separated from the swamp all around by a blue fug of burning
weed. Dangriga's only source of income, so far as I could make
out, came from bussing snapper, lobster and the occasional barra-
cuda to the inland capital. The men who could afford a dugout
or a one-man, flat-keeled dory would put out at night and bring
in their catch early the next morning. Those who had no boats
became assistants to the others, or rastafarians – or both. The
women would pass their mornings gutting and drying whatever
fish were surplus to the day's requirements on long lines of twine,
hung over the doorways of the shacks and serving, incidentally,
as mosquito nets. By two in the afternoon, everyone was asleep.
There would be no-one left to talk to, nothing much to do but
roll up a reefer, tune the radio to the station that played ska and
marimba and settle down to watch the pale brown sea. I spent
many days of distant, peaceless reverie like this.

Absolutely nothing that was not already on show had ever
happened in Dangriga. No wars, no revolutions, no great pas-
sions of any sort. Dangriga's history was without secrets.

According to my map a huge uninhabited atoll group called
Turneffe lay directly out to sea from Dangriga. I would often
sit wall-eyed in front of that brown bay and imagine Turneffe
in the distance as a lush, mudless Eden. Without the listless day-
dream of Turneffe I like to think that I should have gone mad
in Dangriga. I should not have done so, but I like to think it all
the same.

About four years later I met the man who owned Turneffe,
or at least, a little part of it. At least, he managed a little part of
it for someone else. His name was Ray Lightburn, and he had
some environmental project going, he said. Ray was what is
commonly known as a charismatic – huge, commanding, almost
insanely driven. He'd been a prominent trade unionist in Britain
in the sixties, and he possessed a store-cupboard of anecdotes
about political heavyweights he had known and met. Whether

they were true or not didn't seem to matter. Like many charismatics, who are after all expected to be emblematic rather than real, Ray was his own parody. Obviously, he liked it that way. In any case, back in Belize he'd made his political ambitions evident by sinking himself into the environmental movement and conspicuously raising the cash from a Texan oil billionaire with ecological leanings to buy up part of Blackbird Caye in the Turneffe cluster. Blackbird Caye was to all intents and purposes uninhabited at that time; a hippy with too much leisure on his hands had set up a little diving school on one side of the island, but it was Ray who got the money together to transform the Caye into what he envisioned would be an eco-tourists' paradise. As he saw it, the islands' future rested in tourism of one sort or another, and the only means to prevent them from becoming sites for honeymoon hotels and Clubs Méditerranées was to pre-select the market. Ray was a prophet of the inevitable. The idea that the islands might be purchased to be left pristine evidently had not occurred to him, or if it had, he had dismissed it out of hand. Ray had a name to make. The Texan billionaire, Ed Bass, was perhaps his means to this end.

There was a large dolphin population down at Turneffe, which (until Ray stepped in) had enjoyed almost no contact with human beings. Ray's idea was to hire a scientist who would take out crews of paying guests on 'scientific' expeditions to mark and tag these creatures. Ray didn't really seem to know the details. 'What species of dolphin?' I asked. He shrugged his shoulders. 'I leave those things to the scientists. This is a great project. I believe in it.'

The scientist, a singular marine biology student, had accepted the post of tour guide cum researcher in order to complete her Ph.D. In exchange for accommodation and the use of a research boat the student would drag along on her expeditions a pack of dew-eyed puppies who had endowed the neighbouring dolphins with a range of miraculous capabilities, from an ability to heal inner children to the composition of sonic messages that would seek out and shrink malignant tumours. The eco-tourists would put out to sea each day, heady with expectation, and return in the afternoon in a state of mystic transcendence or savage disappointment, depending on whether or not there had been a sighting. The student's job was single-handedly to control the mob in whichever mood, a task she went about with benign and systematic brutality.

Moored a little way off the coast of Blackbird Caye near to the eco-tourist compound was a reproduction Chinese junk, the *Hercules*. According to Ray, the junk was the scientific outpost of a project called Biosphere 2, a futuristic venture based in the Arizona desert. From time to time a limpid woman in a wetsuit would appear on the deck of the junk and wave at the lone scientist and her pride of tourists. The crew of the *Hercules* did not welcome visitors, said Ray.

This was just about all I knew of the Biosphere. I had come across a few speculative articles in the press and a few figures, such as the fact that the project had swallowed the $150m raised by a Texan magnate called Ed Bass (the same Ed Bass whose interests included Blackbird Caye), through a holding company, Space Biosphere Ventures. I knew that Biosphere 2 was the largest experimental closed environment on the planet – three and a bit acres sealed virtually airtight by a metal and glass frame – that eight people had been shut inside and left to get on with things, which they hadn't managed quite to do, because the oxygen levels in the bubble had begun inexplicably to fall, necessitating the introduction of a new supply from outside. There had been rumours that Bass was influenced by a New Age cult led by a charismatic worker-poet whose aim was to begin life again somewhere out in space. Extraordinarily for these times, I had never seen an image of the Biosphere.

The last tourist bus has already left by the time Caboose and I turn off the highway onto Biosphere range. It is June, start of the rattler season – the heat so intense it pushes the air into strange, eddying flues and pulls at the ligaments in the throat. My fingers have fused to the wheel of the car and become woody and aged. Up ahead a paved track runs off the road and leads to a forlorn sentry house with a uniformed guard. Bumping across the cattle grid it feels as though I have crossed a border and am somewhere liminal that is not a part of America at all.

The hotel at the Biosphere is hunched along a mountain ridge above the complex proper, and has a view southward through the Canyon del Oro to the Santa Catalina Mountains beyond. I open my notebook and retrieve the number of Sam, a friend of someone I met in a bar outside Santa Fe. Sam now works at the Biosphere. The switchboard operator intercepts my call and promises to pass a message on.

In exploratory mood I throw off my boots, unpack my camera, take some tortilla chips from the mini-bar, flip on the TV (*Star Trek – The Next Generation*), flip it off, fetch a half bottle of Jim Beam from my suitcase and take off along the deserted paths running across the top of the ridge. To the east a mountain range glows hot from the reflection of the sunset and far below two huge, white-boned dome lungs spin in the shifting light like the eyes of spy insects. From the canyon to the south come the echoes of a woodpecker chipping saguaro cactus. Biosphere 2: two grand glass ziggurats embedded in the lilac rock of the Sonora basin and made insubstantial by the light, like some reinvented Crystal Palace, a grand and brilliant technological announcement. There are lights on in the human habitation tower which illuminate the surrounding metal frame in sodium flare and give the whole the air of an ethereal city. Tatty palms press up against the glass, below the palms floats a miniature ocean encircled by fibreglass cliffs. To the fore buff rocks, and upon them, stringy thornscrub scouring the structure's frame, as if waiting its moment to punch through the glass and reclaim the air. A rustle in the bushes and a mule deer stumbles out onto the path and plunges down the slope of the ridge, leaving only a wave in the mesquite.

Back in room 11, there is no message from Sam. I lock the bolt and chain and call him again. Sam answers. Yes, he got my message, but he thinks I should talk to someone official. I just want to meet up, I say. Oh, he replies, he's very flattered to be asked but he really feels it would be better for me to discuss the matter with a spokesperson. There is no 'matter', I reply, I just want to talk. But we've all signed agreements, says Sam, then clicks his tongue against his palate and hangs up. I ring back, but when he answers the phone I hang up on him too. Not revenge. I just can't figure out what to say.

About two I take a couple of hits of Jim Beam, swallow a unisom and fall into an easy sleep on top of my bed. Towards dawn I dream a series of amorphous dreams linked by their atmosphere of ambient threat. At about eight the telephone rings. Some stuffed shirt in the public relations department says he's heard that I contacted Sam.

'These things need to be done through the official channels.' The roof beams begin to click in the heat.

A press pack mysteriously arrives at the same time as the chambermaid. Inside are a few factoid press releases, some xeroxed newspaper articles and a slim booklet about Space Bio-sphere Ventures. I browse through a couple, lose interest and take the first visitor tour beginning at the Orientation Center with its 'environmental art', followed by a supervised gaze in at the window of the Biosphere 'Test Module' and the opportunity to admire the complimentary tram which runs to and from the car park. I drift off and meander over to the Biosphere itself, where a desultory group of men and women sit in a small square of shade waiting for the official Biosphere tour guide to show up. From the Orientation Center, I have discovered precisely one fact – that Biosphere 1 is planet earth, which presumably makes Biosphere 2 the reissued version. A huddle of us collect in the shade and are rewarded eventually by the appearance of an anxious thread of a girl who busies down the pathway with a large black box slung about her hip, beating the box with the flat of her hand, as if it were a recalcitrant child she has grown too used to admonishing. The box, to which a microphone is attached, is careless of its chastisement and misbehaves from the start, puking up feedback, and spitting out white noise. Pretty soon it caves in altogether, which is no great disaster since no-one in particular is listening. They are eating. The skinny tour guide presses on, shouting bravely over the cacophony of fifteen men and women slugging back Coke and tamping down potato chips.

I am trailing behind with my black notebook and a wetted pencil, waiting to catch a few ripe factoids and conduct a little independent research on the side.

Up close, the Biosphere looks remarkably like the new palm house at Kew Gardens near London. Unlike Kew, visitors to the Biosphere have not come to see the palms but the human inmates, the so-called Biosphereans or 'expedition members'. Sadly for the visitors, the human habitation tower is cordoned off. There is absolutely nothing visible of a remotely prurient nature. Whoever heard of such a thing? There are murmurs of significant disquiet. The crowd, bored, overheated, and – crucially – having eaten all their snacks, are spoiling for a little rebellion. The guide tries her luck at mediating through the incipient mutiny by climbing down beyond the cordon and screwing her head to the glass in anticipation of a sighting. After a minute or so she comes up for air and says:

'I seen one, planting crops.'

A shrunken ghost-face appears at the window and peers out briefly, causing the fattest man in the party to raise his eyes from his Coke and comment:

'Looks damned near dead to me.'

'Surprisingly,' counters the tour guide, supposing she has the fattest man's attention, 'each Biospherean has lost on average only fourteen per cent of their original body weight.'

The ghost-face retreats back into a simulated salt marsh behind the glass.

'What d'they eat anyway?' asks a fat woman dressed in pink shorts.

'Well . . .' pipes up the tour guide. Something in her tone alerts pink shorts to the disturbing possibility that she is staring a lecture right in the face, when all she had been expecting was a sound-bite.

'I guess they eat just the same as anyone else,' says pink shorts, cutting the lecture off at the knees.

'Well, you'd be surprised,' perks up the tour guide. Jeez, she must be new on the job.

'Meat?'

The tour guide smiles. Poor creature. So amiable, so anxious to please.

'How'd they kill it?' asks the fat man, sweating luxuriantly.

The tour guide swallows.

'Gross,' says pink shorts.

And for a single moment we tourers are of one triumphant fraternity, basking in the illusion of a common victory.

Ten minutes later, the tour guide disappears into the staff rest rooms with liquefying eyes. A few stragglers hang around with questions but twenty minutes later there is still no sign of her, which leads me to suppose there must be an escape hatch fitted round the back for precisely such awkward moments.

It has become another damned hot day and the nearest air-conditioned space happens to be a movie theatre in the tourist village showing "Meet the Biosphereans". The quotation marks are important. No-one gets to meet the Biosphereans because they are sealed into a giant glass cage but anyone can "Meet the Biosphereans". Not that anyone other than me actually shows up to "Meet the Biosphereans", but they could have done. At the interactive Q and A after the show the projectionist, noticing a certain vacuum in the theatre, skips down the aisle, proffers an agonizing grin and says 'Oh, oh, seems like you've got them to yourself, ask any question you like,' so I say, 'Wha'd they eat anyway?'

Back at the control desk the projectionist presses a button and Sally Silverstone, co-captain Biospherean, appears on the screen and begins to explain how to make a Biospherean pizza, at which point, under cover of the dark, I slink off to my room like a bad cur, lie on my bed with a can of beer from the mini-bar and watch a Tex Avery cartoon on the TV.

That evening I'm feeling lonely so I ask the man next to me in the Biosphere Cafe if he'd mind my joining him. We natter inconsequentially about this and that for a while. He shows me a scorpion under a prickly pear and mesquite pods lying on the desertic soil like dried-up slugs; 'full of protein for the cattle'. He points out a place where the diamondback rattlers come out to snooze in the sun. I tell the story of Ray Lightburn and the sea at Dangriga, and it turns out that the man I'm talking to knows Ray Lightburn, because the man I'm talking to is John Allen, head of the Biosphere's R&D. He's been out to Blackbird Caye.

'That', he says, pointing to a blue peak illuminated by the sinking sun 'is where Carlos Castaneda found himself.' Allen loves the Sonora. He likes to think of it as the desert-lovers' desert, a man's man's desert. Allen mentions the Biosphere – only to say that it is a gesture that will grow into inventions and gadgets and information, and, eventually, to the human colonization of the universe. I am briefly troubled that a man so wedded to his environment should long to occupy another, but the thought soon leaves me, replaced by admiration for the man's ambitions. We talk on through books and travels, winding skeins of conversation. At about seven the sun strikes a silver lozenge on Allen's bolo tie and projects an orange halo around his face. For those couple of seconds John Allen turns to look directly into the sun and smiles. And then he says, 'So you're one of those indomitable British traveller women.' That really gets me.

A few weeks later I stumble on a paper written by Allen and shelved away in the library at Arcosanti, an experimental ecological community built on the desert uplands north of Phoenix. I take the paper out and read it, for no other reason than a general curiosity. About himself, John Allen writes:

> I acted many roles to avoid creating a personality and by 1962 I was up to four distinct lives a day in Manhattan: a global technocrat, a Village writer working on the 'Great American Novel,' a hip adventurer and a revolutionary. By mid-1963 I added a fifth, an entrepreneur in high-tech and energy corporations and somehow, innerly, everything came to a stop.

It seems he was known as Johnny Dolphin then, or perhaps that was just his *nom de plume*. In any case, the man who is or was John Allen or Johnny Dolphin went off to Tangier and meditated himself out of his fix – a not wholly original activity in the late sixties. Later, towards the tail end of that decade, he put himself 'into the hands of magician shamans', somewhere in Latin America, and lived on strange herbs and his own mythology.

We are twenty-five years on and Johnny Dolphin now heads R&D at one of the most grandiose scientific longshots in history. How'd he get there?

According to his own testimony he 'perceived intimations of a Planetary Mind' around 1967, which he took to be the call of the Noösphere, a mystical realm apparently combining nature and technology in perfect balance. But this was not all that happened, for he also had a premonition 'that the contours of a newer and mightier Mind are beginning to appear. I call it the Solar Mind – it's the Mind capable of foreseeing the evolution of the entire solar system and making provision for the integrated operation of Culture, Life, Matter and Energy on that extraordinary scale.'

He came to the conclusion that the future of humankind lay elsewhere. John Allen began to believe in getting off.

That night at Arcosanti I am lying in bed watching the stars in the Arizona sky, thinking about the ghostly face peering through the half-light from inside Biosphere 2. If the earth must crumble into a poisoned miasmic shell, then I want to crumble with it. Rather that than be shut into a sterile pod and blasted into space to live a simulation of a life on some boiling sulphuric planet. Next morning, driving away from Arcosanti I recall the feel of the thick grey air over the pale brown sea at Dangriga, and I recall the coral sun creeping along the Canyon del Oro and by the time I have reached the freeway I have formed the conclusion that Ray Lightburn, John Allen and their like are prophets of doom, and that, god knows, those are the kind of prophets we least need.

There's a Seeker Born
Every Minute

'Everything you are, except hydrogen, is made of
stars.'

Very Large Array Telescope Visitor Center,
Datil, New Mexico

Polarized light drops silver contours around the rows of date
palms. The dimming sun over Camelback Mountain is bloody
with colour. A Latter-Day Saints temple across the street dissolves into gobbets of rosy haze. It's magic hour in Mesa, Arizona, and I'm in a terrible mood. The mood stole up on me a
couple of days ago. I don't know why it's with me, nor how to
make it go. For the time being we are reluctant fellows. An
endless stream of inner witterings has kept me awake at night,
invading my dreams, tick tick ticking over breakfast. Cheerios,
toast, black coffee. Black. Coffee. And the time is . . . sugar,
sugar and milk. Nip nip nip. Buzzzzzz. Noyz noyz noyz. Tune
out, turn off, drop dead. A terrible, terrible mood.

I'm sitting in the Paradise Cafe reading *Arizona Light*, the
state's premier New Age freesheet. One item catches my attention, an article on the back page about the rise in reported alien
abductions. The article tells the story of a Sedona woman who
claims her foetus was taken from her by some unknown thing
when she was out walking in Secret Canyon near Sedona. It was
an overcast day, but she noticed a very bright light through the
trees, almost as if a shaft of brilliant metal were being lowered
to the ground. After watching it for a while she began to feel
she was locked in some strange form of time warp. Alarmed she
turned back towards the mouth of the canyon, but however hard

she walked, the scene around her remained unchanged. She could hear her own breathing as if it were the breath of a giant. She woke some hours or minutes later lying on the path with a peculiar feeling of emptiness, a little bruised, but otherwise ostensibly none the worse for wear. On a routine visit to her doctor she discovered she was no longer pregnant. Aliens had taken her child, and implanted a chip in her brain to ensure she would never recall in detail what had happened to her.

'Hi.' A woman in beads puts her glass of juice down on my table. She glances at the copy of *Arizona Light*. 'Heading to Sedona?' Sedona is to Arizona what Santa Fe is to New Mexico, only more so. There are more New Agers in Sedona than in the whole of the rest of America, bar Santa Cruz and Sausalito, California.

'Driving?' Her hair smells of Revlon Musk.

'Hmmm.' I feign indifference in the hope she'll have the grace to leave me be.

'Going up tomorrow?'

A minute ago I had no plans. Now it seems as though the plans have come to me.

'Like to share a ride?' She sits down in the chair opposite and begins sipping her juice.

'Uh . . .'

'Great, nine o'clock outside here?'

Nine o'clock it is then.

Nine o'clock sharp the next morning, the woman in beads looks as though she's already been up hours. Caboose and I, on the other hand, are not good in the mornings. I am generally in a foul temper of one kind or another before ten and Caboose requires consideration until its engine has been running a while. Today it can barely cough up sufficient horsepower to get us past the University and on to the Paradise Cafe, even though I've had the decency to fill it up with super unleaded. The ingrate has also switched on one of its warning lights, the one with a picture of a triangle on it. Damned if I have the least clue what that means. Less troublesome to ignore it.

Half an hour on the road and it becomes clear that the woman in beads has two modes of conversation: interrogative and mystical.

'You been to Sedona before?'

I shake my head.

'Sedona is the most magical, powerful place in the world.'

'Uh-huh.'

'After Lhasa. Have you been to Tibet?'

I shake my head

'One of the most amazing experiences of my *life*. And the monks have been put down and suppressed. Like, you must go. You English?'

And so on. Eventually I ask her to read to me from my guidebook.

Sedona, Arizona is an isolated miniature sprawl in the upland Arizona desert, trapped picturesquely between scarlet, high-walled bluffs and the sky. Beyond Sedona the Colorado Plateau runs as far as the Utah mountains three hundred miles to the north. Between its southern most edge and Manti, Utah is a natural Maginot Line of trenches cut from rock by the Colorado River, the greatest and most splendid of which is the Grand Canyon. The region's brilliant red buttes and monumental rocks have long been valued by Hollywood directors and location managers looking for backdrops to western shoot-outs. More recently, crowds have begun to migrate north in summer to the cooler uplands of Sedona and Oak Creek Canyon from Phoenix and the Sonora desert. And for those on a higher spiritual and mental plane Sedona, Arizona, also happens to be the New Age capital of the United States.

JUST WHO WERE YOU IN YOUR PAST LIVES?

New Agers began turning up in Sedona some time in the seventies, drawn by the apparent discovery of power 'vortices' in among the rocks. These spots, not visible to the eye, were proclaimed to be centres of great electrical and magnetic energy, capable of producing minor miracles. The word spread and a remote little town, which was once nothing more than a thirsty farming outpost of the Verde Valley, rapidly gained its current reputation as a curative mecca for victims of chronic post-sixties syndrome. Sedona became an Oz, geographically and symbolically speaking; an oasis of colour and cool and metaphor in the immense desert Kansases to the south and east. What Mount Rushmore is to the spirit of democracy, Red Rock country is to the universal spirit, the cosmic all, the divine within. In August 1988 thousands of New Agers met in Sedona over a weekend with the avowed aim of activating the power of the vortices and lifting the planet to a new level of consciousness, a level without war, or hunger or brutality. For the three days of the Harmonic Convergence they held hands and hugged and chanted and banged out New Age rhythms on drums.

The woman with musky hair puts down my guidebook.

'Then, only a year after the Harmonic Convergence, communism fell,' she concludes, adding

'Well, thanks for the ride,' as we draw into Sedona. She topples out of Caboose beads first, then pokes her head with its musky hair back inside. 'You should get that dash light fixed. See you around, maybe?' No, I'm thinking, you will not. I am still in a terrible mood.

> ## MAKE A QUANTUM LEAP IN YOUR
> ## CONSCIOUSNESS TODAY!

I find a room to rent with a sofa bed, the use of the refrigerator and a shelf in the bathroom out in West Sedona at Sakina Bluestar's place on Pinon Jay Drive. Sakina is not my first choice. My first choice is Dionne, who comes with the recommendation of the cashier at the New Age Drop-in Center. Dionne wants to know if I chant loudly, smoke alien substances or have Virgo in my ascendant. I admit to the alien substances, but am happy to say that Sagittarius is my ascendant. Dionne finds that her spare room is booked after all. So I throw in my lot with a woman called Sakina, who thinks she's an alien, and her lodger Santara, who thinks she's an angel, and a man named Solar who lives in a van parked out in the yard. Sakina Bluestar, without whom this chapter would not have been written, is dedicated to Sedona's mysterious energies. They notified her one evening about ten years ago that she was to give herself up to the Great Spirit.

One of Sakina's most pleasing characteristics is that she makes absolutely no apologies for herself. She accepts she has unusual tastes and asks you to take her as you find her. For example, she has a taste for Barbie dolls and has made a large collection of them. Several dozen blonde Barbies, brunette Barbies, Kens and Sams make her house their home. Some are dressed as mermaids and mermen, others as hippies and cosmic adventurers, but they are all, according to Sakina, first and foremost spirit people, walking spiritual paths, with needs, desires and disappointments like our own.

'They keep me company,' she says, showing me to my room.

Throughout the spring and summer Sakina takes in lodgers like me so that she can afford to head off to California in the autumn and set up psychic workshops.

The room she has to offer is airless and hot, but the light comes in all day, so with a breeze it could almost be pleasant. An old chromium blade fan sits broken in one corner, behind a bookcase. Along the window ledge are a few pictures of Sakina and postcards of the theosophical Ascended Masters done out in lurid colours like Catholic devotional pictures – St Germain, Buddha, Jesus, a woman in white grecian robes, whose profile is hand-labelled in pen underneath, 'The Lady Cavendish'. A photogravure of Byron in Turkish costume sits on its side in a cheap frame between the window ledge and a little table.

Nota bene: if this were a work of fiction you might not believe in Sakina and her friends, but I lived among them and I am simply reporting what I saw. That it is bizarre is undeniable, but then, at the time I had only an occasional sense of just how strange my circumstances were. I don't think anyone is immune to implausible beliefs, however rational and wilful they think themselves to be. It is an easy matter to deny everything you thought you knew and to believe its contradiction rather than to live out your days in bottomless isolation. Only the most rare of individuals will stand up for a belief when all around are declaring its opposite, for most of us feel more anxious to be at ease with each other than we do with ourselves.

A mechanic in a mom-and-pop garage next to the Circle K in West Sedona says that it will take a while to fix Caboose's angry flashing dashboard triangle and cost $150. Since I have not yet eaten I wander over to a restaurant and order the once-through, self-serve salad bar. There is a trick to maximizing the pile of food you can fit on the plate. I can't quite recall how I learned it, only that it is one of those little pieces of informational camaraderie that get passed around among impoverished travellers. The salad bar proprietor, his eye set to turning a profit, puts all the space-taking lettuce and ancient potato salad and so on at the *beginning* of the bar, and all the expensive ingredients such as meats at the *end*, in the hope that you will pile your plate up high with trash before hitting the pastrami. Bearing that single fact in mind it is easily possible to make two days' meals from a single walk through, by first constructing a plate extension using celery and carrot sticks on the cantilever principle then stabilizing it by gluing the bits of carrot down with mayo and weighting the ends with cherry tomatoes. You pile the plate, starting with potatoes, pasta and so forth and following with fruits and vegetables which will stick onto the mayonnaise in the pasta and heap up nicely. Having eaten as much as you are able, you ask for a doggie bag. This is the part when all may be lost, for if your waitperson snitches on you the manager will kick up an unseemly fuss and throw you out, which is what happens to me.

The mechanic, meanwhile, has successfully completed the toilsome job of fixing one wire to another and has pocketed my $150. Every flea has another flea upon its back to bite it.

WHAT ARE YOU WAITING FOR?
YOU CAN BE AN AVATAR RIGHT NOW!

Later that afternoon Sakina Bluestar, clad in full Lakota Sioux ceremonial outfit, runs a dusting feather along the Barbie and Ken vacation van and tickles the breakfast bar at Pinon Jay Drive. 'There just isn't the time to do it all,' she repeats as she goes. It seems churlish not to offer to help, since I have nothing in particular to do, but Sakina will not countenance it.

'Dear, that's so sweet,' she says, 'but the spirits of my things always kick up a fuss if I don't attend to them myself,' smiles affectionately and waves a castigating finger at a Ken who has fallen out of his seat. Sakina has so very many things of a spiritual nature it is hard to imagine quite when she gets the time to attend to all their needs. Over the fake fireplace there hangs a collection of Hopi dream catchers. Crystals sit on every shelf and in every corner. In one alcove is a kachina doll, in another a life-sized statue of Captain James T. Kirk; between the two, sage smudge sticks, mystic texts, relicry, feather headdresses, stylized portraits of Geronimo and other Indian heroes, spirit guide portraits and talismen and spiritual videos and exotic shells containing cosmic messages and every other sort of New Age gizmo. Strangely, though, Sakina is no materialist. She is proud of her collections in the way that children are proud of their gatherings of beach pebbles, not because they have any intrinsic value or are signifiers of intent, but because they are small comfits of personality.

'Are you an extraterrestrial dear?' she asks, later. A little forward for our first day together, but then this is America.

'I don't think so.'

'Ah, that's probably why they won't talk to you,' pointing to the silent Barbie population. 'Never mind. It's all just chitter chatter really.'

'Are you?'

'Of course. Most people in Sedona are.'

In Sakina's kitchen, germinated herbal tea bags (used) hang from an empty bottle of Ivory soap. There is a mystic chopping board which emanates ultra low-frequency signals and protects your carrots and other chopped items from psychic attack. One of the gas rings fires in a semi-circle, the others are dead. In general Sakina recommends enchilada with sour cream and guacamole down at the Copper Kettle on Highway 89A, '$3.89, comes with biscuits, you won't need another thing all day' but she goes there less and less herself on account of the dwindling of her star guide business.

'We had this perfect house in Cape Cod, overlooking the sea, but Philip went into the spirit world and I got out and moved west, thought I would get to San Diego. Never made it,' she says of a life long gone. I'm reminded of a fallen sign in the backyard, partially covered by a stone, which reads 'Philip Comyns, Medical Practitioner,' followed by a series of letters in peeling gold leaf.

'It was a big house, much fancier than this, and he was a dear man, but a Jew, you know, and nobody liked that much on the Cape.'

Sakina collects up the debris of last night's take-out sandwich and flings it out of the window. Armed with a new name in a new town, Sakina started up a business selling pastel portraits of people's celestial guides and channelling their messages. Then she met Randy, who became her second husband.

'But they wanted him back in the spirit world too,' she adds, cleaning the fingernails on her left hand with her right thumbnail. There's not much left that can be said. We sit in silence while the day begins its descent.

Eventually Sakina raises her finger to her mouth and says 'You know dear, Randy's insides got all screwed up. He went to the hospital, he was in a coma for a while and then when he came back he was a starman called Zordache. Randy had gone already. You should have seen it. Zordache had terrible trouble walking in Randy's body. He had no idea how to do some of the most ordinary things. I knew it wasn't Randy, even though it looked like him.'

'I'm not so sure I understand'.

'Randy was called away, like I said. You know, it often happens that way. Zordache recognized things, like Randy's guitar, so he still had Randy's memory banks. But then, after three months, Zordache left and Randy's body just died.'

About eight a brown Honda edges into the drive, the door opens, and an enormous blonde woman dressed in a black catsuit levers herself onto the concrete.

'Oh good,' says Sakina, 'Santara's back. You'll enjoy each other.'

Santara takes a while to wheeze her way up the steps, then another while to recover her breath. She has a smile of rare grace. In her left hand is a quart-sized insulated cold drink dispenser, in her right a book about Sedona's power vortices.

'Hi, I knew someone else would come,' she pants, putting her arms around my head in a misplaced hug. Then, turning to Sakina, 'Wow. They're so strong. I feel like I know why I was called here.'

'Where did you go? Bell Rock?' Santara shakes her head; 'Uh-uh, up to Airport Mesa? You know, I'm not so good at climbing, so I have to go where it's accessible by car.'

'Pity, the Bell Rock vortex is so powerful. Still if you felt it at Airport Mesa that's good. Most people say they get disturbed by the sound of the planes landing.'

Santara needs to take a shower, meditate and go to bed. She asks Sakina to say hi to Solar when he gets back from Cottonwood, and she tells me we'll have a chat in the morning. She says not to expect her up too early.

Four hours later, I am lying on the sofa bed in my room listening to Santara chanting her mantra through the wall. I think it's 'slalom' or 'salem'. It's not just 'om' anyway. I thought it was *always* 'om'. Eventually the chanting gives way to leaden snores, the kind that interrupt the perpetrator's breathing. I grope around in the dark for some foam ear plugs, which have no impact on the noise whatsoever. Two unisom later the snores begin to slip away into a dizzy buzz and I am suddenly at the centre of a surreal submarine. I have reached the point where I can hear the sound of my own anxiety. But I still can't sleep.

After about half an hour I drag myself out of bed and creep onto the porch. Outside the breeze is soft and comfortless. Crickets throb in place of Santara's snores. I stub my toe on a Barbie van and retreat back into the living room. An oxidized light bleaches the sofa to a thin ghost. Beside it, on a coffee table piled with copies of New Age magazines, is the telephone. I think of all the people I might ring and feel bereft and dismal. Either it's the middle of the night for them, too, or it will cost me two dollars a minute. I pick on Fergus in New York. He comes to the phone after fifteen rings and sounds a little edgy, as though he's expecting some bad news.

'It's really late, it's two hours in front here for godssakes.'

'Sorry, Fergus but I can't sleep. I'm feeling scared.'

'Christ, it's nearly *morning*.'

'I'm staying with this woman who thinks she's an alien and talks to Barbie dolls.'

'You can always leave, can't you?'

'I suppose, only I'm frightened I might get sucked in. I mean, she's *nice* and *sad*.'

Fergus scoffs.

'I don't think it's likely.'

'Will you call a couple of times a week and make sure I'm still my usual self? If I start talking rubbish get on a plane, or . . . or call my mother, at least.'

A weary moan slides down the airwaves at precisely the speed of sound and pops my right ear.

'I'm hundreds of miles away, for godssakes. Look, I'll give you the number of my therapist, and if you wake up one morning with one eye and little green feelers then you can give him a call and talk it through. I'll have him put it on my Amex. You can't phase him. He's a New Yorker.'

Sakina has many friends, most of them Indians, although Sakina herself is anglo-saxon, with family still in England. One of her few non-Indian friends is Connie, otherwise known as Shirley. After Randy died, Sakina and Connie took off travelling for a year in a deadbeat RV with no sink. Sakina spent what remained of her Cape Cod savings on keeping body and soul together, and she laundered away her memories. The money ran out before the memories, so the couple returned to Sedona, and Connie now lives in a caravan at the back of Sakina's house with a kitten on a lead called Tom. Sometime soon, Connie is headed back to her roots on the Texas-Arkansas border, if she can persuade her ex-old man to stump up the gas money. She has been cash-poor for some years on account of the Great Spirit telling her in a dream that she was not destined for wage labour, so she lives off what she can call in from friends and blag from strangers.

The days pass slowly at Pinon Jay Drive. Morning segues into afternoon closes into evening. Weeks slip into one another noiselessly, like eggs broken over a cup. Routine is sacrosanct in Sakina's household, even though it consists for the most part in inactivity. I pass my days reading and walking. Usually I take lunch in the Copper Kettle and return to my room to wait out the worst heat of the day. Without habit, the whole place and those in it would fall apart. We have intuitively agreed to become an institution, bound by unspoken rules but otherwise separate and alone. From seven to nine every evening, Connie takes what she calls 'talk time', emerging from her caravan in the front yard with Tom and a little reefer. Tom lays on her lap, nonplussed by the bats and spiders which make use of the porch overhang while Connie puffs and talks, about the Great Spirit and returning to Arkansas, mainly. About one evening in three she rises and gestures with her eyebrows, which is my cue to accompany her to a place more distant so that she can tell me in whispers the things she knows. One of these times she says:

'All this fuss about dinosaurs, *Jurassic Park*, and so forth, I have heard that it's a way to get the kids used to the sight of them before the invasion.'

'So they won't resist?'

'Precisely'.

'Hang, on, just to get it clear in my head,' I say, 'who are *they*? What invasion?'

'The Reptilians. From one of the Orion planets. In any case, it's just something I hear.' She pauses and looks about. 'Listen, they spent forty million promoting that movie. It was all over, the Philippines, everywhere. *Forty million bucks.* There has to be some kind of reason. Think about it.'

She bends down as if to cover her tracks and baffles the sand, making desultory heaps in a circle.

'Unless we all learn to walk in the light, we won't keep them out. The light will save us.'

And with that we stroll back west, towards a bruised cloud hanging in the sunset over Chimney Rock.

Nights are strange in upland Arizona. The sunsets begin vermilion red and end as navy blue, like deoxygenating flesh, and the clouds remain visible throughout the night, even when the sky between is blacker than a new chalk board. What gives the clouds their light, and denies it to the interstitial spaces? The nights are strange.

I leave a message for Santara in the morning to say I'll be out hiking all day, but asking her to meet me at 7pm for dinner. Then I walk out south to Bell Rock, sit in the breeze with my palms turned upward and try to feel the vortex beneath. A Japanese man lies below me on a ledge, completely motionless, his skin as coppered as the rock. I feel quite lost in peace, watching the cloud shade scudding across the Verde Valley below Bell Rock and the ravens stretching into the morning air currents, feeling the powdered rock heating up before the flat bluffs beneath it. The Japanese man rises to leave. He begins to corkscrew down and out of sight. I am disquieted and anxious.

'Hey!' No response.

By this point in my life I should have the guts to admit I'm uneasy with myself, but I haven't. Picking up my things, I follow the invisible Japanese man back down towards the valley.

By five I've done enough walking, taken two rolls of rock pictures and am ready for a drink. There is no-one in at Pinon Jay Drive, so I'm off down Mule Deer Road, turning left at the bottom by the Circle K and swinging into the car park at the Copper Kettle. Happy Hour Bloody Mary in one hand, $2.75 in change in the other. Tip the change into the phone box.

The operator says she'll have to put me through to a long distance carrier. Which would I like?

'Oh, any,' I reply with my eyes on the TV at the bar: *Dr Quinn, Medicine Woman.*

She tells me I have to specify.

'OK, which one's the cheapest?'

She's sorry, she doesn't have that information. OK, I say, put me through to AT&T. 'Thank you for using Western Bell, we appreciate your custom,' she says. 'Western Bell' reaches me as the echo of a voice already disengaged. The AT&T operator asks if I have a US billing address. No, I don't, I'm a foreigner. They can do me a visitors' credit card. It's sixty cents per minute. I ask her to put me through to the operator.

'Which?'

'The cheapest.'

She does not have that information. Come on, I say, you must know if AT&T is cheaper than Sprint, you *work* for them. No, she does not have that information. So I ask for a list of operators from which to choose. She does not have that information. Eventually, we agree that she should probably put me through to the AT&T long-distance division. She says 'Thank you for using AT&T, we appreciate your business' and the long-distance operator says 'Thank you for using AT&T, we appreciate . . .' and then some automated person begins to insist that I put in another dollar, which I do not have. I get through to Fergus long enough to blurt my number and hope he's got a pencil near the phone. The phone rings.

'*You*,' says Fergus, 'Don't they have pay phones in England?'

I want to reply 'Yeah, they do, but we're so backward and inefficient that you get straight through to the person you're trying to reach, and no-one spends your money telling you how much they appreciate your business,' but I keep mum. You have to be careful, even with friends, because culture is like blood; it runs thicker and deeper than water.

'Ferg, do you think that Steven Spielberg is an alien?'

'You mean, it might explain *Close Encounters*?'

'Well, you know, supposing it was autobiographical, with Spielberg as the Encounter?'

'Did you ring that therapist's number?'

I begin to cry without reason. I suppose I'm low. I'm not even the right kind of low for uppers. It's either the Bloody Mary or something in the air. Tears do not affect Fergus. At least, he doesn't let them bother him.

'Sorry Ferg, the temperature hit 108 today. I'm not depressed, just you know, listless.'

'Why?'

'I don't know, I feel uncomfortable.'

'He couldn't be an alien for godsakes, or he'd have taken the money back to Mars.'

'Who?'

'Spielberg.'

'Oh, yeah? How do you know?' I ask, brightening.

'Tax haven. They say that if you look carefully at Mars you'll see the mark of a human face on it, you know. What does *that* tell you, eh?'

Good old Fergus. I do love him.

Santara appears at 7.00, looking fragile. In this heat it is a categorical imperative of hers to eat her weight in ice cream; she says she's so prone to overheating that ice cream is the only thing coming between her and the county morgue. At the age of twenty-nine she discovered that she was an angel, and that all those vague, uncertain longings her therapist never cured were the result of being stuck in the wrong body in the wrong place with the wrong life. Sometimes she catches sight of her wings in the mirror but she has never been able to make them fly. One time she tried they put her in a hospital and fed her daytime television and little yellow pills. You know, if Santara *is* an angel (and I don't see I've got the right to say she's not) then the time has come for a redefinition of the word, for Santara favours black attire, is only blonde because she tries and cannot play the harp. Under the current definition it's difficult to know quite where to place her.

Back in LA things were different for Santara. There was air conditioning everywhere and sea breezes and a thousand flavours of frozen yoghurt and she was happy sometimes.

'I escaped from a dysfunctional love affair,' she begins as the waitress arrives with Rocky Road (two scoops), Double Chocolate Cookie Crumble (two scoops), Pecan Almond with Swiss Chocolate Ripple (one scoop), whipped cream and two spoons. Santara holds one out to me.

'Uh-nunh, thanks, I don't do chocolate much. Maybe some whipped cream. Mind if I dunk?'

'Go ahead.'

'You know,' I find myself saying, 'People say that you can't run away from things forever, but it's not true; it's something therapists tell you to keep them in work and parents and lovers tell you to avoid the pain of rejection. Sometimes you can leave and just keep on going. The things, whatever they are, never catch up.'

'Oh, I'll head back to LA in the end, but I have work to do here.' She shrugs her shoulders. 'It's just, like, there's so much I miss already. Spirit has something big in mind for me.'

'Like what?'

'Like you know, really knowing who I am, honouring the angel thing. Don't you ever feel that, you know, like, you just want to be sure?'

'Of course.'

'Doesn't Spirit send you messages?'

I look up from my whipped cream.

'Yeah, I suppose, but I don't ever expect to discover what they are, or what it is, or anything.'

'Chocolate has the same chemical in as an orgasm, I read it. Serotonin. Weird, huh?'

'Which is better?' At that moment I can't remember.

'An orgasm, I guess, but you can get chocolate any place.'

Santara is trying for the impossible – a job in Sedona that is not cleaning or waitressing and pays more than minimum wage. She applied to be a tour guide for a jeep rental company when she first arrived but they told her that there were ninety applicants and that she wouldn't fit in the jeep. Back in LA Santara was promised administrative work with the Ashtar Command

Ascension Activation and Christ Healing Center, world HQ, Sedona, Arizona, but by the time Santara arrived in Sedona, the job offer had disappeared.

She thinks it's too hot to live in the house any more and she's upset that Sakina won't turn on the swamp cooler. Doesn't she suffer from the heat? I tell her I think Sakina's done enough suffering, and she's just squared her jaw, dried her eyes and decided not to do any more. I ask her if she really believes that Randy turned into a starman and she replies that she's never heard it happen to anyone else, but she knows enough about things to be sure that anything is possible. She thinks that Connie might have some weed. That's got to be right, I reply, about anything being possible, except people rising from the dead. Death is final, I say, and Santara agrees, but adds that I seem to have forgotten about reincarnation.

Connie isn't in her trailer, so we kidnap poor little Tom and carry him a hundred yards or so out into the sagebrush and watch him playing with the night beetles. Life blooms on the rocks in the empty hours. Even where the topsoil gives up single-celled plants grow as a verditer crust on nuggets of flaky streusel stone. If left undisturbed, the plants will break down the stones into topsoil. Santara and Tom and I wander out a half-mile or so, and have to direct ourselves back by the position of the moon, which lies slumped in a lurid smear over the porch overhang at Pinon Jay Drive like one of Dali's clocks.

Tom catches sight of Connie before we do, claws his way from my arms and runs towards the red and yellow circle of her reefer. Solar, the man who lives in the driveway emerges from the front door with a T-shirt and a towel around his belly. Holding out his hands to Santara he strokes her hair behind her ears, his eyes straining to catch sight of something moving on the road outside. She begins to shake.

'It's this simple,' he says. 'Love yourself because you are perfect. Every one of us is perfect. Don't even consider tomorrow. Live in the moment. It's all taken care of. Whenever you need something, just visualize it.'

'I don't feel perfect,' replies Santara, eyes clouding with tears.

He stops her lips with a finger. 'Me is or I am?' His voice is almost indistinguishable from the sounds of the night.

'I am,' mouths Santara, smiling.

'Always remember,' says Solar, 'that nothing matters. You can affect nothing in this world, you have no responsibilities, except to live in the moment.'

'You're right,' says Santara. 'You're just always right.'

According to Santara, Solar was Napoleon in a past life and before that he was Merlin and an unspecified emperor of Rome. Evidently, other lives leave their impressions.

'Sometimes it just doesn't feel that easy to me. I guess I'm not meditating enough.'

'Yeah,' says Connie, 'Too much thinking is a psychological condition.'

After solstice, I have decided to move along. Sedona is an unlovely little town, a brand on the rocks around it. The west sprawls along the 89A out towards Prescott, a mess of shopping malls and tract homes like any other desert strip, while uptown has been given over to the kind of booster tourism so beloved of bureaux of commerce in one-horse western towns which are themselves unremarkable but have the good luck to be prettily set. The rubrick includes packing two hundred yards of false-fronted, western-style boardwalk stores with cheerful miscellanea, providing easy access to a few selected beauty spots connected conveniently to this commercial district, inventing a couple of heritage spots, and throwing in an art gallery or two to attract the high earners. There you have a viable small-town economy providing sufficient minimum-wage jobs to prevent its population from turning their backs and heading for the nearest metropolis.

Contrary to my expectations the solstice creeps up on Sedona almost unnoticed. In the New Age Drop-in Center they have received details of only one event – an all-night drumming session up on Airport Vortex, led by two incomers from California who are asking for a $15 per head 'love donation'. Some days previously, Sakina had promised to provide an unforgettable solstice. She did not reveal what she had in mind, but I'm confident that it was not the all-night Californian drumming fest. Still, no plans are evident by lunchtime when she and Connie return jubilant from a workshop on Philippine psychic surgery.

'The surgeon messed around with this guy's auric field and there was all this gore, like red ectoplasm,' thrills Connie, spooning up a Basha's lime jello salad for her lunch. 'He also operates telepathically, with similar results.'

'I think I may have a problem with my duodenum, like that guy in the video,' muses Sakina. She envisages a time when the entire health industry will be controlled by the will of aliens conducting psychic surgery from Venus. Connie says 'You can operate psychically with success for the common cold.' Sakina contemplates this for a moment.

'How much would a cheap rate call to the Philippines cost, approximately?' she asks, then turning to me, 'Be back for seven. Don't forget, dear.'

At the crossroads separating uptown from West Sedona, beyond the last ice cream store, there is a path which disappears into a knot of feathery mesquite and cottonwoods and continues along the inside of a drainage tunnel running under the 89A highway. Where the tunnel opens, the earth breaks down to mud and slopes into a silent green pool, fringed around with cottonwoods and rushes. I've been there a couple of times during the afternoon. Today a water bird shrieks up into the piñon pine at the far edge. The water itself is frigid and thin in places where the sink holes lie, but warm and soupy in the shallower reaches. I float naked on my back, until the sun begins to stretch my eyelids and the water bird returns to feed.

At 6.45 Santara's Babemobile rolls up into the yard at Pinon Jay Drive and out rolls Santara in a purple catsuit, looking flushed.

'There's a portal, get in the car.' We motor out past the Chapel of the Holy Cross as far as a sign to Back O'Beyond then on to an unpaved road and just behind Cathedral Rock, there it is, splitting the clouds, a smudge of shifting pinks and blues rising like a mushroom from a hole in the sky, a sunbar, the kind of visual bomb that leaves an indelible fallout on the inner eye. The Hopi say that the sky is a shell and their ancestors entered this world through a space in the clouds of another, less colourful place.

'It's a sign that they're coming to take me back, you can say what you like. I belong with the angels,' says Santara in maudlin tone, easing herself back into Babemobile.

Something tells me it is time to ring that therapist in New York City.

'Fergus? Oh, yeah, he told me about you.' Bad beginning.

'It's just that I'm living with this woman who thinks she's an angel.'

'Yeah . . . ?' asks the therapist, expecting me to continue the story and not realizing that I've just hit the punch line.

'Well, she thinks she's an angel, and it gets to me.'

'How does it get to you?' Therapists, all damned questions, questions. Never any answers.

'Let me ask you something. What makes you think she isn't an angel?'

'But that's the point. That's just it. I know *she* thinks she's an angel, and I'm sure I'm not, but I've thought about it and I've come to the conclusion that there's no way of knowing that she isn't. I mean, there is no way, is there?'

'What if she were symbolically an angel. What if the angel were her inner child? Would that help?'

I think about this for a second or two, and then I realize the conversation is hopeless because it's headed straight for some mawkish little episode in my childhood that I haven't given a thought to in twenty-five years and I'm thinking existentially.

'No, that would make it worse.' We end the conversation amicably enough and the therapist adds a few more numbers to Fergus's account.

Remembering Sakina's promise I have prepared my nature-goddess within for a druidic solstice ceremony of naked Wiccan dancing and intriguing mushrooms. I am to be disappointed. Among New Agers, as in the wider population, there are those who do and those who don't, *ingénues* and recidivists. While some contentedly fill their days honouring their interior children and giving birth to drums others pass the time in ritual toad-sacrifice and group sex. A proportion regularly leave the planet altogether, having ascended to a higher plane. Among these will eventually be the entire weirdo congregation of the Ashtar Command Ascension Activation and Christ Healing Center, which is where the residents, lodgers and pets of Pinon Jay Drive are headed for their solstice celebrations.

Arriving late at the Center (a suburban home on the edge of town), Santara and Sakina take up places on the sofa at the far end of the room, leaving me in the company of a single woman, quite mute and possibly a little mad. Still, she's smiling.

Commander Lady Athena, the Center's guiding presence is beginning the introductory remarks as we settle ourselves. 'Welcome starseeds,' she says, 'Are we ready for the song?'

Commander Lady Athena Ashtar-Athena of the Ashtar Command Ascension Activation and Christ Healing Center, or ACAACHC, preceeds to strum upon a two-stringed lyre. Ashtar, it should be explained, is an Ascended Master, which means that he has risen to a higher plane of consciousness than our own, lives in a mothership and supervises our lowly comings and goings from a position of literal and spiritual elevation. His channelling vessel Athena is, without doubt, a captivatingly beautiful woman, possessed of china-blue eyes, thin, imperially-arched eyebrows and skin of poetic luminescence. She is costumed in a boudoir robe of lavender crêpe de chine left partly open, and partly covered by a chiffon pelisse the colour of a blush. Without doubt Lady Athena is spectacle enough. We are already in her thrall. No matter that she cannot sing in tune, for the ACAACHC's signature theme seems to fall from her mouth in a single silken motion:

> We are the Eagles of the Ashtar Command
> (*response*: Yes, we are the Eagles)
> We are the Commanders of the Ashtar Command
> We are the Space People
> (We are the people from space)

We have come to follow our path
We have come to see through the Plan
Then we'll go back to the ships
(We long to go back to the ships)
We are the Eagles of the Ashtar Command
(Yes, we are the Eagles)
We are the Commanders of the Ashtar Command
We are the Space People
(We are the people from space)

'You are all that is and that which is the all and the eternity is also you. Do not heed the voices of others for you have come for that which you must do, and what you must do is that which your heart tells you is the path,' says Athena.

This is more fun than girl-guide camp.

Athena channels Commander Ashtar by closing her eyes, twitching and waiting for the Ascended One's spirit to come to her. Fortunately for his audience Ashtar is always remarkably punctual in this respect.

'Ha,' says Athena in Ashtar's voice, raising a blanched hand to her forehead.

'Ashtar speaks through his beloved Athena, and wishes to know if you are well. You have questions?'

A smothering silence before Sakina makes the first contribution.

'Will my journey be the right one?'

Illuminatus Ashtar nods in consideration of his tiny starseed Sakina. Oh Melchior. Oh Solomon. Oh Periander.

'The itinerary is indeed correct.'

A second or two passes, then Sakina's voice again, a full octave higher and rather too loud for the room.

'But I don't *have* an itinerary.'

'Ah, but I can see the direction you will take.'

'It could be anywhere,' says Sakina, brow creased.

'To the south, my little starseed.'

A deathly pause precedes a sudden anguished howl.

'SOUTH, why would I go SOUTH? South is MEXICO. I've

67

never even BEEN to Mexico, I don't LIKE Mexico. I don't speak SPANISH.'

'The direction will come to you.'

'Couldn't it be north?'

'Uh, you must know it for yourself,' replies Ashtar, a little shaken.

'Now I'm confused.'

'In the midst of confusion there is light' Ashtar recovers his (or her) composure. 'Focus on the white light, my Eagle. Soar above the third dimension and you shall see. Oh, once all was clouds, now all is clear. Ashtar has spoken. I say to you that your purpose on this earth is to assist in the ascension of the planet to a higher dimension, that which is the dimension of love and healing. For the time is near, and when it comes, the unenlightened will be carried to a distant planet. In order to work with the Divine Plan you may be forced to leave your home, discard old friends and family, travel around. All this and more may come about. That which is is as it must be, for you cannot resist the Plan, you can only be drawn along in the divinity of its light. Ashtar has spoken.'

Ashtar sneaks a look at Athena's watch, shuts his/her eyes, begins to shiver and falls seemingly into a torpor, upon which cue Assistant Commander Solariel reaches out and puts a bony hand on Athena's head. The eyes open, the lovelocks tumble, the Lady Athena blinks in the light, pants and puts a hand to her breast.

'What did he say? What did he *say*?'

Whereupon the crowd expresses its collective emotion by exchanging engaging looks of metaphysical content. Later, after a break for orange juice, Athena sits us in a circle and asks us to repeat the incantation: 'I serve the Ascendant Masters, the one true light, the divine being, that which is holy, that which is love, the place that is surrounded by the white light, the great Ascended Ones, the most sacred of all that is, the place from where we came, the divine which is within, that which we are, all that we must fully be,' and when it comes to my turn I say 'I think I got a little lost. Could you repeat it please?'

On the 89A cutting back to Pinon Jay Drive, Santara suddenly points to the sky: 'Wow, it's a mothership.' Connie and Sakina both peer out and up at the void above, their eyes following the same track. I can see nothing other than the usual puddle of stars, not even a moving meteorite or aeroplane. The moment passes without comment, as if it were commonplace for three people to fix upon, or believe they have fixed upon, the exact locus of an invisible spaceship in the tremendous confusion of the night sky.

Santara leans back and begins to plait her hair.

'Athena's put *on* like you wouldn't believe.'

'Do you think?' asks Sakina

'Fifteen pounds *at least.*'

'It's the energies around here,' says Connie.

'I guess that must be it, 'cos I am *not* the shape I was in LA and I was wondering how that could have happened.'

'What shape was that, dear?' asks Sakina

'A kind of thinner shape, I guess.'

VISUALIZE WHIRLED PEAS —
IT'S MORE THAN JUST A BUMPER STICKER!

Back in May, at the western edge of the Texas Panhandle, a country and western song played on the radio and has stayed with me ever since. I can't remember who sings it, but the refrain goes: 'Well, you've got to stand for somethin' or you'll fall for anything.' I am humming the tune, half unconsciously, squatting on the rock above Pinon Jay Drive and watching the sun melting into a pulp of cinnabar and wondering why it is that the red rocks stripe across with blue-black lines towards the end of the day. When the sun sends its final light in cords, the edges of the stone harden to a cadmium shimmer against the skyline, as if steeling against the day's departure. Between the first intimations of dusk and the onset of the night the plain of buttes and mesas dissolves into a Man Ray print, textured like bone and ascetic in its outlines, almost an uncompleted city. A shooting star passes briefly, dies somewhere out of view, beyond Boynton Canyon.

Santara is not happy. Her rent is paid through to August but she can't get a job, she has no friends and she's missing Santa Monica. Her Babemobile won't start and Spirit says she has work to do in Sedona, if only she knew what. If only. If only the heat would subside, for just a day, she says, it would give her time to think. She cries most evenings now, saucing tubs of Choc Praline Candy Crunch with her tears. All she knows is that she is an angel from another place, and that Los Angeles calls her back to a home that is not a home but merely the giant smoggy terminus in a terrestrial waystation. A few times I am tempted to drive her back there myself, in Caboose, but, but . . . each time, but.

'Solar says everything is perfect, but I'm sorry, it's not fucking perfect. In fact it's a mess, right? My wings don't work, my wheels don't work. All I can think about is my ascension into the heavenly realms. The ships have gotta come pick me up real soon,' she whimpers one night, poking her finger into a spider's web.

'Uh-huh,' I reply. I don't like myself much when I'm around Santara.

'Listen, I think I'm gay,' she says.

'Oh,' I reply Why only 'oh'? Why not 'great' or 'terrible' or even 'how do you feel about that?' What kind of a response is 'oh'?

'I thought maybe . . . ?'

'Er no, I don't think so.'

'I see. I just thought.'

'Yeah. But if you want to talk . . . ?'

'No.'

'Um, what can I say?'

'No, that's fine. Really, really OK.'

'Really?'

'Well, uh . . . I have to go meditate now.'

Fergus calls later. He's just got in from a publishing party for

Marianne Williamson, whose book about discovering Jesus in the higher self (or something) is hitting the bestseller lists.

'Everyone was there. Some anorexic got me up against the wall with a tray of canapés and asked me about my favourite spiritual practice. What a line!'

'Which is . . . ?'

'Bourbon, lots of rocks.'

'Jeez, Ferg, why are you such a disappointment?' I reply, thrilled.

'Oh I don't know, spirituality seems such a chore.'

'Ferg, you know this alien abduction thing?'

'Sure. Popular pre-millennial mass hysteria.'

'Whatever. There's this place near here called Secret Canyon. They say it happens all the time out there. I've got an urge to test it out.'

'Do it. But from a rational perspective, it's bullshit. Right?'

Sakina does not think that Secret Canyon is a good idea at all.

'I don't know, but you hear of all sorts of things happening there; abductions, brainwashing.'

I must have giggled involuntarily, for Sakina looks at me with contempt and says, 'Yes, dear, and what makes you so sure?'

PROTECT YOURSELF FROM PSYCHIC ATTACK

Most hikers walking around Sedona begin at Boynton and fetch up at Cathedral Rock, where the paths are cut clear out of the piñon pine and there are no steep inclines or footholds. On the other hand Secret Canyon, the most isolated part of a finger mesa system in the east of the Red Rock Secret Mountain wilderness is, as the name suggests, seldom visited.

From West Sedona, Dry Creek Road leads off north past Coffee Pot Rock and the treacherous crags of Capitol Butte, dwindling to a pitted, coconut-coloured rocky track, barely wide enough for a single car at Secret Canyon. At the mouths of more accessible canyons there are visitors' books so that rangers can keep track of hikers, in case of flash floods and sudden changes in the weather, but so few people come to Secret Canyon that there is no book, only a patch of earth cleared of juniper trees for hikers' cars. One sound echoes at the mouth of Secret Canyon, the airy whirr of wings.

Now, I have never seen or heard a UFO, or, for that matter, an alien, but I have always felt that it would be good to have done so, just as it would be a comfort to have seen the Virgin Mary floating above the bath or met and killed the Buddha on a country road. At least you'd *know*.

I read somewhere that every Hopi boy has to bring a piece of moon rock back to the ceremonial kiva before he may be regarded a man. The journey is meant to test the young man's courage, and supposedly reconcile him to the advantages and limitations of home. I was five when the first pictures of the planet taken from the surface of the moon were transmitted to TV sets round the world. I was too young for those pictures to mean much, but to the generation before me, the Baby Boomers, the event would have been quite different, I suppose. To them the transformation of their familiar streets and cities into the intense blue abstraction of planet earth must have seemed the perfect metaphor for the journeys they were then making through adolescence. I often wonder how anything in their later lives could have begun to match the potency of the unblinking iris-image of the earth.

The path into Secret Canyon runs across a dry river bed, then rises gently over soft sand between two slabs of rock, red as carcasses. Ancient waterfalls, long since dried, have left their bold stains upon the sediment and where there are ledges staring open-faced into the sun, a few juniper bushes have put down anxious roots. In China rocks are admired for their three essentials – holeyness, hardness and flakiness. A rock having none of these is somehow a pretence, not worthy of contemplation, whereas a rock with all three in abundance is truly a piece of nature's art. The rock at this southern edge of the Colorado Plateau is brittle and frail, divesting itself of its skin as a lizard sheds its tail. It crunches to powder under the boot, but there is no doubting its holeyness or flakiness. So the Chinese might consider it two-thirds rock, one-third nature's trick, cooked up from volcanic belches and the ruptures of tectonic plates. This paradox of impermanence in a land millions of years old is one of the defining qualities of the southwest. You can stand on the time-worn plains or under the massif of canyons and still never be quite sure that the earth will not swallow you up and leave you imprisoned in its scorching belly until an earthquake spews you up again. The Hopi who live out on the mesas to the northeast of Sedona say that the southwest is the earth's vagina, birthplace of souls and the gateway through which the spirits of dead people must pass in order to gain entry to the spirit world.

MAGIK HAPPENS

Twelve dollars does not buy much tent. It buys precisely this; one summer-weight plastic sheet, one plastic awning, a length of polypropylene rope and eleven plastic pegs (one missing). It does not appear to buy any form of instruction manual or leaflet. Luckily, I can recall a few of the rules from my girl guide days. First, select a convenient patch devoid of scrub. To avoid flash flood do not camp in dry river beds. Do not camp under single trees; do not camp on exposed plains or cliff-tops for fear of wind, sand storms and dust devils. Next, so far as is possible, clear the area of all spooky bits of nature; in the southwest this means scorpions, black widow spiders, Gila monsters, rattlers, sidewinders, centipedes, wolf spiders, coral snakes and tarantulas.

Collect firewood to ward off such nighttime prowlers as mountain lions, skunks, coyotes, porcupines. It is important to exclude the possibility of any living thing intruding under the ground sheet or appearing in terrorizing, poly-legged silhouette upon the awning. Interlopers are not welcome. Insect killer must be sprayed vigorously inside the tent and roach traps set along the sides. There are trenches to be dug for electric lanterns, flypaper to be nailed to all surrounding trees, branches to be painted with quicklime. Guy ropes should be coated with anti-climb paint and rodent traps set throughout the area. As an extra precaution it is possible to line the outside of the tent with trays of caustic soda, before setting a strict watch rota and being ready should any nature-enemy break the fortifications and appear over the breach. Throughout the preparations it is important to behave in a normal and relaxed manner, for the moment you become tense and over-anxious Nature has won its first little victory. And remember, wild things have their own agendas.

For several hours I sit and read Edward Abbey's *Desert Solitaire* and suck on the occasional smoke, thrilling to the fact that no-one has the least idea where I am. In time, even the ravens forget my existence and start up their screaming and choking.

I suppose I have been sitting for six or seven hours accompanied by nothing more alarming than ravens and rodents when of a sudden, through the dwindling fragments of cloud cover there throbs a distant muffled hum, which ebbs for a moment before swelling to a loud clockwork buzz. In all these high places of the southwestern desert, the dawn air is thin, thickening up in the sun only to become scratchy and contingent again at dusk. Sights and sounds have substance at noon but at either end of the day you cannot trust your eyes or ears, or any physical sense. All that remains is intuition and an intense, smoky light. I drop Abbey, run out onto the path, and look about. No presence in the sky but the sun, burning itself out. The noise persists, begins to boom and shiver, repeating off the sandstone. For a moment the sound is omnipresent, but still there is nothing in the sky but sun and a whorl of ravens. I am suddenly overtaken by a fantasy of terror. In my mind I am already rehearsing my abduction speech. Adrenaline cuts crisp as electricity through the arteries of my limbs, my stomach flutters, heart drums to the vacant sky, but the thrill doesn't last, for within seconds a little Cessna comes into view, rises up on the canyon slipstream and disappears to the south, heading for Sedona.

YOUR HIGHER SELF NEEDS HEALING

In June 1947, rumour has it that an alien spacecraft crashed just outside Roswell, New Mexico, more than four hundred and fifty miles to the southeast of Sedona. The military authorities recovered several alien bodies, one of which was alive, and the wreckage of a mothership. From time to time, witnesses (mostly retired military employees) have come forward to tell their stories. Although the military authorities deny all knowledge of the event, and have done their best to discredit witnesses, many people in Arizona and New Mexico continue to insist that the night sky is punctuated with strange objects and unexplained mechanical noises and so the tales of the crash at Roswell rumble on. A few weeks after I left Sedona, I met a journalist in a bar in Albuquerque who specialized in covering defence stories. We began talking about the Roswell crash and the journalist mentioned that several respected scientists were currently searching for alien craft in Chaco Canyon, an ancient Anasazi ruin up in the Four Corners Area of New Mexico. During our conversation it became increasingly clear that the journalist was assessing me, as though he had something to say but would only say it if given a particular cue. As we talked he became more agitated until finally he said;

'Listen, I have been to places in New Mexico that don't exist, places that are not on any maps and that no-one will acknowledge. Some of them are supposedly ranches, others are on federal land, and I have seen things I could never report because no-one would ever admit to them. I'd be discredited and I'd be waving goodbye to my career.'

'What, you mean *spacecraft*, UFOs?'

'I don't know. All I know is that I've never seen anything else like them in all my years of defence reporting.'

He told me this on condition I never mention his name, so let's just say I have forgotten it.

I walked out of that bar in Albuquerque into a silver night lit by the moon, with an image of the blue earth iris taking shape in my mind's eye and I thought about Sakina and her star people and I began to envy them their journey in search of the wonderful wizard of Oz.

Highway 666

'This road don't carry no gamblers,
Liars, thieves and big-shot ramblers.
This road is bound for glory.'

WOODY GUTHRIE

A few minutes ago I was rolling along state highway 666, which runs south from Shiprock to Gallup, New Mexico, with nothing more on my mind than green chile taco chips and Chet Baker's version of 'You Don't Know What Love Is'. Beside me lay an almost empty can of root beer and a piece of fake beef jerky. The three of us – me, root beer and jerky – were cruising along feeling the sun through the glass, humming the Baker tune, planning on keeping going until we reached our destination, wherever that turned out to be. About a mile back a chromium RV with a loose fender passed, heading towards Four Corners, metal plinking on metal, but up ahead the road stretched out flat like an opened vein. It's a pretty remote road, state highway 666. A little way past the Chuska Mountain range I noticed Caboose was dragging its heels, but I put it down to an incline in the road. A few hundred yards on Caboose slowed down by another five miles an hour or so. A cranky old station wagon appeared from over the brow of the hill, pulled up behind then shaved past us to give the driver a chance to peer in and take a closer look.

Caboose's engine problem was no longer possible to ignore. I sat for a minute or two with the accelerator pedal slammed hard down swaying forwards and backwards in an attempt to create momentum, hoping with fervour that there was some kind of blockage in the gas tank that would clear if I slooshed it around. No warning lights were on, the gauge was indicating there was plenty of oil and plenty of gas; even the temperature seemed OK. Nonetheless we were drizzling along at 15mph and slowing at a rate of about 5mph every thirty seconds. Another station wagon with a fat old redneck inside caught us up and zoomed by, blowing its horn. Evidently, the redneck had got it into his head that I was rolling along at 8mph in the middle of a million square miles of desert sod because I liked it that way.

Eventually, we grind to a halt. From highway 666 open range yawns off north into the epic plains of the Navajo Nation. Some distance away to the south are the badlands of Cibola, a sinkhole full of volcanic lava beds. The horizon is unmarked by tree or habitation. By pinching my hands together and squinting through a hole between my fingers I can make out most of the letters on the sign up ahead. Twin Lakes 16, Yah Tah Hey 20, Gallup 29. That's a long walk, in every direction. A nervous tic starts up in my left eye. This is not looking good. Driving alone across the void is one thing, breaking down in the void feels significantly different, worse in fact. Looking down at the tyres I notice a piece of jack rabbit – timely intimation of mortality – lying smeared on the verge next to Caboose and awaiting the attentions of the raven demolition crew circling above.

Out on the northeastern New Mexico plains it is possible to hear a tumbleweed tripping along the highway five miles back, but here in the west, where mesas and buttes string out along the plateau like terracotta beads, there are only two sounds persistent enough to carry beyond the next dip in the road; the sound of thunder and the wind's vacant hiss.

At this moment I am looking at the root beer can in the passenger seat and reassessing yesterday's decision, made in an air-conditioned motel in the cool mountains of New Mexico, to throw away the bottle of radiator water. I think of the emergency CB I never quite got round to buying, and I think about what happens to a dehydrating body before it gives up the ghost. Competent inner self says 'This situation is an opportunity.' Voice of unreason (also within) replies 'Whoever heard of a no-win opportunity?'

From somewhere to the north or east a rocky outcrop breaks the boom of a thunder cloud into spiny sound-shards. A soupy rain-cloud dips towards the horizon, suggesting the possibility of a twister developing later. A breeze shuffles some shale about on the soft shoulder. Far off, six or seven thin rainbows stack up beneath gaseous and chaotic clouds and bring a little hopeless comfort. A thunderstorm is building. The membranous sky starts to clot into mildewed cream; dark blue cirrus clouds bleed in spots overhead. A brown column of rain above the horizon line evaporates and vanishes before it has wet the ground. Every so often a white electric nerve splits the sky. Rain from the Dinetah begins to crawl across the plain like the uneasy procession of melted grease, beating as it goes the shrivelled bodies of dead yucca blooms which can only rustle their seeds in supplication to the rain-bearing wind and endure.

One thing: I am not good on my own at the beginning of a thunderstorm. This is an admission of considerable feebleness on my part, but it is also, unfortunately, the way things are.

I have a number of choices: one, walk back or forwards to the nearest town, risking death by dehydration, lightning, or an encounter with an imprecisely driven juggernaut; two, wait and risk pretty much the same; three, give up and prepare for the other side. I consider my epitaph; she kicked her last kick on route 666. Not bad. Actually, I don't mind the thought of being dead, it is the process of dying that troubles me. How long would it take? How much would it hurt? Would my remains be discovered before or after anyone who ever knew me had long since forgotten who I was?

I decide to walk. I wish I had taken better note of the last town which, as I recall, consisted in a few empty mobile homes and a hogan with a mean, starved dog tied up outside. I start off at brisk pace in the direction of Gallup. The road continues flat for a while, then begins a long slow incline up across a mesa. At the brow I begin to feel a little panicky. Below lies a stripe of tarmacadam stretching about ten miles along the plain to another hill. At the horizon silhouetted against a heat haze is a fringe of trees and beyond that perhaps another endless road cutting through the open range down into Gallup twenty miles beyond. No ranch, no town, no village in sight. Even the road is empty.

A while further up the road an immense, ancient Oldsmobile steals up from behind, slows down and a fat, sweating cowboy type with a plum-coloured face leans out.

'Need some help?'

'Car broke down.'

'Little thing a mile back? Oh, we'll fix that,' says the cowboy, looking for approval from the woman sitting next to him.

'D'ya think it's gas?'

'No, it might be a blockage though.'

'We'll go back home and fetch up some gas.'

The woman winds down her window and shouts something like 'Be right back' but the words have peeled away before they reach me. I squat on the verge and start up a few tunes on a bazooka made from some old couch grass. I am on to the second verse of 'Amazing Grace' when the white Olds pulls up and Cowboy Plum leans out; 'Forgot te ask. Unleaded?' and, receiving my answer, swings round and speeds off along the empty track below, leaving a cloud of blue smoke rising on the heat current. Just then a lump of hail the size of a kid's fist lands at my feet. The weather in the southwest specializes in such tricks. People die in hail sometimes. The white Olds rolls along below catching the sun and flinging out light, too far away now to summon back. Looks like a metallic tick settling itself on the plain. Fifteen minutes later it's back again.

'Git in,' says the woman, shifting along the front seat to make room. I am struck by Cowboy Plum's hands, swollen as a salmon's roe with one fingernail oozing from a blood blister underneath.

We fill Caboose's tank with gas (unleaded), soak the carburetter, check the sparks, fix the fluid levels in the battery, push-start, bump-start, jump-start. zip. Caboose remains in persistent vegetative state. Cowboy Plum turns to me and says, 'Nope. Let's give ya a ride home,' which he pronounces 'hoom', 'and then we can git someone come out and pick up the car.'

The Plums live in a mobile home in an informal trailer park

on the verge of Interstate 40. A fence keeps their stinking white and liver spaniel from straying out onto the freeway. The fence is also, of course, a symbol of proud ownership.

'You from Texas?' asks Mrs Plum. Caboose has Texas plates. Not waiting for a reply, she turns to the cowboy until he catches her eye and his face lines up a little. The mobile home is small and dirty. The lights don't work, though Mrs Plum still switches them on. Looks as if nothing much works any longer, and anything that does is held together with duct tape.

'Where you headin'? Won't be no mechanics out today.'

'Flagstaff.'

An identity parade of immense Plum children sits on the sofa in the middle of the room and stares vacantly ahead at a cartoon on the TV. The youngest-looking is transporting a mountain of popcorn from bag to mouth while belching over a bottle of Gatorade. The rest appear to be pupating. Mrs Plum waves me a seat near the door – 'Alright?' – and disappears behind a partition.

'I got a friend got a tow truck. Reckon you'll have te stay in Gallup tonight. Ya won't find no mechanics workin,' says the cowboy.

Minutes pass in silence, broken only by the cartoon on the TV, and by one of the Plum pupae waking from its dreamless sleep to open a bag of potato chips. Eventually Mrs Plum reemerges from behind the partition clad in brand-new WalMart overall.

'Gotta git goin'.' The cowboy nods, puts on his hat and turns to me.

'They'll be along te pick ya up, but ya won't make Flagstaff today.' I hold out my hand, but the cowboy simply stares at it.

'Thanks very much.'

Peewee Herman begins singing on the TV.

The railway runs through Gallup, New Mexico. My history book suggests that the Blue Goose Saloon arrived at the spot first, drawing people from all around and the town of Gallup followed after, but it fails to mention that the Atlantic and Pacific railway stopped right in Gallup, and that, if it hadn't, Gallup might not have existed at all. The passenger service went long ago, but a few abandoned carriages still sit in the sidings, waiting for some locomotive to appear and pull them back to California. The railway brings little business and still less excitement these days but the town has grown used to being with it. Main Street still hugs the contours of the track and town and railway are as dependent on one another as Darby on Joan.

Caboose is to spend the night in a mechanic's forecourt, awaiting an early morning assessment of its condition, which means that I'm stuck in Gallup for the night at least.

The Hopi Motel, cheapest stopover downtown, is owned by a Gujarati couple from a village north of Lahore. In the concrete car port beyond the Hopi's baby blue walkway stands the biggest billboard in the street. It reads 'Viva El Whopper, Viva El Mejor.'

About six a caravan of heavy-duty bikers roars into the car park around the Hopi Motel, runs a circuit around the cars and lines up in front of the diner next door to the motel, where I am sat waiting for a *chile relleno* to arrive. SoCals, SoNevs and Nomads, about thirty all told, mean age let's say forty-two. By my reckoning that adds up to 1260 years of machismo. What a thought. Laid end to end, it would reach back into the Dark Ages.

'You open?' asks the Chief Nomad poking his head round the door. I take the precaution of jotting a few observations in my notebook: 'Chief Nomad: red neckerchief tied tight around head, powdery chops, black leather Harley jacket' to make the cops' job easier in the event that the Chief leaves no fingerprints, sperm, beard fragments, or other identifying marks.

'No,' replies the waitress

'*Not open?*'

'Closed all day.'

'How come she in here, then?' he asks, glancing over at me.

'She's fam'ly,' replies the waitress, cocking a thumb in my direction.

'Oh, 'scuse me' says the Chief without irony, closing the door behind him.

A minute or so later he's back.

'Er, can we just get, like, some eggs, or somethin'?'

'Look, there's no cook here,' she shrugs her shoulders 'Nothing I can do about it.'

'Fuck,' says the Chief and goes back out into the light.

A man appears from the back room.

'You wanna call the police?'

'Nah, they'll back off,' says the watress, unruffled.

Just then someone bangs on the door hard enough to break it and crashes into the diner. It's the Chief again.

'We got fuckin' *veterans* out here, lady.'

While I'm eating a blue night gradually takes root in the places where the sun has died back. Across the road from the diner perhaps a dozen figures sit on a wall, smoking. One of them is wearing a red neckerchief on his head, edged in white. He is half in shadow, half in the neon light from a store. Flipping his smoke into the gutter, he shouts over to me: 'You the family?'

'Uh, yeah.' I keep my eyes on the pavement

'How come you staying in the motel?'

'Uh, it's a family business.'

'Oh.'

He flicks his wrist in my direction. I don't know what kind of a gesture this is, but I calculate it's best to pretend not to have seen it.

'When they gonna open up in there?'

I shrug my shoulders.

'Thought you wuz fam'ly, man?'

'Yeah, uh, visiting family.'

I can just make out the silhouette of the Chief's fist in the store lights, as he reaches into his pocket, leans towards one of his compadres and murmurs something. The compadre looks back at me.

I am contemplating the probability of being pulped and left to stain the sidewalk when all of a sudden a huge irridescent blue spray cracks in the sky over the Hopi motel, showering the roof with sparks. Then, high above the billboard in the parking lot an immense vermilion bloom opens, drowning the words Viva

El Whopper in a meaty light. Even before it has faded dozens of brilliant-coloured stripes appear against the sky across its path, cross one another and fall away, twisting round like the wires in a phone box. Fireworks for Independence Day.

Postcard Home

'And now we stare astonished at the sea,
And a miraculous strange bird shrieks at us.'

W. B. YEATS

So much has already been said about the Grand Canyon I feel I
have little to add.

The canyon is an awesome, seductive, deceiving spectacle. Its
lunar cliffs and peaks, made to appear supple by the dance of
light, are in reality unyielding, treacherous and indifferent. The
deepest and therefore oldest of the canyon's fractal crags has
played its tricks with the light for more than four billion years,
that is two-thirds of the age of the planet. Slow red Colorado
river mud continues to cut the crag and will eventually expose
the primal silence of the beginning. There is nothing more allur-
ing under the sun than the immortal power of that river. And
yet, from the rim at the edge of the plateau only a thin line
marks its path, the rock, as if in envy, diminishing it. But the
hot-blowing wind falling white over the rim at Bright Angel
Point still sings in anticipation as it tumbles towards the bluegreen line.

I really don't have much to say because the Grand Canyon is
no longer a place, but the representation of a place. Over the
years of photographs and films and home movies and books and
merchandising, the canyon's *image* has come to stand in for what
might once have appeared as real. Who can assert with confidence
that the view they see from the rim is the thing itself, rather than
a familiar reflection of it, the memory's recollection of a poster
or a silk-screened towel? More people visit the gift store and the
canyon movie theatre than walk the rim or climb the canyon

paths, and that, to me, is not surprising. The scale of the gorge is too great to process, and too fearful to contemplate, which is in part why we seek out its image.

Staring out across the red and blue rock at Yavapai Point in the clear midday light of a June day, I was approached by a man with a fancy camera who shuffled up beside me and said in a voice both awed and disappointed: 'It looks just like a picture postcard.' All I could think to reply at the time was 'Yes, it does,' but the words were taken up by the wind and thrown down over the numbing precipice, and I am not sure if he heard me.

God's Country

'God has been replaced, as he has all over the West,
with respectability and airconditioning.'

IMAMU AMIRI BARAKA

A small huddle of mormon kids loiters outside The Golden Loop Cafe in Escalante, Utah, talking and chewing on Baby Ruths. One of them, a blonde boy, about fourteen, leans on a red and yellow mountain bike with an air of grand insouciance, while the others, on foot, kick the dust up around and pretend not to care. From where I am sitting, inside the Golden Loop, a radio blurs their conversation, but I can catch enough of it to know that it is one of those intensely convoluted disquisitions on life's purpose favoured by adolescents.

Everything at the Golden Loop bears the reeky must of age but the cafe is, all the same, as ordered and spartan as it might have been twenty or thirty years ago when the fittings were first fitted and the tables first filled. The floor is lino and the tables formica-topped. The women's toilet is labelled 'ladies' restroom' and has a picture of a woman in the New Look on the door. Balanced on the counter is a glass and chromium spider-legged cake cabinet, full of donuts protected by tupperware fly covers. The cash machine has a side lever, like a one-armed bandit, for opening up. A poster of a Rocky Mountain scene in Technicolor hangs over wood-look panelling behind.

The waitress comes by to refill my coffee mug and deliver the day's special, a steak sandwich. On Sundays it's chicken, on Mondays omelettes, on Tuesdays ground beef, it's been that way ever since the waitress started working at the Golden Loop and that's a good deal longer than she cares to recall.

87

I pull out from the pocket of my shorts the leaflet someone left in my room at the Padre Motel. The leaflet claims that Escalante was one of the last frontiers to be explored or settled in the continental United States. Two Spanish priests meandered through the area in the mid-eighteenth century looking for a route from Santa Fe to California but the area was not settled by whites until the Mormons moved there a hundred and twenty years later and made it the pert little community it is today. A town map fills one page of the leaflet, each road on the tiny chequerboard laboriously labelled: Main Street, First Street West, Second Street West, First Street South, Second South, First East, and so on. Marked in the heart of downtown is a Christian gift shop and a general store. A stock feed market, another general store, a burger shack, an LDS church, a few residential streets, an auto mart and three motels – two of which appear to be shut – make up what's left of Escalante. There's not much else to remark upon. The first real road to the nearest town, Boulder, twenty-nine miles to the northeast, was built by the Civilian Conservation Corps in the 1930s and each year the eight hundred souls of Escalante mark Independence Day with a flag ceremony, and the anniversary of the entry of Mormon Pioneers into the Salt Lake Valley on 24 July, 1847, with a parade and rodeo. There is no crime in Escalante, no delinquency and low rates of out-migration. In short, the town is as every small town would like itself to be – safe, conventional and proud to be set in its ways.

Outside in the street the boy with the mountain bike is now spinning wheelies around B&R Burgers Plus, making eyes at a couple of kids parked in cars close by.

Finishing my steak, I take a stroll across the road to the general store for a carton of milk, where I am informed by the proprietor that only heat-treated milk is available in Escalante at the ends of months. Full cream milk and chocolate milk sell out during the week following the supplier's monthly consignment. If I'd care to wait, the supplier is due in a few days. If it's not at the general store, no-one will have it, and in any case, everywhere else is shut on a Saturday at this time. They have tinned cream, heat-treated milk and the kind of yoghurt that tastes like sperm gone off. If I'd like to come by in a week or so . . .

When I step out of the store I find the blonde boy hanging around waiting for me out on the street. He says: 'What d'you buy?' so I offer him a choc chunk cookie and a swig of Seven-Up. He takes the cookie and refuses the drink.

'You from Texas?'

I shake my head: 'England.'

'How come your car says Texas, then?'

'That's where I bought it.'

He looks at me with half-closed eyes, making a silhouette from the shape in front of him.

'Do you know the Queen of England?'

'No, no, I don't.'

His face reveals incomprehension, followed closely by scepticism and finally, by downright suspicion. I claim to be English but don't know the royal family – a contradiction surely?

'Like my bike?' he ventures. I nod.

'You ever seen her?'

'On the TV.'

'Wow,' he replies, unconvinced. A map of England presents itself in his mind's eye as a minuscule blip at the end of a remote and unknowable continent. He takes another tack.

'Does she smile? I heard she wasn't allowed to smile.'

'I don't know . . . anyway, why would that be?'

'Considerations of security,' replies the boy, replete, quite sure now that I am not English at all but a pretender.

Someone has been in to my motel room and left a copy of the *Book of Mormon* bound in blue leatherette. As the night draws in, a few lights snap on around Center Street and fewer still beyond. There is no bar in Escalante, no cinema and no bowling alley. Even the Golden Loop shuts early. From my window I can see a couple of teens illuminated in a strip light outside B&R's talking with each other through their car windows. Around ten one of them glances at his watch, they start up their engines and peel off in different directions along Center Street. One drives slowly towards the Golden Loop and the other heads out of Escalante on the Boulder road.

The blonde boy's red and yellow mountain bike lies on the pavement outside B&R the next morning, early, but the boy himself is nowhere in sight. The same waitress who was on last night's shift at the Golden Loop offers me eggs and coffee. Eggs is all they have for breakfast. Each day is an eggs special day. Sunday is eggs scrambled up with ham, Monday is omlette, Tuesday is eggs any style. The blonde boy appears from round the corner of the general store, alone, picks his bike up out of the dust and sits on the pavement with his legs widespread, flipping at something on the road. Seeing me sat by the window in the Golden Loop he walks over and opens the door.

'Wanna see what I've got?'

A few dozen tan caterpillars lie in an empty styrofoam burger tray next to the mountain bike. The boy picks one out and flicks it with his thumb and index finger at speed towards a drain in the road. The caterpillar lands on the grate, squirms violently for a few seconds, topples and finally slides down into the sewer below. The boy grins and studies me in hope of registering signs of shock.

'Do you like it here?' I ask him, thinking of my own childhood spent wandering around the semi-rural fields outside my home on the outskirts of a village on the outskirts of a town on the hinterland of a suburb on the periphery of London.

'Sure,' says the boy. 'Escalante is cool.'

'What do you do?'

'Bike. Watch TV. You know.'

He doesn't want to leave when he gets older. He wants to stay and fish and watch TV and maybe work in the general store at the weekends. Older is sixteen, or maybe seventeen. Anyway, his mom works at the school part-time and his dad hunts jack rabbits, so where would they go?

A ten-minute drive from Escalante northeast along Highway 12 towards Boulder brings you to the Death Box wilderness area, a stretch of rock pitted with the roots of piñon pine and juniper. A mile or so beyond, the road takes a precipitous bend before opening onto a milky brown cliff from which a plain of magnetic slickrock extends into the distance as far as the eye can see, fifty or sixty miles beyond. A dried-up river cuts two bloody zippers into its nap. This is the Aquarian Plateau. All about is the rubble of mesas and hoodoos, rumbling the reddened rock into a boiling stew. Viewed from above, there is something sinister about the arrangement of sandstone towers, as if each had struggled to submerge another and rise above it. Somewhere there must be water, for there are scattered about the slickrock contingent little desert plants and the tracks of animals. A few ravens cough among the rocks but it seems to the eye that every other creature must be lying low and waiting for death, for nothing else is visible beside the tracks, and strangely for a road in the southwest, there is no roadkill in sight. Beyond Boulder lie the half-abandoned villages of Torrey and Grover and Hanksville, each consisting of a gas station, a few shotgun sheds, some with sheep inside, a Latter-Day Saints church and a cluster of whitewashed single-storey houses. From Torrey to the junction with Interstate 70, a distance of a hundred miles or so, I pass no other vehicle on the road, and none passes me.

It is a strange journey, that drive from Escalante to Moab across the San Rafael Swell. The Swell and the mountains around it must count as some of the most alienating terrain on the planet. From the road you look down upon the grotesquely exposed geological viscera of the earth and it is difficult not to feel in the odd position of being both voyeur and violator of inanimate rock.

By Hanksville I am running low on gas, so I stop off at the station a little way from what used to be the town. A skinny man in a stained stetson hat and cowboy boots wanders up to the car with a German Shepherd dog and asks if I want the tank filled. Being anxious to stretch my legs, I step onto the forecourt and look out over a completely flat plate of basalt extending about fifty or sixty miles around. That's one hundred and twenty miles of view taken in a straight line. In theory it is said that one can see one hundred and sixty-eight miles, before the curvature of the earth makes a horizon. Aside from a scar in the plain where the Dirty Devil River is supposed to run, and the miniature habitations I have just passed, there is nothing standing from the sod but the dome of a cloudless sky.

I ask the skinny man if he lives in Hanksville. It is a stupid question. Why would anyone commute to Hanksville? Sure, he lives right round at the back, he says, with the dog.

'I'd go mad, being so cut off,' I remark without thinking much about it.

'Don't trouble me,' replies the man, handing me back change from a ten-dollar bill. 'Don't care if I see folk, don't care if I don't.'

He strolls back into the garage and pulls a blind over the window for shade. The dog returns to its place in the doorway, leans its head on its front legs, and pants.

The stretch from Hanksville to the junction with the Interstate really eats away at me. I turn the radio on, but there are no stations close enough, so I push a tape in the player but it makes no difference to the road; the road just keeps on being straight and black and wickedly long. I move around in the sweat under my buttocks just to keep awake. I give myself fictitious reasons for carrying on – to check out a fragment of tyre on the road, to compose a non-existent frame, to make sure of the car's ability to hold a corner – because the flatland gives me no markers of its own. It remains apparently boundless, unchanged. From time to time I consider that I might be trapped in an eternal present, repeating the same moment over and over, never living beyond the same blink of an eye, the same one breath.

To cross the Swell in a car requires courage. At least, it took some from me. That anyone ever did it in ox wagons or on foot defies belief. But the Mormons did do it. All over the dismal and fantastic terrain of southeastern Utah they drove their cattle and worked their land and built ordered little towns like Escalante and kept the rocks around at bay.

The Grander Purpose

'After prosperity, what?'

MAX LERNER

'They're saying in the papers that the billionaires are buying up the real estate in Aspen and forcing the multi-millionaires down the road into Carbondale. It's just crazy. Before long the millionaires'll have to pack up from Carbondale and come down to Moab, and where will it end?'

Shift change at the Westerner Grill. The late shift waitress, Ellen, comes on at ten and works through until breakfast. At some point or other during the night all the hidden people of Grand County, Utah, end up at the Westerner Grill, the nightshift miners, the drunks, the insomniacs and the folk like me with no-one warm to go home to. Ellen's job is to pour our coffee and let us think she's on our side. She doesn't have much time for the early morning crowd who come in just as she's winding up her shift and expect their big breakfast specials to be served just so. And she doesn't like the ones in fancy boots and designer outdoor gear, whatever time they come in. Tip like vagrants, she says.

Disposing of my order on the spike, Ellen shuffles over to the counter, picks up a faded side salad along with a jug of greasy coffee, comes back, and in a single well-honed motion slides the salad bowl off her forearm, onto my table and moves along to the booth next door, where an old man in a straw hat is trying to remove his teeth from a piece of chicken fried steak.

'OK there, hon?'

The man replies indistinctly through gristle.

'Nope, all out,' says Ellen in response. 'Some hikers come in a coupla hours or so ago, ate the batch.'

93

'The hell!' replies the old man, ejecting cow cartilage onto the plate in front of him. 'That's the third time this week. Goddammit, strangers have gotten just about everything worth having round here.'

Something tells me all is not well in Moab, Utah.

Ellen brings over a T-bone, too well done, but resistant to the teeth, which is how I like them, with a side of home fries, the grease from which makes a sauce for the steak. She returns a couple of minutes later with a basket of saltines and bread on the grounds that I need feeding up. I don't much like saltines, but I stash a few away in my pocket before I leave, for luck.

My room at the Off-Center Hotel has been themed by the owner to give it the feel of a noir movie. On the dresser sit a kooky bakelite phone (non-operative), a Zenith radio set (also non-operative) and two copies of *The Lady in the Lake*. Next door a wholesaler of mountain bikes from California, called David, is putting up at Butch Cassidy and Sundance. He's got a life-sized, glass-fibre pinto pony in there; I saw it through the keyhole.

Page 245 of my guidebook has it that Grand County, whose principal town is Moab, is bigger than the states of Rhode Island and Delaware put together. Around and about is some of the most empty, most spectacular desert in the United States – architectural buttes, arches, columns and frilled hoodoos formed by ancient earthquakes and eruptions or else melted into shape by eons of rain and wind. Through Grand runs the Green River, the last explored major river in the lower forty-eight states, and the Colorado, still thin, fast and brown. This stretch of terrain is now known as 'Canyonlands' and over the past ten or fifteen years it has been vigorously marketed as a kind of huge outdoor sports arena. There is hiking, microlighting, bunjee-jumping and mountain-biking to be done in the hills, fishing and white-water rafting in the rivers, snowmobiling and skiing during the winter months. Canyonlands is 'a world of activity' according to the guidebook.

David, the mountain bike salesman, promises to take me up to Arches National Park several miles out of Moab and show me some of the places the tourists don't get to. At the weekends, he says, it's hard to find a bed in Moab and the main drag becomes jammed with RVs and jeep convertibles, coming down from Salt Lake City and across from California.

The following morning, wandering around trying to find a mail box, I stumble on Moab's little civic museum, which is set behind Lombardy poplars just around the corner from the Off-Center. I love these places, with their proud noticeboards and chaotic, irrelevant paraphernalia. During the last great war, a team of military mineralogists began digging about under the sandstone around Moab looking for deposits of a mineral they called vanadium, which was a military code name for uranium. This they found in plentiful supply and in 1947 the atomic energy industry was put into the hands of the American Energy Commission, who promptly guaranteed the market for uranium ore, thus sparking a uranium boom. Moab became a frontier-style boomtown sixty years after the frontier closed. Prospectors swooped down on the town like a storm of locusts, bearing Geiger counters. Radioactivity became a kind of craze. Stakes were swapped and dealt all over Grand County, and there wasn't a scrap of sandstone about that wasn't claimed as someone's own. Hawkers set up stalls in the street to peddle heavy water, which was purported to cure hayfever, diabetes and bronchitis, and Moab took on a new double identity as a mining boomtown and an odd, fatal sort of spa.

The boom was short-lived, for sometime in the sixties the price of uranium ore was floated and subsequently fell, leaving Moab to re-establish itself as the quiet, conservative little Mormon town it had been fifteen years before. The period of crazed prosperity left no great or lasting stain on the town's soul, on account, in part, of its Mormon foundations and in part because the extraction industry had always shared with the town's population many of the conservative values of frontier culture.

But Moab did change or at least, change was forced upon it, when, sometime in the mid-seventies, Grand County found itself becoming Canyonlands. Whether this sudden popularity was due to the proficiency of the National Park Service in promoting itself, or to the general increase in leisure travel, or because middle America was becoming conscious of the finite quality of its natural resources and thus placing a greater value on them, or to a combination of all three of these things, it is difficult to say. In any case, Moab became the playground for outdoors types who liked to think of themselves not as lowly visitors, but as lovers of the land, and later, as conservationists. The Park Service responded by setting up hiking trails and signposts and the area became a draw to tourists from abroad, particularly Germany. So popular is Canyonlands these days that the hiking trails have bitten into the desert's crypto-bacterial crust, and every byway is littered with metal boxes carrying self-guiding tour booklets, and at each turn one passes some permission sign or interdict: 'No fires here'; 'BBQs welcome'; 'This area for picnics only'; 'Take only photos, leave only footprints'; 'Please take time to notice the petroglyphs to the left of the slick-rock'.

An article in the local paper predicts that the population of Grand County will double and the number of tourists quadruple before the century is out. Real estate prices have already increased twofold since the early eighties and some of the older and poorer residents can no longer afford the property taxes on their homes. Six months prior to my visit, the Grand County Commission, a three-man clique of elders dominated by Mormon interests, was thrown out and replaced by a new seven-member council. In as sparsely populated a district as Grand County, tossing out the well-known representatives of stability and conservatism and replacing them with, among others, the owner of the local Subway franchise, amounted to a bloodless revolution. The members of the original commission were Moab men with what they still considered to be old Moab values; they were on the side of extraction, ranching and farming. The new team, by contrast, wants to encourage 'clean' money into the county, which means attracting more recreators (but not too many), raising the prices of beds in the town's motels (but not by too much). They have no objection to gourmet ice cream stores, or to fencing off hiking trails or to putting up boat houses along the Grand River. There is even talk of a new desert golf course.

Naturally, they don't want Moab to become another Aspen, Colorado with its trashy exclusivity, but while their private plots of land appreciate in value and their livelihoods grow fatter on the proceeds of kit stores and literary muffin shoppes they see no reason to resist 'the inevitable'. And if an old man can no longer look forward to his apricot cobbler in the Westerner Grill because a pack of hikers have eaten it up, well then, so what?

David and I drive up to Arches National Park a couple of days later in David's Mitsubishi. According to David the road through the park has been recently repaved to accommodate the flow of traffic, and some of the sidetracks, which were previously dirt, have been metalled. Tourists of all kinds – backpackers, tourers, package holidaymakers – scrabble across the grand red sandstone arches to take pictures of themselves posing underneath. A brilliant full moon has risen early over the La Sal mountain range to the southeast and from Devil's Garden, a strange concatenation of arches and hoodoos, it is possible to see out over the Grand River Valley to the banks of the Colorado. Pinned up alongside the car park at Devil's Garden is a Park Service notice reading 'Disappointed? Arches not as big as you'd expected? We hope so, because you're standing too far away. Walk on over. It only takes fifteen minutes to see that the arches are BIG.' But we don't walk on over, and David does not keep his promise to show me the further reaches of the park, the places tourists don't get to, because he has to get back into Moab in time for an appointment with a retailer who, he is hoping, will become one of his best customers.

A few days after leaving Moab, I'm driving through the suburbs of southern Phoenix, looking for a Jiffy Lube, with nothing of consequence on my mind. The further I drive, the seedier the surroundings become, so I decide to stop at a garage just off the freeway and ask if anyone there knows the way to the nearest lube shop. The cashier doesn't know, so he calls the mechanic, who doesn't know either, but rings through to someone in the carwash, who neither knows nor speaks English. A customer comes in to the store to pay and says that he lives right down

the street from a Q-Lube in Tucson. The cashier points out that
we're one hundred and sixteen miles from Tucson.

'Hell,' replies the customer, 'There's a Q-Lube everywhere.'

Then the mechanic has an idea: 'Try the guy in the bookstore,
he knows pretty much everything.'

One block north from the garage, on the opposite side of the
road, is the Alpha Bookstore. Inside the Alpha sits a sack in its
fifties, tight around the gut, hair grown long and little-washed
and with traces of gold filling in the gaps between the teeth, and
inside the sack is a man called John Rodgers.

Rodgers doesn't know of any lube shops; his pick up's so old
there wouldn't be any point in spending money on it.

The Alpha Bookstore is not so much a bookstore as a warehouse for New Age flotsam. Rodgers sells crystals and magic
wands and tarot cards, even pieces of dried animal. He admits
he's become a bit of a pariah among a certain section of the
Phoenix New Age community on account of the dried animal
pieces, but while they sell well he'd be a fool not to stock them.
Every month or so he and his wife write and print a New Age
paper which covers the news that its rival, the *Arizona Light*,
dare not print, such as Elvis sightings. Rodgers invites me to
take tea, and I accept, so he closes up the store and gets me to
follow him out to the back room, where there's a samovar boiling and a couple of chairs pulled in around a cheap plastic table.

Rodgers is a hell of a talker, brusque, self-obsessed, rude,
without guile. His family were Mormon converts from Minne-
sota who settled in Arizona to be nearer Zion. Why they had
not moved to Utah itself, I don't know.

He was active in the church from an early age, and his missions
as a young man took him first to Oregon then back to Arizona.
He was preaching at an LDS temple in Mesa one Sunday when
a naturist came in and invited him to visit a nudist camp somewhere north of Scottsdale. Quite what brought the naturist into
a Mormon temple, Rodgers doesn't know. Perhaps the naturist
was on a mission to convert Mormons to nudism. In any case,
Rodgers mentioned the proposition to the bishop who informed
him that he would be excommunicated from the church if he

had anything further to do with the naturist, or indeed, with nudity in general.

'I thought, why, what do *you* know, so I asked his authority and he said 'the Bishop's Handbook' and I discovered there was this whole book of scripture that people like me didn't know anything about.'

In deference to the bishop and his beloved church, Rodgers didn't go nude, but they excommunicated him anyway, for entertaining the idea. He woke up one day to discover that, so far as the church was concerned, he was no longer a Mormon. Nonetheless, still *feeling* like a Mormon, he went back to the temple and signed up and began again as a novitiate.

'And the bishop said, well that's OK, but we don't want you to talk.' And that was just too much for him.

So he quit the Mormon Church and set about reinventing himself, which was easy because this happened to be the late sixties. He met a girl who said she'd date him on condition that he learn the tarot. So he taught himself the tarot. The girl dumped him a while later, but the tarot told him his life had a grander purpose. Given his past history and skills, he assumed that the purpose must be to set up a New Age church.

'It's a small church because we preach truth, and who in hell wants truth? Fantasy's much better. Lies and fantasy you can sell all day long. And the truth is that there is no devil, and that you are responsible for everything that happens in your life. What-ever happens, you choose it, if not in this lifetime, in some other.'

Chief among Rodgers' subsequent record of achievements in public life was his success in forcing a repeal of the Phoenix municipal law against psychic reading, which had been on the city's statute books since 1913, and, though rarely enforced, rep-resented, as he saw it, a transgression of the rights and dignities of psychics everywhere.

Nonetheless, in 1992, feeling that the grander purpose his tarot cards predicted for him had not yet been fulfilled, John Rodgers ran as an independent candidate for the presidency of the United States of America on the following platform:

NO INCOME TAX

LEGALIZATION OF ALL DRUGS

PRINTING MONEY TO PAY OFF THE NATIONAL DEBT

NO GUN CONTROL

SENATORS TO SERVE ON STATE LEGISLATURES

NO CENSORSHIP

If Rodgers had been elected he would have been the first libertarian New Age ex-Mormon minister ever to occupy the White House. But he was not elected, on account of the fact, he says, that the electorate were not yet ready for him.

'Most people are looking for answers, but you can only give them the answers if the time is right. There's an answer to every question.' He reaches for an incense stick. 'Would you like some tea?'

'If that's true,' I say, 'Then I'd like you to tell me the meaning of life, because it seems to me that no-one has the answer to that, whatever the time.'

'The only purpose for existence is to be happy,' he replies, 'and now, I have to open up the store again.'

I buy a jar of Poseidon incense and a book called *How to Make Yourself Invisible* from him, out of courtesy. And then I leave the Alpha Bookstore and head back up in the direction I have come. Two blocks down from the garage there is a Q-Lube with a special summer deal banner flying from its signpost. I can't quite see how I missed it the first time round.

Two Cities

'Two vast and trunkless legs of stone
Stand in the desert . . . Near them, on the sand,
Half sunk, a shattered visage lies . . .

P.B. SHELLEY

Home-grown frontier mythology has for so long promulgated the bizarre idea that deserts exist solely for the purpose of testing the ingenuity of irrigators that many people, among them inhabitants of the desert states, are quite put out at the more recent discovery that deserts in general exist for no purpose at all, beyond the simple fact of their being.

Strewn across the wide range throughout the southwest are small wood or metal windmills, pumping up water from the underground table into holding tanks on the surface. Without these mundane little turbines, the west could not have been settled; the water they pumped kept cattle on the range, kept miners and prospectors watered and made homesteaders from migrants otherwise headed for the fertile valleys of California. In many southwestern yards model windmills stand as talismanic reminders of the fragile grace of the god water.

Settlers to the southwest, the vast majority of them from well-watered land to the east of the 98th parallel, have been reluctant to accept that the southwest's most persistent quality is aridity, even though everything we know of the history of the region's human inhabitants suggests that their adaptation to the lack of water is the single common thread linking them all together. Over a thousand years ago the Sinagua ('without water', the Spanish called them), who lived in the Verde Valley in the northern upland desert, near Sedona, were constructing stone-lined ditches to divert streams to their farmlands. Their geographical and temporal neighbours, the Hohokam, dug the most extensive prehistoric canal system in the world right through the Salt River Valley, over which Phoenix now sprawls, and grew sufficient cotton and barley on irrigated fields to support an estimated population of a hundred thousand souls. The name Hohokam, incidentally, was given to these people by the Pima Indians. It means 'the vanished ones' or 'all used up'; they were so named, because they disappeared.

In 1867, newly released from the losing side in the Civil War and feeling he didn't have much more to lose, a man called Jack Swilling fetched up in the Salt Valley Basin and noticed what seemed to be the marks of ancient trenches cut into the sod. At that time, a few farmers in the Salt Valley grew hay to supply the army of the union, but the Salt River only watered a strip of land on either side of the bank. Beyond that the soil was dry and impenetrable. In those days, the Salt, the Colorado, the Green, the Rio Grande and a few other southwestern rivers provided settlers close-by with reliable, year-round sources of water. Whoever controlled these of necessity determined how the southwest developed and the kind of place it has become today. Swilling figured there was money to be made uncovering the ancient irrigation trenches and putting them to work again, so he raised $400 from an eastern financier to set up the Swilling Irrigation Canal Company, hired sixteen hands and began in December 1867 to dig out Hohokam ditches at the north bank of the Salt across from present day Tempe. Hitting caliche the troupe moved location and began again a little further north at a place called Smith's Station, eventually opening up an irrigation channel a mile and a half into the desert. By 1870 164 men and 61 women were living at Smith's farming the newly watered land. The little community was to become the city of Phoenix, and it arose, quite literally, from the ashes of the Hohokam empire. Phoenix was given the title of capital of the Arizona Territory, over the town of Prescott further north in the cooler uplands, but soon successive flooding and drought in Phoenix created whispers of counter-revolution from the residents of Prescott, and it became clear that Phoenix's future as a prominent administrative and governmental centre depended upon gaining proper control of its water supply, without which it risked dwindling back into the remote little supply station it had been when Swilling dropped by just a decade or two before.

Phoenix, City of the Sun, is the southwest's great hubris. Today around a million people work in its chilled offices and shuffle through its miles of shopping malls, kept comfortable by banks of air conditioning units and the mist from overhead water coolers. For about nine months of the year the bowels of the city are cooled to a pleasant 72 degrees, while outside the ambient temperature can reach 110. Heat produced by air conditioners and moisture from misters and swamp coolers makes the streets of the city hotter still and humid. Over the past twenty years or so, Phoenix has reinvented its ecosystem. In every public space, in office plazas, in private yards and in hotel gardens the colours of the desert – browns, soft purple, olive drab and umber – have been replaced by a deceiving verdancy; middle eastern palms line the boulevards, the roadside verges are kept plush with Bermuda grass, the golf courses filled in with astroturf. Waterfalls tumble down brand-new Italian Renaissance statuary in shopping malls named Il Borgata and the spacious lawns of Shea Boulevard and Joan d'Arc Road are daily ploughed by Chicanos watering, mowing, watering. Most of the city's inhabitants are strangers to desert life and wish to stay that way; they grew up among the waving grasses of the Great Plains, they tramped rainy Chicago streets, they remember the Mississippi mud. To these people the desert scape is as unforgiving as a wrathful god. Greening the land is become a Pheonix obsession, or rather, what goes on in Phoenix is a reflection of a national preoccupation, for lawns occupy more land than any single crop in the USA, including wheat, corn and tobacco. In the west, where aridity is a persistent problem, they suck up sixty per cent of the water pumped to the cities.

Phoenix seems to regard itself as a triumphant monument to the strength of human ingenuity, a great whorl of life where all around is dead and dry. In 1958 the city won the All-American City award in *Look* Magazine; the aspirations of that aggressive, neurasthenic decade matching the cosy suburban grids, the wide, auto-friendly expressways and the jousting braggadocio of the City of the Sun. Phoenix is the only city I know whose natural features have become nothing more than yard landscaping. When confronted by mountains, Camelback to the east, Squaw Point to the north, the wanton suburbs have spread their creeping roads and grown around them. Between the glittering resort hotels in the north and the empty lots of the hispanic south are dotted shopping malls counterfeiting urban bustle. The mammon virus throbs everywhere, extending its spidery legs into the lowliest corner of the city and poisoning its soul. The metropolis that supposedly rose from a voided desert basin like a brilliant mirage has become little more than a phantasmagoria of isolation, greed and nihilistic materialism. And as it grew and thrived, the Salt River Valley Basin on which it stood began slowly to die.

Some crazy things have been done in the name of the Colorado Doctrine and the Homestead Act, but none much crazier than the agricultural development of the Salt River Valley. The doctrine, which was designed to encourage settlers on the frontier, said that every man (or woman?) had an exclusive right to the water on his land, so long as he sank the wells and built the windmills to pump it up. The doctrine held no regard for the principle of sharing; if your land lay upstream from your neighbour's there was nothing to stop you bottling the entire river, taking it out to the sea and pitching it in, if the mood to do so came upon you. The Homestead Act was introduced in an attempt to dispose of public land for farming, in the days when the federal government held most of the land out west. Each family of settlers was given a plot of 160 acres. The rule applied equally to wet, fertile plains land as to the semi-arid sagebrush and desert laterite west of the 98th, so the homesteader, given the right to suck up as much ground water as he could often didn't distinguish either and planted the west with fool-headed crops completely unsuited to the semi-arid conditions; thirsty cotton, citrus, leafy vegetables. Alfalfa, a low-value crop used for cattle feed, grows in the Salt River valley today on water sucked up from the Colorado River and piped over 150 miles of arid mesas and sunburnt plain.

Aridity calls for adaptation and implies limits to development, population growth and agriculture. The equilibrium of an arid land is so delicately maintained that it demands attentiveness from those who wish to live in it; it cannot give of itself for long without being nurtured in return. These are the qualities that deserts share with rainforests.

The Hopi, who live on the mesas east of the painted desert in northern Arizona, pay homage to the kachina spirits they say control precipitation and moving water and to snakes who look after pools of water and the ground water supply. Rain and snake dances call up these spirits and assure that the order of the cosmos is kept. If there is drought, it is because the Hopi have not been diligent in their dancing and they must start afresh with renewed vigour. Hispanics, who have lived for many centuries in the deserts of the American continent pray to Santa Barbara for hail and lightning, to San Isidro for irrigation, to San Juan Bautista to bless baptismal water and hot spring spas and to the Virgin herself, to intercede and beg for rain and clement weather.

According to the Hopi, the Hohokam and Sinagua didn't disappear at all, but became so decadent from their years spent farming fertile, irrigated land, that their spirits died, their culture failed and they were forced to move to the thirsty hills of the painted desert to rediscover their souls. Anthropologists say that the Hohokam survived years of drought, but were defeated by the flooding which followed and washed away their irrigation canals. In any case, water was somehow or other the most likely cause of the Hohokam's disappearance.

Without the Salt River the city of Phoenix would most likely scorch into dust. Dams on the Salt – Granite Reef, Diversion Dam, Mormon Flat, Horse Mesa Dam, Steward Mountain Dam, and the Roosevelt Dam, the nation's first reclamation project – regulate the natural dwindling and flooding of the river and bring the Phoenix suburbs of Mesa, Tempe and Scottsdale and much of the city itself sufficient water to keep the roadside verges green, faucets running and the yard pools full. In 1963 Arizona won a claim against California in the Supreme Court, giving the state in addition, a right to Colorado River water, and the construction of hundreds of miles of pipeline and pumps began, to bring water to the south and west of the city. So Phoenix divided into two; in the north and east water brought in from the Salt is cheap, and used as if infinite. In the south and west, also the poorest parts of the city, dependent on the Central Arizona Project, water is expensive, lawns are smaller and there are fewer boulevards of palms.

Not so long ago Scottsdale was a convalescent spot for consumptives, who came in from the newly crowded slums of New York and Chicago. The air in the Salt Valley was said to be among the driest and purest in the country. Barred from entering Phoenix proper, the consumptives pitched their tents just outside the town in what is now Scottsdale. Although I have never seen any pictures from that time, I have an image in my mind of Scottsdale as it was then, a mountainous city of white rope and canvas biting at the blue sky, its inhabitants lying within, gasping and bloody. Scottsdale has particularly poignant associations for me, because my mother was consumptive all through her adolescence, and being born in one of the poorer boroughs of East London, spent her convalescent years in the mid-forties lying on a balcony at a sanatorium near Wanstead Flats, breathing in all the filth and smog of a ruined city and struggling to live. The once-dry air of Scottsdale is damp from the mist of swamp coolers, and contaminated with car exhaust and pollen from Bermuda grass. Ironically, the population of the Phoenix metropolitan area, which includes Scottsdale now has one of the highest incidences of hay fever on the continent.

Driving south along Interstate 17 towards Tucson, past whirring windmills, alongside rich, black, abandoned loam, I saw great splits in the land running east to west, a foot wide in places, where the underground water table has been sucked dry and earth has sunk. The little wooden windmills still turn, but there is nothing much left for them to pump.

It's different in Tucson, according to Mark Myers, who is trying to change southern Arizona's water policy. 'You should have seen the city fifteen years ago. Palm trees, huge yards planted to lawn back and front. That's all gone. We've taught ourselves to like the desert purples and browns. We're a desert town. No-one's pretending anything else any more.' I looked out of the window of his office over the web of the city and saw that what he was saying was right. Bounded at its northern and western edges by the Rillito and Santa Cruz rivers, and all around by high desert mountains, Tucson seems to have come to terms with itself. No banks of Bermuda grass or weeping medieval fountains set on marble plazas attempt to hide the truth, which is that Tucson is built on the desert. The reasons for this are complex and historical. The proportion of hispanic people, whose roots run deep and long in southern Arizona, is higher in Tucson than it is in Phoenix. Perhaps this accounts for the southern city's quiet self-confidence. Hispanic culture tends to value community and family above wealth-creation, and perhaps because it remains a sacred culture hispanic people seem more accepting of their surroundings than anglo-saxons. In any case, Tucson has a kind of freedom that the state capital, a much larger, richer and more sprawling city, lacks. Phoenix appears to be a city under silent and persistent siege; its sprawl an act of defiant self-defence. In some profound way, the desert has defeated it.

The planners – if there were any – who oversaw the building of Phoenix have allowed a creeping tumour to take over the Salt River basin, a canker that swells but does not live and does its best to kill the life around it. Phoenix continues to grow and although it is unlikely to run out of water faster than it has already run out of life, Phoenix is *hohokam*, quite used up.

In the end, the great southwestern deserts will tend towards what deserts have always doubly been; no man's lands and nomads' lands.

Standing People

'Why are deserts so facinating? It is because you are
delivered from all depth there.'

JEAN BAUDRILLARD

There was a rumour going around the bars and cafes of the
southwest in the summer of '93 that during the filming of *Thelma
and Louise* a year or so before, the movie's location managers
had stripped a large acreage of southeast Utah desert clean of its
sagebrush, creosote and mesquite trees in order to make it appear
more authentic.

We in the West have some strange ideas about deserts, and
that is, I suppose, because we have come by them strangely.
For the most part desert lands are geographically and culturally
remote places for westerners, belonging as they do to the Middle
East, to Africa, and to Mongolia. Our colonization and settle-
ment of the great American, Australian, and even African deserts
is so recent and has brought with it so much repression and
butchery that we are still too busy recovering from our collective
guilt to have been able to form a settled opinion of what desert
occupation may mean for us, having in those colonized countries
literally whited out the more ancient cultural conventions of the
original inhabitants, and replaced them, if at all, with a series of
stereotypes. I don't quite know why, perhaps as a defence against
the hostility and strangeness of the terrain, but we westerners
routinely choose to ignore the richness and complexity of desert
scapes in favour of a psychological archetype which represents
them as dead zones, liminal purgatories, symbolic of the border
between life and death, between Christianity and Islam, between
ignorance and wisdom, between rationalism and magic. The

desert – for all deserts are become 'the desert' – still remains for many of us the ascetic stereotype gleaned from the diaries and paintings of western adventurers in Egypt and the Arabian peninsula. No matter what our actual experience of deserts might be, the cultural memory persists of an expanse of sand, heaped at intervals into a waved sea of dunes, on which single palms are to be found wilting with picturesque abandon over blue oasis water. Likewise, we have chosen to imbue the lives of most indigenous desert-dwellers, which are exquisitely adapted to their harsh and delicate environment, with nothing more complex than a romantic wistfulness. Whether we are speaking of Australian aborigines, American Indians, Mongols or Bedouin, it has made little difference to our summation of all desert-dwellers as lawless, fierce, exciting, uncommitted people, as though by the same account all inhabitants of temperate climates could be categorized as law-abiding, phlegmatic and dull.

The Great American desert isn't a singular terrain of course; it consists of many different scapes and ecosystems which together make up a number of discrete environments. There are vernacular deserts with their plains of sagebrush and yucca, and monumental deserts with their architectural buttes and sandstone reefs. There are low deserts and upland deserts, cold and hot, desert made from laval Navajo sandstone, soft, white gypsum or ferrous laterite; deserts of green hills and valleys and deserts of burned, brick-hard plain thinly dotted with couch grass. Four great deserts stretch across the southwestern states of New Mexico and Arizona: the Yuma, Mojave, Sonora and Chihuahua, each quite different to the eye and in fact, but remaining indistinct and muddled in the western cultural codex. Of the four, the Sonora is perhaps the best known and loved, not least because it is the sole North American habitat of the saguaro cactus which has become the supreme symbol of the American southwest. In many people's eyes the saguaro is the definitive cactus, tall, perpendicular trunk, coloured dull leaf-green, spiny along the vertical ribs. Although the real things often have no branches, or many branches, the saguaro always appear in cartoon images with a pair of arms set parallel to one another and lifted up to the sky in supplication. In one way, the saguaro is a strange choice of symbol, for the cacti grow only over a relatively small area of the Sonoran desert, and within that area, generally only on bajadas, the slopes of desert mountains. They cease altogether at the elevations north of Phoenix and in many places, cattle grazing has reduced them to a thin population. Nonetheless, as advertisers know well, our image of desert America is incomplete without them.

Caboose and I passed through the Sonora from the south, in April, and then again three months later, in late July. On the first occasion we were heading down towards Robles Junction on the 86, across the flat basalt chaparral of the Tucson basin towards the Papago Indian Reservation and the town of Why, Arizona, making the journey slowly, over several days. Beyond the soft shoulder of the road, the desert stirred in the beginnings of the spring heat like a marsh monster. The odd roadrunner skimmed across in front of the car, leaving its tracks but there were no indications that other vehicles had been by. We ran over a thin film of powder which had gradually settled into a baked cast in the centre of the track, at either side of the road divider markings.

The saguaro were in bloom, and where the road dipped it was fringed with supple bunch grass growing in the drainage ditches either side. Although it had not rained for many days, there was evidence of precipitation. We passed through Green Valley, Queen's Well and Miracle Valley, and came out the other side into fields of red-blossomed ocotillo branches. Waxy white saguaro flowers made bridal veils of the bajadas and appeared as sombre teacups balanced at the tip of green columns where the road cut through low-lying plains. At night, longnose bats came out to sip their nectar, and by the next afternoon the blooms would be dead, pushed aside by new buds eager to meet the sun which would next day vanquish them also. Occasionally, a Gila woodpecker hollowing out saguaro flesh for its nest would send the sound of machine-gun fire echoing across the hills. On that first visit, I remember being shocked by the greenness and complexity of the Sonora. Perhaps I was even a little affronted that this hottest, driest of the great American continental deserts had so confounded my expectations. There were no palms, no oases, no honey-coloured dunes. Instead there were highway medians lined with immense green ocotillo, palo verde trees and green-leaved mesquite and saltbush and greasewood and barrel cactus and prickly pear and furry cholla.

When I returned along more or less the same route in late July, the saguaro bore brick-red fruit, some of which had already fallen and reduced in the sun to a figgy compote beneath. The summer rains were late that year and the woody ribs that keep the cacti vertical had dried and were creaking in the heat like ancient gables. Cactus wrens scuttled in and out of the spines and headed for the shade of the holes cut by the woodpeckers back in the spring. By day, sparrowhawks hung as still as pictures in the sky, and screech owls sang the nights through.

At the junction onto the 286, in the direction of Sasabe and the Mexican border, on the return journey there was a whole coyote, hours dead, end-up and barrel-fat. Six or seven raven-surgeons rose in front of the car, flapped noiselessly round and landed back on its belly, each waiting for another to make the first incision. Further south the road dissolved out to a line of glossy light before being lost below the curvature of the earth. To the west a range of low hills obscured the horizon and to the east was a small disturbance of dust, most likely where a group of cattle had gathered around a water pump. Across the monumental sweep of land in view there were saguaro, extending up to the horizon and watching sightless the progression of day to night, night to day; waiting for nothing, but seemingly waiting all the same.

Part of our fascination with the saguaro must be that they are the only living things of great size out in the Sonora. There are no large trees – palo verde and mesquite are squat in habit. And part must also be that there is an ancient stillness about them, along with a particular kind of stoic dignity. Together they seem to make up a strange and silent tribe. The Hopi call them the standing people, and ranchers in the Spanish Land Grant ranches south of Tucson towards Nogales often refer to them as citizens.

Unlike us, the saguaro are so finely attuned to their environment, that any change in circumstance kills them. An unexpected frost will destroy them, even though they can habitually withstand the 40° C changes in temperature imposed by burning Sonoran summers and freezing winter nights. If cattle trample the nurse plants – palo verde and mesquite – that shade saguaro seedlings and protect them from predators then the seedlings will perish. The roots, which snake out just below the surface as widespread as the cactus is tall, are capable of sucking up two hundred gallons of water in one rainfall and holding it for a year as a viscous jelly deep inside the pleated trunk. Yet a strong wind or lightning will defeat them. Their skins are waxed against transpiration and spined to ward off animals, but many of the more mature plants are pitted with the disease-ridden holes made by Gila woodpeckers or insects. They can take fifteen years to reach a foot high, and yet cactus rustlers can, and do uproot them in a matter of seconds with shovels.

On the second visit, I drove down to the Saguaro National Monument just outside Tucson, left the car on the east side of the park, near the Desert Museum, and took off on one of the short hiking trails, an old mine road twisting up through King's Canyon into the Tucson Mountains. It was late morning and the temperature was hitting 110, too hot for most of those who had made the drive over from the city. Of the six or seven cars parked in the lot, only one party looked as though they had any intention of walking. The others left the comfort of air conditioning for as brief a moment as possible, in order to get from their cars to the exhibit room, gift store and cafe. Even the museum's small botanical garden was empty. I like heat as a rule, particularly dry heat but the combined heat from the sun and rocks up at King's Canyon that morning was as intense as a charcoal grill, so hot it brought on a pounding head, breathlessness and heart palpitations. The brilliant green that coloured almost everything in the spring had faded, and the ocotillo leaves had fallen, but in compensation, there were prickly pears and cinnamon-coloured saguaro fruit. At the top of the path I disturbed a jack rabbit hidden under the shade of a mesquite bush. Looking down across the red hills, spiny with saguaro and into the deep blackened green of the horizon, I became aware of the mythical quality of the image in front of my eyes and it was suddenly clear to me just how satisfying a symbol the saguaro are, for a panoma of saguaro rising from heat-crazed hills is as perfect a picture of the desert as you will ever see.

The Death Cult

'After all, what's a cult? It just means not enough
people to make a minority.'

ROBERT ALTMAN

A letter from an Italian prince arrives at Fergus' apartment in
New York in late July. The prince is a friend of one of Fergus'
acquaintances. According to Fergus the prince's family own a
palazzo on the Corso in Rome and count popes and dukes and
statesmen among their ancestors. In his letter, the prince explains
that death is pointless, he sees absolutely no reason why he should
die and so he's decided not to. Being immortal, the prince himself
will be the family terminus.

Fergus faxes the letter through to a bureau near my motel in
Albuquerque with his own message scrawled in uneven hand
along the bottom: 'Is this some kind of joke?' The next day an
accompanying book arrives in the mail, by someone with the
moniker CBJ, called *Together Forever*. Along with the book
comes an invitation to the Annual Convergence of the Flame
Foundation in Phoenix, Arizona, a gathering of people who, like
the prince, are physically immortal.

At the time of the letter's arrival I've been in Albuquerque
only three days, and I like it. It's not impressive but it is stolid,
in the same way that parts of nineteenth-century London are
stolid. Roads in Albuquerque are called Iron and Coal and Lead
and there is a serious, mildly aspirant, burgher aspect to the city
I find pleasing. In any case, it's a huge distance to Phoenix. I'm
tempted to skip the Flame Foundation Annual Convergence. On
the other hand, eternal life is probably not something at which
I'll get many cracks so on balance, I'll go. I resign myself to the

drive and call the number on the prince's letter which gets me through to a public relations firm in Los Angeles.

A man on the line introduces himself as the publicist.

'I've been invited to the Annual Conference of the Flame Foundation, could you tell me something about it?'

'The prince said you'd call,' says the publicist 'Uh, it's a convergence, not a conference. A convergence.'

I take it upon myself to ignore this and continue.

'You know, I'm just a friend of a friend of the prince.'

'Oh,' says the publicist 'I think it's best to go through me anyways.'

Showing up at the convergence as a part of some kind of press corps really doesn't appeal to me at all.

'I didn't know that this number would be a PR agency.'

'Well it is,' replies the publicist.

'Couldn't I just come along as an ordinary person?'

'Sure,' says the publicist, 'but I'll be looking after you.'

'Is this thing a big deal? It sounds like it's a big deal, what with a PR agency and all. I mean, how many people will be converging?'

'Eight hundred, a thousand maybe. Listen,' says the publicist. 'If you had awakened to eternal life, would you think it was a big deal?

'A *thousand* immortal people? You mean to say that there are a thousand people who really think they're not going to die, ever?'

'Actually, there are three times that, but two-thirds of them can't come.'

He gives me a number to call and fix up my hotel reservation. An Australian woman called Carol answers the phone and says

'It's so important for you to be here. I am having a good feeling this could change your life.' And that is incentive enough for me.

The next day a press pack arrives along with another copy of the book by CBJ which reminds me that I have yet to look at the first copy. A ticket to the convergence costs $895 plus travelling expenses. $895 x 800 delegates = $716,000. That's tax free. The Flame Foundation is registered with the IRS as a church.

According to the publicity brief, Charles Paul Brown, founder of Flame, was at one time a minister of God, fashion buyer and nightclub singer as well as being the world's first physical immortal. Back in the late fifties Chuck, being spiritually curious but unsatisfied (like most of the rest of us), found himself at a lecture given by a Dr O. L. Jaggers who was running around the US trying to persuade people to live forever. At first Chuck thought the notion was baloney, but then he had a cellular awakening. What happened apparently, was that the death genome in the genetic material in Chuck's cells underwent a change, and, Chuck realized almost overnight, that he had become immortal. Sometime after he became immortal, or perhaps it was in the same moment, Jesus Christ came to see Chuck and told him that everyone on the planet could enjoy the same cellular awakening as Chuck had himself experienced. Chuck was amazed. No need for anyone to die at all, said Jesus. 'When the visitation of him came to me . . . it was not as I had been taught to believe,' Chuck said in a press interview. From then on, he knew he had to spread the message. Nearly thirty years later, Chuck has brought three thousand beings to the realization of their own physical immortality.

Chuck's immortality theory says that if a sufficient number of people discover eternal life then nuclear war and eco-terrorism and family dysfunction and dolphin slaughter and all those other contemporary evils will stop happening because no-one will want to do them any more. According to the theory, if everyone lives forever there will be no ethics, because there will be no moral choices. And there will be no moral choices because we will all be so wonderfully, deliriously *good*. The number of immortals required to form the critical mass is unclear, but it could be as low as 150,000.

It has never occurred to me to give the apostolic calling much consideration, but I seem to be meeting apostles of one sort or another in such quantity right now that the time has come to put my mind to it, and to consider, for example, how tough the apostle's life must be, how physically arduous, peripatetic and without end. The apostle packs a bag and heads for the road like a commercial traveller, tearing himself away from the ties and solid comforts of his home, to pound the lonely road with his spiritual sample bag, never knowing where he might end up, relying solely on his epiphany for support and company. There must be times in an apostle's career when he is laughed and jeered at, disbelieved and disrespected. And so it must have been for Charles Paul Brown. Fortunately, it was not long before he met BernaDeane, an ex-model and singer from Salem, Oregon, with two generations of Seventh-day Adventist preachers in her blood. The couple were married in Mexico and before long BernaDeane had a cellular awakening, and realized that she too was physically immortal.

A few years later, at the end of the sixties, Chuck and Berna-Deane brought James Russell Strole, a young real estate agent into the immortality movement. Within a short while, Jim too had physically immortalized. The trio settled in Scottsdale, set up an administration and came up with the name Eternal Flame (which then became the Flame Foundation, and, most recently, United Forever). At some point Jim got married and the trinity grew a limb and became a quadriparty. Then Jim got divorced, and Charles, BernaDeane and James now live together in a house with a pool and a jacuzzi at Pinnacle Peak Estates in the glamorous wastelands of northern Scottsdale, known by their collective marque CBJ, or ChuckBernieJim. They have a white Cadillac, and, reputedly, a Harley Davidson painted coral pink.

Two days after the fax I set off from Albuquerque early and drive like a wild thing for 470 miles or so, stopping only once to pick up gas, beef jerky and root beer. For eight hours Caboose thunders along the Interstate, gas pedal flat to the floor with the odometer climbing to a cool sixty-two on a decline, every rivet begging for indulgence; poor Caboose wonders what has hit it and shakes from roof-rack to road. For part of the way the route twists up through ponderosa pine forest and green alpine meadows. On the flatter stretches, across the southern tip of the painted desert, for example, I prop a copy of Mark Twain's *Roughing It* on the steering wheel and read. By the time I reach Phoenix that evening, I am several hundred pages in without knowing quite how I got there.

The Flame Foundation's convergence hotel is one in a chain of bold purgatories sprawled along Scottsdale Road to the north-east of the city. It is hard to imagine a more creative celebration of banality than that afforded by these 'homes from home' with their valet parking, their polypropylene fountains, their corridormuzak, their elevatunes, their hovering uniformed persons as bored and pitiful as organ grinders' monkeys and their open-all-hours themed brasseries offering Custer's Last Stand Cookie Crumble Pie and The Alamo All-American Double Cheeseburger. Imagine an eternity here, a future of pay-per-view, french-milled deodorant soap, maxi-bars and wilting goodnight chocolates. A future yawning through the eons.

By the time I arrive, I'm too tired to socialize, so instead I lie in bed with an uneaten complimentary liqueur chocolate and a copy of the Flame Foundation press pack for company, grazing on room service sandwiches and channel surfing from game show to talk show to sitcom and on to game show again. At nine the prince calls and wishes me goodnight. Half an hour later, the phone rings again; this time it is the publicist.

'You know, there are people who aren't very friendly to the Flame Foundation and who have said all sorts of kooky things about cults.'

'It's not a cult then?'

'Oh jeez, that is so ridiculous. D'you think that a hotel like this would have them if they were a cult? That is so ridiculous. Chuck, Bernie and Jim are three of the nicest people I have ever met. I mean ever.'

'Are you immortal?'

'Uh no, now you mention it, but, I'd sure as hell like to be.'

I pass the rest of the evening contemplating an eternity of Oprah Winfrey. Would she run out of battered wives, pregnant teens, compulsive eaters and impotent husbands, and if she did, could she interview the same ones over again on, say a five hundred year cycle, without anybody noticing?

At the end of 1990, my father died. The evening it happened, I dressed, washed my face and walked down to a cafe where I ate a piece of battered plaice, a pile of salted chips and two pickled eggs. My head was light and sore from crying and all I could do was to sit in this red plastic chair watching the paint on the wall, trying to reconstruct in my mind my father's smell, knowing I had forgotten it already. Sometimes this memory unsettles me, but then, it's not possible to keep on and on feeling. There comes a point at which some unconscious survival mechanism pulls the numbness switch, and shuts down everything but the motor functions and the senses, so, although there may be nothing left to feel, there is always something left to see or touch or smell or taste or hear.

The following morning the publicist rings through to my room.

'Uh, there's been a press article in one of the New York style mags. It's really not worth reading. The usual flim flam, cult blah. The journalist had some problems, oh jeez, I should tell you about that woman.'

'Look,' I say emphatically, 'I'm just here out of curiosity. In any case, does it really matter if the Flame Foundation *is* a cult?'

'CBJ is *not* a cult.'

'Yup, right.'

'It's so ridiculous. ChuckBernieJim are wonderful people. Wonderful! Nice! Ridiculous!' the publicist has a habit of carrying vowel sounds on so long you wonder if they will end at all, or simply continue on forever as musical notes.

'If you're gonna write anything,' he says 'it's not customary to quote the publicist, you know. Nothing the publicist says ever gets attributed.'

'OK.' This is new to me, but I don't feel like taking much notice of it either.

The prince and I have agreed to meet for breakfast. I get to the hotel cafe early, take a seat and help myself to a cup of cold coffee at the breakfast bar. Most of the tables are full, and most of their occupants are wearing Flame Foundation name badges. One of the odd things is, that no-one is on their own. Perhaps that's not odd; but it seems odd right now.

'Hi,' a woman with Sally on her name badge, shouts across from the table next door, waving with her fingers and giggling a little. Her companion, sitting with her back to me turns and grins. I grin back for as short a time as is polite, then bury myself in my coffee. Actually I'm rather nervous. The first time I came across royalty on this trip the whole thing didn't go down so well. Ten minutes after our agreed time the prince arrives with casual but unmistakeable *langueur*, trailing behind him a bronzed, somewhat other-worldly latin type with bee-stung lips. I don't quite know what I should be expecting – someone older perhaps? Colder? Less cherubic? The prince and his companion are dressed in pressed white jeans and navy blazers. Their hair is oiled and pushed back, their skin is newly shaved and perfumed, their fingernails buffed. The effect is to lend them an air of sinister insouciance.

'And how is England?' enquires the prince, 'Is your suite comfortable?'

Suite? I smile a nervous smile and say nothing.

'The grand piano in my room is a little out of tune, but they are sending someone to fix it.'

The prince and his companion fly in to Phoenix for Flame Foundation meetings a couple of times a year from the Venezuelan island of Margarita, where they raise coconuts. They also follow ChuckBernieJim around on their international tours.

From somewhere unseen a waiter rustles up and places a cafetière of coffee in front of the prince's companion, Eduardo, who pours it, first for the prince, then for himself. The prince explains that he does not eat breakfast.

'Immortality has taught us to care about our bodies.' He invites me to look. Trim, well-muscled, smooth-skinned. But then he's only twenty-nine. What about when he's 29,000? The prospect doesn't bother him, for he's sure the ageing process will go into reverse after a while. I wonder silently if he will eventually become a million-year-old foetus.

'This gathering here is just one example of cellular intercourse,' says the prince, referring to the breakfast room of immortal people. The phrase 'cellular intercourse' was coined by CBJ to describe the quite innocent desire of immortal bodies to be in close proximity to other immortal bodies. It has caused a few misunderstandings in the mortal community. And most particularly among the press. In any case, since they discovered the secret of eternal life the prince and Eduardo have been having regular cellular intercourse both with each other and with their three thousand or so fellow immortals.

We sip our coffee in pensive silence for a while before the prince remarks: 'Death is something that you've been doing all along in small things, in not being everything you could be, censoring yourself, all these things are death. By the end, by the time people die, all they need is a little push.' This rings true to me. 'He knows death to the bone,' said Yeats. 'Man has created death.'

The prince and his lover wear wedding bands. Eduardo explains: 'We used to be promiscuous, but now we are together forever.'

In the hotel bookstore there is a copy of *that* New York magazine. The writer of the article on CBJ spent time at a Flame Foundation convergence in Tel Aviv and has no doubts that the Flame Foundation is a cult fostered by a charismatic trinity of spiritual entrepreneurs whose mission is to manipulate wealthy brainwashees out of their greenbacks. It's a curious thing, but there are more immortals, as a proportion of the population, in Israel than anywhere on earth. Is immortality another promised land, I wonder, less embattled than the first? The publicist catches sight of me in the store, and, taking me to one side, murmurs 'I don't know what got into that woman,' referring to the writer of the article, 'one minute she was having a great time, and then she just went all cold on us. She was out for some sleaze story and she wasn't about to stop until she got it. Jeez, people like that . . . Listen, go anywhere you like, talk to anyone you like. We have absolutely nothing to hide.'

'CBJ?'

'Sure, I can fix that,' replies the publicist, taking my arm and drawing me closer. His breath smells faintly of cornflakes. 'You're not going to like me for saying it, but maybe she had PMT or something.'

I make no response. The publicist is right, I am not going to like him for saying it. Actually, I am not going to like him for much else either.

The prince has a point I think. Death does reach back into our lives to stifle what it finds. We have sent out our stories and our fierce technology to bait it, and yet, at the same time, the law, politics, money, the family, most of our institutions are constructed around its inevitability. And what else is America's history, or Europe's, or Africa's or Asia's but a rack of tales whose beginnings and ends are death and death and always death?.

Out in the foyer, the massed realms of immortals gather for the day's events, exquisitely dressed, groomed, bejewelled, handsome, huggy, goddamned perfect. After all these months in scalding temperatures with no money and little company, I am forced to admit that I have gone to seed. My body's scrawny, my clothes are shabby and my hair is dyed in Brazilian Dreams. I'm intimidated. I lose my nerve and bolt off to the foyer to pay the Flame Foundation my hotel bill, where I discover that my credit card has been stopped for non-payment. Carol, the Australian, remembers my voice and throws me a look of tender disdain. She knows Brazilian Dreams when she sees it.

The CBJ manager Art corners me on the way out and introduces himself. He says he wants me to meet his daughter, who is as beautiful as himself, dressed head to toe in DKNY and almost inevitably, I suppose, immortal.

'How do you *know* she's going to live forever?'

'Because both her parents are. See, if you look better this year than you did last, you've had a cellular awakening. If you don't, well, you're doing something wrong,' replies Art, inviting me to admire his limpid eyes, his honey-coloured skin, his Donna Karan playsuit. Eternal life in lieu of plastic surgery.

'Some people have experienced what we call a cellular awakening, and then gone off and thought they could do the rest of it by themselves.' He shakes his head, and his daughter shakes hers.

'They didn't make it.'

Today is science day at the Flame Foundation Convergence, but most of the convergers have gone shopping, because most of them have plenty of money to spend . . . because all of them have had a cellular awakening. Who needs to sit around listening to some dreary boffin expounding on the virtues of immortal brain cells. Hell, if you can afford Ralph Lauren you *know* you're special.

I take a seat in the lecture theatre next to an elderly lady who turns to look for my badge, and not seeing it, asks:

'Are you . . . ?' I nod.

She lowers her voice to a soft whisper

'I'm worried about my husband.'

Suppressing an in-bred tendency to embarrassment, I shuffle closer. There are surprisingly few elderly immortals. Maybe the ageing process makes such self-deception harder, or perhaps the elderly are just wiser than us, after all.

'I think he has his doubts about whether or not he's had a cellular awakening,' she whispers. 'And it's making him sick.'

Five minutes later she is fast asleep and snoring in her chair, while some mad scientist delivers the day's keynote speech on the pointlessness of ageing. The Flame Foundation has invited some pretty respectable names to its science day – physicians, eminent immunologists, biochemists – as well as a few New Agey rent-a-cranks. The cranks and the boffins differ in one crucial respect; none of the boffins ever suggests that human beings can live forever.

That evening, I run into the prince and his lover relaxing by the pool having spent an arduous day out shopping. They want to be sure I will turn up to hear CBJ speak the following morning.

'You'll see, ChuckBernieJim are the most sincere, most loving, most supportive people on the planet,' says the prince, sipping a mineral water.

'We follow them around because we just want to be with them all the time,' echoes Eduardo, squeezing a lime into his partner's glass.

'CBJ have made us whole,' adds the prince squeezing my hand.

'Believe us. You won't find a more amazing group of people.'

'Our family,' says the prince, mystically, raising his glass and watching the ice swivelling inside.

A moth annihilates itself in the neon lamplight around the swimming pool. Eduardo puts down his glass, reaches out to hug me, misses and squeezes my arm instead.

'When someone – anyone – does something bad we don't talk about the reasons, we don't apologise, we just look at it and let it go. Whatever it is, we won't let it divide us,' continues the prince. Whether this remark is aimed at me, I don't know, but it seems a strange thing to say nonetheless.

'I used to call myself a gay man. I used to say I'm gay, I'm this and that but all those labels are limiting now. I'm me and I'm immortal.' Lounging by a palm-fringed pool in the middle of a warm summer evening sipping cocktails and expounding your own virtues to attentive ears is about enough to make any-one feel immortal, I should think. You might expect a certain mysticism to cling to people whose will to live is such that they are prepared to believe they will never die, but it doesn't.

'We leave it to others now to deal with symptoms. We deal with the cause. We're scratching the surface of what it means to be human. We're in the lab stage but we're contagious.'

Bleah bleah bleah to that.

I'm back in my room, fanning off the heat.

The phone rings. Anticipating the publicist, I hesitate to answer, but after a dozen rings I pick up. It's Fergus.

'How are they?'

'Don't ask. I have brain meltdown. It's all I can do to force myself to leave my room.'

'Think positive,' responds Fergus, half-ironically.

'OK,' I ruminate on positivity. 'The hotel has three pools and a cute cocktail waiter.'

Stifled laughter. Fergus is friend enough to get my jokes, even the bad ones.

'To my mind there's something really rather hubristic and faustian and enchanted about it all,' he says, 'people who actually think they'll live forever, like Greek gods. Reminds me of *The Picture of Dorian Gray*; splendid in a crumbling, ruined sort of way.' Fergus is in grandiose mood and I feel wretched. We are ill suited at this moment for conversation. After a few superficial pleasantries he rings off. I sulk for a while, then collect my thoughts. There is something very weird going on. It is as though I have descended into a sort of limbo without having time to pack a bag. I am in new and dismal territory. I am gradually becoming quite confused and nervous. I begin to sense a presence hanging around the room. I check inside the wardrobe, under the bed and behind the shower curtain, but of course, I don't find anything, or anybody. However and whenever it happened, there is no doubt in my mind that I have been separated off from everything familiar. The morbid presence grows and begins to feel like panic.

The phone rings. This time it's the publicist.

'Just ringing to remind you about the CBJ event tomorrow. I've organized for you to meet them after. Once you meet them you'll realize all this cult stuff is nonsense.'

I go to bed repeating his words as a refrain. All this cult stuff is nonsense. All this cult stuff is nonsense. All this cult stuff . . .

No-one wants to live forever, not really, do they? Aren't we simply frightened of the process of dying? And aren't we afraid because we are self-conscious, and aren't we self-conscious because we are human? There doesn't seem to be much of a way around it.

At breakfast the next morning, after a long, profound sleep, my perspective has returned, and I am feeling less vulnerable. Whatever uncertainties came upon me during the night seem to have dissipated. Next to me in the line for cereal is a man who informs me that if oxygen became scarce as a result of pollution his body would adapt because it is immortal. He'd grow eighteen lungs, a pollution filter, gills, an extra head if it were needed. Ageing is just the process of morphing into other forms, he remarks, spooning some raisin bran into a bowl. There's not much I can add to this byzantine prophecy. Maybe a three-thousand year-old human being *would* evolve quite naturally into some poly-lunged, multi-headed fish-person. Who am I to discount the possibility? I've never met one.

Sally approaches me at the fruit juice bar, puts a hand around my waist and says, 'My want for you is to feel that you want to be here.'

CBJ do not give talks or put on performances, or lecture; they have 'happenings,' which for the purposes of the convergence take place in a lecture theatre at the hotel. The 'happenings' are always full, and many people in the audience have come a long way for them. A premium seat for the duration of the convergence, including all the 'happenings', costs a great deal in 'heart money', and is the privilege of the rich and very committed. A big day for the publicist who is up at the rostrum, fussing around with the sound system. I mention that there are a few things I'm not clear about and since he has to change for the 'happening' at ten he suggests we walk over to his room and talk them through.

Is it true, I ask in a casual sort of way, that members of the Flame Foundation live in communal houses in Scottsdale, and if I discover the secret of eternal life, will I get a place in one?

The publicist throws me a look of despair, as if to say 'Haven't you been *listening* to me all these days?' then sighs and settles in for the long distance. We wander past the pool and through a side gate to a row of casitas looking out over the courtyard. Yes, some immortals live together, but immortals are all friends, and it's natural for friends to help out other friends, and get them settled when they move to Scottsdale. CBJ never asks anyone to come to Arizona, there's no weird compound or anything, but they just do, you can't stop people being where they want to be. What about the money? The publicist shakes his head. They'd earn more being *dentists* for chrissakes, and here they are opening up the world to the potential for immortality. Jeez. He raises his eyes to heaven, stops in front of casita number four and is just about to put his key in the door and end our conversation when his wife pokes her head out of the room, throws me the devil's glance and tossing her sweetheart blonde hair, says to her husband, 'Honey, we need to speak.'

The publicist's wife is not just a trophy, she's the championship. I wonder vaguely how he hooked her. He's not rich, he's not young, he's not handsome. He *is* tenacious, though; terribly, terribly tenacious.

'You know,' he continues in confidential mode, 'my business was in a mess. Jeez, it was the end of the eighties, really tough times, and then I landed this contract with CBJ . . .'

'Honey,' repeats his wife 'I'd like to speak with you now.'

The publicist shoots a momentary pleading glance in the direction of the blonde curls, before returning his gaze to his pumps.

'So I landed this contract with CBJ and things have just been great ever since. The business has picked up . . .' he glances at his wife '. . . everything.' Then drawing me closer to him he whispers 'That journalist, you know, you're not gonna like me for sayin' this, but she was about forty and not married or anything and jeez, I think maybe the frustration went to her head.'

Back in the lecture theatre, the crowd has grown several hundredfold and transmogrified into a mob. Raised above them on the stage sit the progeny of Charles and BernaDeane; silent daughter, apostolic son, immortals both, while at the back of the room, behind the very rich and very committed the rabble squabbles over seats with the usual assortment of tricks; left luggage, icy stares, scribbled notices, strings of clothes, latent violence. The prince and Eduardo are seated at the front, fanning each other. Piped MOR ballads tinkle out of the speakers on the stage and a roadie fiddles with the mikes. The publicist has disappeared. The lights dim, the lights go up and Art the office manager appears at the front of the stage, beaming.

'How are you all?'

'Yeeaaahh.'

'Feeling OK?'

'Yeeaahhh, right on.'

'Welcome.'

'Wooowee.'

'You know, this morning we are really happy to have a CBJ . . .'

'Right on.'

'. . . Happening'

'Yeeearrggghh.'

'And I'm sure you'll want to let them know how much of a praise you have for them.'

The crowd begins to clap and whistle and stomp until CBJ enters stage left, a multi-dimensional being made up of thousands of perfect pixel points of light, and moves to centre-stage before suddenly, almost shockingly, separating out into Chuck, Berna-Deane and Jim. The crowd gasps. Chuck is wearing an Andy Warhol print silk shirt, leopardskin waistcoat, and creaseless glazed shoes, while Jim is dressed in raw silk pants pressed so sharp you could commit a murder with them, and a silk shirt with double cuffs. BernaDeane, a vision in designer jeans and low-cut T-shirt with a girlish gingham dress pulled over, moves over to the mike.

'I think we should all sing a song,' and so we do, all of us, in perfect unison, and while we sing, some of us take the opportunity to have a little weep, others to hug each other. The woman seated next to me says 'I love you, you're a beautiful person.' We've never actually met before, but I'm glad she's already seen my better side. Up at the front Kevin, the immortal son of C and B, grabs the mike, a little choked, and shouts: 'Hey, I don't care what the fucking press has to say about us, we fucking *know* who we are, and we *like* it.' Art, the office manager, meanwhile, scans the crowd like a search light, beaming.

A man in the corner of the room shouts back. 'That's *right*' And the mob adds its general approbation: 'Yeah, yeah'; 'That's the *truth*'; 'Right on'.

Another man from the opposite side of the room stands and opens his mouth to speak. In an instant Art catches his eye, points to him and says 'If you have a judgement about what's being said, drop it and keep on *feeling*.'

'Hey, that's *right*. That's great.'

'*Just keep on feeling,*' shouts Art.

'Tell it like it *is*.' 'Yeah, way to go.' 'Right on.' 'We have a praise for you.'

'I *feel* you with me,' says Kevin, addressing the audience, 'We're inside each other.'

'Hey', Art continues, taking up the theme, 'I *need* you, all of you. We have such a *need* for each other.'

'Yeah. That's the truth,' pipes up Chuck, dabbing at the corner of one eye with the cuff of his Andy Warhol shirt.

A lean man with long hair tied behind stands up and says he wants to make a declaration. Silence falls.

'Go ahead, brother. You can be anything you want to be. We're so alive here.'

'I owe these people everything', sighs the man, 'I just want you to know you are the three most wonderful people I have ever met,' he mumbles before bursting into tears.

'Right on,' shouts the crowd en masse, clapping to a beat.

Up on stage, modestly sat, with legs crossed and arms at its sides, the CBJ creature bows its heads and smiles shyly.

'Yeah,' says Art 'Keep on feelin' it.'

As I've said before, I am not afraid to be dead, I'm only fearful of the moment of death, the instant not of the final breath, but of the last thought. I once knew a woman who became so ill that she lost her desire to continue living. She began to refuse food, but she was still afraid of the pain of dying. I asked her if she had any children and she said yes, two, born in 1929 and in 1931. Can you imagine pain greater than that of childbirth, I asked. She thought about this for a little while then said no, she could not, but the pain of childbearing is forgotten in the joy of its consequences. It may well be the same with death, I said.

'Now's the time to give these people heart money'. The financial director of the Flame Foundation is a millionaire business-man. 'It doesn't matter how much but it's a feeling. We want to set targets for people. I don't know *anyone on the planet* like CBJ. They move money from a point of inspiration. I feel abundant when I'm with them.'

'And I feel abundant too,' adds his wife. Maybe that's because you're rich, I say to myself.

'People are trying to put the label cult on us, but it's our daily movement, our daily passion. We're just so alive it *scares* people.'

'Yeah, right on.'

At that moment Chuck shifts in his seat on stage, begins to scratch his crotch and mouths, 'Really, alright, yessss.'

'If they don't see how you can be immortal then leave 'em because they don't love you enough to know the truth,' shouts the financial director's wife, which unsettles the crowd momentarily as they think of the husbands and mothers and children and friends they have left back home. 'Leave them all, they're not worthy.'

'Right on,' responds the woman, who loves me.

James Russell Strole lifts himself to his feet, holds his palms out to the audience and asks for quiet.

'We are out to get people to hear what we're about and to have the opportunity to choose whether to live or not. Anyone can leave. You want to leave? You can just walk out that door, or you can stay here and *live*. You've got people here that care and will support you. All this cheering, this isn't hype. We're excited about each other.' Well, I think, I'm damned glad someone is, because, believe me, you don't make it easy. And with that Jim swings off into some diatribe, the exact point of which is lost on me since it meets absolutely no opposition, about CBJ's right to make their own decisions on how to spend Flame Foundation money.

'We don't tell you what to do with your money, no-one should fucking tell us what to do with ours. You should trust us to use it in the best way,' says Jim.

'Right on,' 'That's great,' 'Yeah, we're with you,' shouts the crowd, dizzy with righteous anger at the mythical enemy.

'They try to label us a cult, but they are in death cult, which is the biggest fucking cult of all.'

Yeah, Yeah, Yeah, they say, like a mouse trap shutting SNAP on reason, SNAP on dissent, SNAP on ambiguity, Yeah yeah yeah, SNAP SNAP SNAP.

Later, in their suite, complete with white grand piano, white marble floors, white spiral staircase, the three parts of CBJ explain to me that they are not a cult, that they earn almost nothing for their endeavours and that they are simply on a pretty humble sort of mission to save the human race from having to die.

'Uh, wasn't that Jesus' job?' I ask, troublemaking.

Chuck, a man of admirably resplendent convictions begins to explain that what Jesus was trying to say during the resurrection was that no-one had physically to die. Even though Jesus did. Because he had to. Just to show that no-one else had to. Which is why the whole Jesus story has been radically misinterpreted. Or misjudged. And anyway, immortality and immortalism and immortals are completely compatible with Christianity, and he used to be a preacher, so he knows that, and Jesus, is you know, on the side of life, or something. BernaDeane, lying on a chaise longue opposite my chair and purring, looks up at me with her big eyes and snickers charmingly. She is fiftysomething, looks thirty-five and the publicist tells me that she still has her period.

From my room that evening I can hear the crowd joining together in some rousing old MOR number before the convergence disco. I'm reminded of Susan Ertz's words: 'millions long for immortality who don't know what to do with themselves on a rainy Sunday afternoon.' Exhausted by the effort of pretence, I black out peacefully into a dreamless sleep.

The next morning, I rise early, put on my swimsuit and head down to the pool. At the bottom of the stairs is a large chick obviously fallen from its nest during the night, alive, not visibly injured, but frightened. The nest is out of sight. An hour or so later I am on my way back to my room when I notice a cleaner wheeling a trolley of towels towards the bird, and I call to him to watch out for it, but instead the man bends down to take a closer look, then without further thought squashes the animal under his boot. BLAM, bird dead. He lifts his boot to inspect the creature's guts still clinging wetly, with indifferent curiosity, as though they were nothing more than his customary breakfast order of scrambled eggs.

'It was dead in any case,' he says breezing off with his trolley.

At ten I ring the prince to say goodbye and a man answers the phone, who is not the prince, nor Eduardo. The prince picks up an extension line, feigns not quite to remember who I am, then wishes me well with the most exquisite *politesse*. This is the last I ever see or hear of him, but I assume he and his lover are living still on an island off the coast of Venezuela forever watching over a grove of coconut trees.

A few months later, back in London, someone from the British branch of the Flame Foundation calls me up and asks if I'd like to come to one of their weekly meetings. How did they get my number? It's a wet, dark afternoon, I am cold and on my own, half tempted.

'Hey,' says the man on the other end of the line, 'we never put pressure on anyone.'

'I hear that,' I reply.

'Right on,' says the man.

'I think I'll go some other time,' I say.

'We're always here for you,' answers the man, 'Always.'

La Jornada

'The most beautiful thing we can experience is mystery. He who does not know it, and does not marvel at it, is, one might say, dead; and his vision extinct.'

ALBERT EINSTEIN

Hardly a day passed during my travels when I did not stumble upon some desert place named for death, mortality and dying: Dead Horse, Skull Valley, Dangling Rope, Death Valley, Hell Canyon, Camino del Diablo, Devil's Backbone, Skeleton Canyon, Murderer's Grave, Deadman Flat, but one of these places served as symbol for them all; Tombstone, Arizona.

The real Tombstone is now a town of shabby bars, seasonal unemployment and souvenir stores. It began as a tiny mining camp in 1879, and by the 1890s fifteen thousand people lived there, making it the fastest-growing city between St Louis and San Francisco. These days Tombstone has a permanent population of 1200, most of whom make their living from the Japanese, German and American tourists who tramp the boardwalks on Allen Street. In place of the whorehouses and gambling joints there is now a sterile row of bric-à-brac stores, selling overpriced paperweights made of scorpions encased in perspex, and drab little jars of cactus jelly. Staging posts have become coach parks, grocery stores frozen yoghurt parlours. The Courthouse is a museum, the Bird Cage Theatre an attraction, Boothill Cemetery an excuse to pass off second-rate Indian jewellery and Western 'art'. During the high season, around Christmas, the locals stage shoot-outs, and vigilante knock-out contests. There is even a mock lynching every now and then. Tombstone makes its living from its myths, and without them the town would die, as have many of the mining and processing towns around – Contention City, Dos Cabezas, Charleston, Pearce, and Paradise. According

133

to the tourist brochure put out by the chamber of commerce, Tombstone is 'as authentic now as it was a hundred years ago'. The town has gone full circle; from camp to camp with barely a breath between.

It is the middle of the low season now, and the town has the forlorn air of all abandoned places. The sky is overcast, and stewed air moving in from the south threatens rain. Having arrived a few hours earlier and found myself a motel for the night, I am throwing in my lot with three locals in a bar on the north side of Allen Street, drinking Bloody Marys and waiting for the storm to break.

'Humid,' remarks a man in a wheelchair, in an attempt to strike up a conversation 'You visitin'?'

'Uh huh.'

'Which motel?'

'Larimar.'

'Bin to th'isotrama show?' The Historama is a three-dimensional tableau of the Tombstone story. A billboard outside advertises it as 'a presentation of the town's factual history', as if there were any other sort.

'Uh nhuh,' I reply, and am about to change the topic of conversation when the barmaid catches my eye with a mildly threatening gesture which suggests that it's just going to be a whole lot easier to keep shtum and order another Bloody Mary and buy the man in the wheelchair a beer.

'Vincent Price does the narration,' says the man, as if offering incontrovertible proof of the show's quality.

The thing with Bloody Marys is they always make me drunk.

'What happened to your legs?' I ask the man. A weathered-looking woman looks away from her conversation on the other side of the bar, glances at me, then returns her gaze to the wood panelling. 'Damned steer fell right on top o'me. You never seen such a mess.'

'Jeez, that's terrible.' A sudden wave of drunken melancholy washes over me. A whole steer, that's just too sad. That's a fucking tragedy.

The man drains his bottle of beer, starts up his wheelchair and without glancing back whirrs out into the summer rain. The barmaid watches him go, pours herself a bourbon then turns to me and says:

'Full of bullshit 'bout cowpunching. He came up from Bisbee 'bout ten years ago. Don't think he ever went near no steer.'

'Damned terrible,' I say.

I stumble out of the bar about thirty minutes later in the vague hope of catching a few of the tourist sights. The rain has cleared and left a pall of humidity smoking the air. A lone teen in a white Toyota calls out 'Yo, baaaabe,' and the sound of his voice parallaxes past the souvenir shops like a fart and dies somewhere up by Fourth Street.

The gunfight at the OK Corral for which Tombstone is mostly famous must count as one of the most overrated events in history, for in actuality it was an affair of seconds, and an accidental one at that, a sort of tragedy of manners. Just before the shooting began, Virgil Earp cried out 'Hold!' but by then it was too late to stop the show. Today, papier mâché models, two-thirds size, more mummy-children than men, have been erected inside the corral where each of the shooters supposedly stood. Tourists can take a picture of a wall laced with bullet holes and a reconstructed gibbet. A tape on a thirty-second loop explains who fired which shots and when (but not why), and then starts over again. The corral's proprietors must have figured that the average visitor spends just enough time in that corral to grab a snapshot and get out. In any case, and whatever the truth of the matter, without the reinvented history of the gunfight, a significant part of the myth of the west would need rethinking, which is something few Americans are willing to do. A dramatic consensus, a theatrical suspension of disbelief keeps western myths alive.

Although Wyatt Earp and Ike Clanton are popularly represented as opposing forces, both men were actually patsies operated by enemy puppetmasters. They served their respective masters, as puppets do, but I'd be willing to bet that they remained ignorant of the larger picture. For if the shoot-out is representative of anything at all it is the victory of extraction interests over those of ranching. Now, ranching on a commercial scale has a longer history in the west than extraction, having been brought north by Mexican cowboys a hundred years or more before Earp and the Clantons were born. The members of the Clanton clan, which loosely represented ranchers, were either killed or driven away. Extraction interests won out. Though it must have seemed pretty conclusive at the time, the extractors' victory was a partial one, for it pitted the interests of ranching (hispanics) and extracting (anglos) in direct opposition to each other, which is so often where they remain today.

Back in June I found myself sitting at a military roadblock in the San Augustin Pass in southern New Mexico watching a missile, its tracer and a fighter plane chase across the basalt plain of the Jornada del Muerto and on to White Sands Missile Range. Quite what I was doing stuck in a roadblock on the San Augustin pass I don't know. I have asked myself the question more than once, because I am in general, an impatient, rangy person and tend to avoid any situation which involves waiting anywhere for anything. One answer might be that I was headed for Jicarilla Apache country and there was only one road leading in the right direction, but this suggests a purposiveness that did not exist at the time. A better answer would be that the enormity of the landscape had eaten up my plans. I could no longer remember what I had to do or where I wanted to go, so I allowed the road to direct my journey. Over the months I wandered too many days to count, made some small discoveries as a result, and bedded down in strange, bone-dry little towns which otherwise I would scarcely have believed existed. In the southwest you can find your rut and follow it to eternity. Every so often en route I roused myself to take stock and the road-block was one of these occasions. Reaching for my root beer, I took out a map and studied the plain below. A few distant white pods on the horizon suggestive of horse bots marked out the military surveillance and testing stations at Holloman Airforce Base. Otherwise, there was very little to see excepting the never-ending sheet of sagebrush and yucca that typifies the Chihuahua desert.

Aside from the whine of the missile the plain was silent. A

military policeman patrolling the line said it would be a long wait, so I switched on the radio, settled back in my seat and drifted off into a hypnotic doze. I don't think I lost consciousness, but with the air conditioning turned off the car became so stifling that it was impossible to remain wholly awake. Probably I dozed for fifteen minutes or so, and I was brought back to my senses by a newsflash announcing the seventh or eighth unexpected death of the week in the Four Corners area. A few days previously, it had been discovered that some kind of virus was stalking the region, but no-one knew quite where it was coming from. A dozen people had died, most of them Navajo from the reservation at Four Corners. Fear of the virus had permeated through to the most minute detail of people's lives. Everyone was affected, either because they restricted their daily comings and goings or because they felt it necessary to keep up a kind of blusterous denial. Some people didn't show up for work, others took vacation time and left the state altogether. Up in the north a journalist spotted a family from Los Angeles emerging from their RV clad in protective plastic surgeons' outfits. They said that they were determined to continue their vacation and this seemed the best way to do it and get back alive. Twelve deaths in a state the size of France. For a month the Santa Fe *New Mexican* and the *Albuquerque Journal* carried hand-wringing pieces from their editors chastising the national media for focusing their attentions on the state of New Mexico, when there had been deaths in Arizona, Utah and Colorado too. They in turn focused their attentions on the Navajo, on whose reservation most of the deaths had occurred. The more traditional of the Navajo elders said that the whole sorry situation had arisen in part because the tribe had neglected its sacred dances.

It occurred to me that perhaps it wasn't so much the idea of death that had become embedded in southwestern culture, but the archetype of the quest. From what I could recall from anthropology classes a few years back, the quest myth emerged from the shamanic tradition, in which a seeker took off on a journey, spiritual or literal, to uncover wisdom. Often the seeker would have to confront and overcome death in order to complete their journey. Sometimes the seeker would lose to death, but be transformed by it and become a hero in the process. In any case, the presence of death in the archetype helped make the quest seem bolder and weightier, and the prize, whether it be money, or wisdom or power, more precious.

Americans hold quests in high esteem. A culture like America's can not only select its myths and archetypes from the multitude brought to it by an immigrant population but can also manufacture new ones and locate them on the magic surfaces of movie screens and in the heightened landscapes of its empty places. In these places, mysteries are dreamed up from the drabbest tales; a virus becomes a spectral stalker, a hunt for gold becomes a search for self, a gun fight turns into a metaphor for the transformative qualities of death. The desert southwest is one such enchanted kingdom, a place, at least symbolically, beyond the ordinary limitations.

Sitting in Caboose, humming something or other as a distraction from the heat, my attention was drawn to a band of clouds pitched up bruisy black on the horizon line with their grey raintails strung out beside them like guy ropes. Rain was falling onto the carbon droppings left by the missile and its companions but the mechanical troupe itself had long disappeared north across the salty plain of the Jornada del Muerto, the journey of the dead.

Juan de Onate came this way or rather a little to the west of it, along the Camino Espejo, in 1596. By all accounts Onate was a spectacle of a man – rich, ambitious, swaggering and insanely driven. Just south of what is now Las Cruces at El Paso del Norte, he planted the royal Spanish standard, nailed a cross to a tree, renamed the Camino Espejo the Camino Real and claimed all of New Mexico for the Spanish crown. His entourage of four hundred men, their families and seven thousand head of livestock took off across the Jornada towards Santa Fe. For the most part the Tularosa Valley in which the Jornada lies is an arid plain encircled by badlands to the east and phosphorescent mesas to the north and south. To the west the Rio Grande waters cottonwoods in a lush riparian stripe, but out in the basin itself you have to dig for water, and what little you find is briny and undrinkable. According to the Parks Bureau there are mountain lions in the hills around and antelope on the plain. If there are, I did not see them. Cacti flourish, it's true, but the Spaniards, Mexicans, and later anglo settlers all lost men and women and livestock along the Jornada del Muerto.

A number of Spanish argonauts had been lured into New Mexico before Onate by the quest for seven mythical golden cities, called Cibola, stories of which passed into Spanish folklore from the Moors. The Jornada was the first obstacle they encountered north of what is now the Mexican border, and so it became one of those liminal places in the history of hispanic exploration, a boundary beyond which unknown treasures lay. So far as we know, the first of these bounty hunters was not strictly speaking a Spaniard at all, but a Moorish slave, called Estevan, who led a scouting party of men into the region in 1539. The leader of Estevan's expedition, a Spanish priest called Fray Marcos de Niza stayed behind on what is now the Arizona-Mexico border waiting for Estevan to report back. As it turned out, the slave was killed by Indians somewhere in Arizona, but before he died, he sent word to de Niza saying that he had seen glittering cities spread across the desert plains. Estevan's tale has puzzled historians ever since. One theory has it that Estevan was taken in by the glint of mica, a slate-like material which the Indians used for windows in their adobe houses, another suggests simply that the slave was anxious to please in order to earn his freedom, and that de Niza was equally anxious to believe him. To my mind the promise of riches which brought so many people to the region was itself a metaphor for a greater seduction; the allure of an awesome, transcendent, inhuman landscape. In any case, de Niza himself had no appetite for heroics, so instead of checking Estevan's story out he returned to Mexico and repeated the claim, adding suitable embellishments.

And so the myth of the golden cities flourished. A year later Francisco Vasques de Coronado took a party of men north from Mexico City to rediscover Cibola and make himself a name. In what is now New Mexico, Coronado met a plains Indian slave of the pueblos whom he called El Turco, who persuaded him that the cities were to be found to the east of the present New Mexico border, in present-day Texas and Oklahoma. Acting as guide, El Turco ran Coronado's party a merry goose chase as far north and east as Kansas, but the cities were never found, Coronado had El Turco executed and he and his dishevelled followers headed home to Mexico empty-handed in April 1542. It was to be another fifty years before Onate conquered the territory for Spain. A few miles southwest of present-day Grants, Onate left a message carved symbolically over Indian petroglyphs, which reads:

Paso por aqui el adelantado Don Juan de Onate del descumbrimiento de la mar del sur a 16 de Abril de 1605.

Governor Don Juan de Onate passed by here on 16 April, 1605, from the discovery of the Sea of the South.

It came to me as I was driving past this notice one day in May that Onate must have understood something Coronado did not and that was this: heroes need hero-makers. In democracies heroes are made by the media, or by political, military or economic interests, in true monarchies they are made by kings and queens, in totalitarian regimes by incumbent presidents or heads of ruling political parties and the military; but always, in every circumstance they are made by the creation of a myth so strong that it passes into the culture. Perhaps this fact partly explains why Onate conquered New Mexico when Coronado gave it up for a barren waste; Onate knew that by returning to his king and country empty-handed he could never become a hero. If there was no gold to bring back and fill the royal treasuries in Spain, then he must bring back some other thing I suppose he reckoned that the territory of New Mexico would do the trick, which it did, at least for a while.

The land reveals its secrets only gradually. By 1975, the grey porphyry hills near Bisbee in Cochise County, Arizona, over which Estevan tramped almost 450 years before in search of golden cities, had yielded 3 million ounces of gold, 97 million ounces of silver, 8 billion pounds of copper, over 270 million pounds of zinc and 304 million pounds of lead. Yet Estevan found nothing of value but the moment of his death. Now, had he known what Non-Assessable Smith discovered, he would, perhaps, have become one of history's heroes. I found the story that follows in a guidebook, and to me it serves to illustrate the symbolic value of the southwest, as a place where quests are undertaken, and men made immortal by them. According to the guidebook, Non-Assessable Smith was a resident of Cochise County during the great mining days of the late nineteenth century. He used to tell the tale of how he struck it lucky while out prospecting with his drunken partner Bill Bolger.

One summer day, Bill Bolger, whose eyesight was none too steady from years of boozing, purchased a hatful of small eggs from a wandering Mexican, and feeling hungry, he cooked a few, by frying them on a flat rock in the full sun. When his partner Smith turned up some hours later, Bolger was rolling around in agonies clutching his stomach, saying that the eggs had got him, so Smith took off on his mule in search of a doctor. By the time Smith returned with the doctor, Bill Bolger was dead. Beside the corpse lay the few remaining eggs from the Mexican's hatful. The doctor recognized these at once as lizard eggs, laid by a Gila Monster, which carries cyanide in its body. There being nothing much else to be done, Smith bundled up the body of his friend, loaded it on the mule and set off for the local morgue. Then a strange thing happened. Bolger's corpse gradually became heavier and heavier, so heavy in fact that by the time Smith got into town, the mule could hardly carry it. When Smith opened the sackcloth he had used as a body bag to try to discover the cause of the weightiness, he could see that Bolger was shimmering in the light. Recognizing that something unusual was going on, Smith hid the corpse in his shed while he tried to figure out what it was. After a few days he thought he understood. Bolger had cooked his lizard eggs on a gold lode; since cyanide purifies gold ore the cyanide in the eggs had absorbed the gold, while killing off Bolger. As he was digesting the eggs, Bolger's body had become a sort of alchemical mill. Smith could barely contain his joy. Instead of burying his friend, he stored away the body and whenever he was in need of ready cash, he would hack the odd piece off. Now, it would be hard to imagine a less heroic figure than Bill Bolger, but he achieved a sort of immortality nonetheless. All it had taken was the desert rock and a slice of luck.

For the best part of a century, Hollywood has churned out mythical images of western vistas and dealt in mythical western themes as if the frontier were the continent's whole history. For many Americans frontierism has, as a result become as transcendent a narrative as the sacraments once were. The myth pervades all forms of political and economic life – what were the Reagan years if not the playing out of a grotesque and ill-scripted global western with its good guy versus bad guy tropes? The western writer Stan Steiner tells of a conversation in 1974 between Leonid Brezhnev and Richard Nixon who were flying over the Grand Canyon en route to a summit meeting. According to the story Nixon leaned across to Brezhnev and pointed out the spectacle down below, but Brezhnev was unimpressed, saying that he had seen the Canyon at much closer quarters in a number of John Wayne movies. Nixon, evidently accepting the rationality of this response, then drew an imaginary pistol from his pocket and with one eye closed as if taking aim he cocked it at Brezhnev, who responded by drawing his own finger weapon; whereupon, over that most symbolic of geologic formations, the two men shot each other dead.

Frontier myths have stuck to the west for three reasons; first, because North America tends to be forgetful of anything but its most recent past and its most recent past is the history of the west; second, because the landscape of the west encourages them; third because myths have to attach themselves somewhere and the west is as good, if not better, a place as anywhere else.

The enormous spans, naked, elemental crags and plains west of the 98th have come to symbolize the archetypal oppositions of life and death, truth and fakery, good and evil, so that the west still stands for everything America could and would be and to have passed through the west even today is to have matured and come of age.

Driving through the Jornada that day in June, I decided to pay a visit to the site where the first atomic bomb exploded, a site, I could see from my map, situated deep in the grounds of the White Sands Missile Range. I rang the range and got put through to someone in public relations who told me that the site was only open to the public for two days each year, in April and in October. Since I knew that I would be back in London by October, I asked the woman on the phone if she could make an exception to the rule.

'Why are you so interested in Trinity Site?' she asked, which made me realize that I hadn't thought why, I only knew I was.

'I don't really know,' I said. 'Because it's mystical?'

A while later a man called Jim Eckles phoned and said that on account of my having come so far, he would take me to ground zero at the weekend.

Jim Eckles was not born in New Mexico, like so many others in the desert states he's a transplant, but he rooted happily and has been working for the US army at White Sands Missile Range for sixteen years or so. Unlike many publicists, who are by and large a low breed, there is no guile about Jim, just a sharp mind and a little playful disingenuousness. It was Jim who told me about the gold buried in the Jornada del Muerto, at Victorio Peak on the White Sands Missile Range due north of the San Augustin Pass. It fits my purposes well, so I shall use it. Just whose gold it might be, if it exists, no-one quite knows. Some stories say that it was mined by a French Jesuit priest, Felipe La Rue, and his followers in 1796 or thereabouts. Others claim that the Germans paid Francisco 'Pancho' Villa, the Mexican revolutionary, gold bullion to stir up trouble between Mexico and the United States and by doing so keep the United States out of the First World War. Yet another version is that General Patton stashed away a horde of Nazi gold just after the war to protect the military from post-war budget cuts.

Jim's tale starts with Doc and Ova Noss who first laid claim to the bullion buried at Victorio Peak. Today Doc Noss would be called a New Age podiatrician; a man who doctored feet and practised soothsaying on the side. He and his wife lived in Hot Springs – now known as Truth or Consequences after the fifties TV quiz show – which lies to the west of the Jornada, about half-way between Socorro and Las Cruces. Before the Second World War the area was rich in game, and Doc Noss used to spend his weekends hunting up in the mountains. One day in 1937 he was out with his gun when the wind kicked up a sudden thunderstorm and he was forced to shelter in a nearby cave. Down a shaft in the cave he discovered an underground store 'big enough to hold a freight train', or so he said, and in the store were gold bars, stacked up high, the remains of several Wells Fargo chests and twenty-seven skeletons chained to wooden stakes. Imagining this to be Felipe La Rue's gold (even though the padre would have been in the ground some decades before Wells Fargo started up), Noss managed to remove a few of the bars, a crown and a statue, before the entrance to the shaft inconveniently caved in, burying the gold under tons of rubble. For the next ten years the Nosses worked to clear the shaft, even bringing in outside investors to defray the clearance costs. Ironically enough, Doc Noss was shot and killed in 1949 by one such investor who had sunk $28,000 into the venture and was growing tired of waiting for a result. The man was brought to trial for Noss' murder but was acquitted on grounds of self-defence. In the west of gold and silver rushes, boomtown morals and instant fortunes, it is a well-understood principle that there will always be a death or two before the earth yields up its ores.

Twenty years passed by before the padre's gold was redis-covered, this time by an officer in the US Air Force, Leonard V. Fiege, who claimed that, after finding the stash, he covered the entrance to the shaft to prevent anyone else from discovering it. In 1961 the head of the White Sands Missile Range gave him permission to go back to Victorio Peak and open up the site. The trouble was that Fiege couldn't relocate the shaft, so a search began. Doc Noss' widow, Ova Noss didn't like the idea of any-one claiming her gold, whether or not they could actually find it, so she kept making a pest of herself until the US Army agreed to call the search off.

However, the mystery did not die with Fiege's departure from White Sands. On the contrary, it is the perverse nature of mysteries to reassert themselves each time someone attempts to resolve them. By 1963 the Museum of New Mexico had been named custodian of the state-owned land on which the treasure supposedly lay. Under pressure to make a 'find' the museum brought in the Gaddis Mining Company of Denver, Colorado, to look for the gold. At the end of thirty days there was still no sign of it, so the Museum extended Gaddis' contract for a further month, at which point a quarter of a million dollars of public funds had been spent chasing a myth and not an ounce of gold extracted.

According to Jim's tale, neither Leonard Fiege nor Ova Noss gave up their belief in the padre's gold. In the late seventies a Florida-based buccaneering company called Expeditions Unlimited conducted an electronic survey of Victorio Peak with the help of Stanford Research Institute and under the eager eyes of Fiege and Noss. Again, nothing was found, but a survey of the area using radar reportedly showed the possible existence of a large underground cavern. Four or five years later Ova Noss died. So far as I know, Leonard Fiege, like the legend, lives on.

A new frontierism has in part replaced the old in New Mexico. That frontier is science, in particular the science of destruction, and its heroes are not cowboys or explorers but physicists and rocket scientists. The National Laboratory at Los Alamos is as fertile a symbol of this new frontier as the OK Corral at Tombstone was of the old. The laboratory's activities have diversified since the breakup of the Soviet Union, but its principal interest is still in endgames, which is to say, in death. Nuclear death, neutron death, scientific death, non-lethal death, death by other names, necessary and defensive death, all the manufactured deaths that have ever been rationalized were born or nurtured at some point or other in the laboratories at Los Alamos.

Of all New Mexico's secrets the development of the atomic

bomb at Los Alamos was probably one of the best kept. Head of operations back in 1942 was a man with the prophetic name of Graves. This man Graves hired as head of research Robert Oppenheimer, who, as everyone knows, headed the Los Alamos team which built the A-bomb. Oppenheimer became a folk hero, symbol of great American patriotism, not for his brave rebuttal of nuclear warfare, but for its invention.

Pinned up on the corkboard at home is a picture of me at ground zero, the spot where the first atomic bomb went off, dwarfed by a sooty lava obelisk. I am holding one hand against my breasts while the other fends off the hair in my face. I am very thin and my eyes are screwed up against the sun. It must have been 100 degrees that day, but I am wearing a leather jacket which has caught the wind and ballooned outwards. You can't see it in the photo, but I have a piece of greenish trinitite in one hand. When the bomb went off at 5:29:45 on the morning of 16 July, 1945, the heat from the blast turned the sandy topsoil into radioactive glass, or trinitite as it became known, and this is the only remaining evidence of the momentous transformations wrought by that bomb on the desert. The crater itself was filled in, the green lawn of trinitite bulldozed, the huts and buildings of the base and scientific outposts taken down and disposed of. If there is radioactive dust remaining, then it is indistinguishable from the other sort. Everything of the steel bomb tower but a single concrete sump evaporated away and fell as metal rain, somewhere over the Tulorosa Valley, along the Jornada del Muerto. The refashioning of history begins when that first most crucial evidence is blotted from the land. Eventually the story of the A-bomb test will simplify into archetype, like the gunfight at the OK Corral, the Seven Cities of Cibola, Bill Bolger's body, or the padre's gold, if, that is, it has not already done so.

Millions of years before the A-bomb, volcanoes had made a wasteland of the Tulorosa valley with their ashes. That yellow pall of radioactive A-bomb dust might have changed our world, but in geologic time it came and went in the blink of an eye. Long before Coronado appeared, before the Indians, before life itself, the Jornada del Muerto was a fragile, entropic place, a *terra nullius*, an imaginative void swept clean by a wind already whispering mortality.

Jim Eckles mentioned that he knew of someone who had worked with Oppenheimer on the Manhattan Project and who settled in the area after the war. Jim could not recall the man's name, but I tracked him down in Socorro, New Mexico. Like many southern desert towns Socorro's heart is Mexican. Behind the strip of home-style Mexican restaurants and cheap motels is a little green plaza where a Spanish church sits immaculate, while the town's stores and services gently disintegrate around it. Beyond the church are a few mobile homes and beyond them, thousands of square miles of desert. Up on a hill, a little away from the worst of the heat, is the campus of New Mexico Tech, which used to be the School of Mines, and that is where I found Marvin Wilkening.

In 1942, the year of the first successful controlled nuclear fission experiment, Marvin was a twenty-four year-old student at the University of Chicago, the amanuensis of Enrico Fermi. He was responsible for a device which monitored the activity of neutrons during nuclear reactions and it was the importance of this device to the work of the Manhattan Project which saved Marvin from conscription. Marvin can't imagine why I should be interested in him, so he keeps trying to tell me about his neutron device, and I keep trying to ask him about the night the bomb went off, and eventually, after an hour or so, I win. Marvin was lying in a bunker on that night at base camp to the south, looking out at ground zero through tinted spectacles.

'It was a thrill,' he said, 'The first mushroom from an atomic explosion. I remember seeing this thing go up and into the clouds and drift away from us. It was an overcast night, broken clouds all around. You could feel the heat, you know, in your bones.'

For a while he sat still, no doubt he was sifting through the images in his mind's eye, then he began to mumble, turned track, and added:

'You know, I don't think we thought too much about it.

There was so much to do, you just didn't have time to think
. . . so much to do.'

He began to remove a biography of Oppenheimer from
the shelves in his office, then changed his mind and replaced
it carefully, dragging his finger over the spine to remove
the dust.

'But did you think that the bomb would end the war?' I asked.

He took a sip of coke.

'It was in the back of our minds, but, you know, on the night,
we weren't thinking about who it would kill, or what it might
save, we weren't thinking about anything much except to see
that it was a successful mission,' he replied, looking at me
with an unflinching eye. To me, born two months after the
death of John Fitzgerald Kennedy, into a world, I am told, in
which certainty – of the moral, political and spiritual kind – had
been finally extinguished such directness was unsettling and
unwordly. Marvin represented another age, one in which there
were still heroes to be made.

From an ill-fitting drawer buried behind some books, he
pulled out a polished wood box labelled 'Trinity'. Inside the box
was a cardboard shoebox, and inside that, buried under thick
cotton wool, there were two slabs of trinitite, bubbled and shiny
on top and rough underneath with the imprint of unmelted flints.
He took the pieces from their wrapper and we both admired
them for a while.

'Do you believe in god?' I asked

'Yes, in a different way from most people I guess. Folks die,
and the spirit lives on, somehow,' he replied.

Marvin is a nature-lover. He watches the Jornada change
colour from roan and purple in winter, to the summer's brown
and olive drab; he sees it becoming crystalline in the sun, sullen
at either end of the day. He listens to it moaning after rain.
Every day he takes his binoculars out and looks out for birds
and creatures in the sagebrush. The thing that strikes me most
about Marvin, given his experience, is that he doesn't see the
desert as a place of death, even though it is the place where he
will meet his own quite soon now. He expects nothing more

from the Jornada than a skyful of ravens, and a plain strewn with tumbleweed and yucca. Every so often he spots an eagle skimming the plain, and when he does, he considers himself particularly fortunate.

The Firm

'Jesus
he was a handsome man
and what I want to know is
how do you like your blueeyed boy
Mister Death.'

I've read plenty of books about Billy the Kid, but I've never read two that agree on the facts; what facts there are, that is.

The man was born Henry McCarty, to an Irish couple. Maybe it was in New York, but it could have been out in Indiana.

Damn, writing history is so difficult, it's easier to stick to legend. But then again, which one? I've been through them all, and none of them comes out right.

William H. Bonney, alias Billy, Billy Antrim, William Antrim sometimes known as the Kid, otherwise called Kid Antrim, Billy the Kid. Jeez, Henry McCarty, whatever your name is, you've defeated me.

Outlaw supremo of the purple sage, a 'frontier Robespierre' someone wrote. Sallie Chisum said years after Billy had crumbled away that he was always the pink of politeness and a damned fine dancer to boot.

Michael Ondaatje wrote a book about him, poems mostly. It says in the book that 'if you dug him up and brought him out. You'd see very little. There'd be the buck teeth.' If we only knew that much it would be a start. I have a picture of the tombstone. William H. Bonney, Tom O'Folliard and Charlie Bowdre: Pals, it says. They've put it in a wrought-iron cage to keep the tourists from trampling it down. The headstone got stolen, then recovered, twice, and there's a rumour that they dug the Kid's corpse

up and took him along to Santa Fe. By now, he could be anywhere. You know, Pat Garrett who killed him also presumed
to write about his life and swore that Billy the Kid's body lay
undisturbed in the grave. But that was nearly a hundred years
ago, and things change. All we can say now is that the lifeless
bones of Billy the Kid are most likely buried somewhere in New
Mexico dirt, unless the coyotes have dug them up and eaten
them of course. Pete Maxwell heard him die. It was dark but he
knew from the voice. He and Pat Garrett.

How do we remember the Kid? A hero? Hell, no, he was loose
with his gun, didn't mind much who he shot down and rustled
cattle from the greasers. I don't think he had much integrity to
speak of. Some kind of villain then? Well, not that either, quite.
Look at his portrait and you'll see a shell with a man behind it.

Picture Laurence Stallings and King Vidor pitching the
screenplay of the Billy the Kid story to Irving Thalberg in 1930
on the way to Mabel Normand's funeral. Thalberg chews over
the themes, the audience potential, then shakes his head and
whispers along the pew, just in front of Mabel's coffin, 'Too
many murders.' They made the movie anyway. Vidor hired
Sophie Poe as a consultant on the grounds that she knew the Kid
when he was running about Lincoln County but when she saw
what they had in mind for Billy, she said that he was a 'little
buck-toothed killer' and they'd got him wrong, so they took her
off the picture.

'The experience of tragic drama both gives in the figure of the
hero an objective form to the self of imaginative aspiration, and
also, through the hero's death, satisfies the counter movement
of feeling toward the surrender of personal claims and the merg-
ing of the ego within a greater power' says Maud Bodkin in
Archetypal Patterns in Poetry: Psychological Studies of Imagination
(1964). Well, Maud Bodkin, maybe you are right, but where
does that leave us?

I was there at the grave with the sky dimmed to the colour
of cuttlefish ink. From where I stood, I could look out to the
remains of the Bosque Redondo concentration camp, Pete Maxwell's ranch as was. It was there that Billy died.

I was thinking, what happened to the bodies of the Navajos and Apaches over there? The ones who could not hold on to life, in the freezing winters with no food, the ones who died in their wikiups rigid with cold and disintegrating from disease? All the promising young men and women, whose lives were cut short by Kiowa and Comanche raids, where are they? How many was it? Three thousand, it was three thousand died there in the concentration camp at Bosque Redondo under Brigadier General James H. Carleton. Ending the 'Indian problem', or so he thought. It was a final solution as barbarous and as futile as any.

Outside Adkin's dance hall at Bonito, Arizona, Billy the Kid killed a local blacksmith known as Frank P. Cahill. They got into a fight over a card game; Cahill, who was the bigger man by far, laid into Billy so the boy pulled Cahill's own gun and shot him in the stomach, at point blank range. A witness said 'He had no choice . . . he had to use his "equalizer" . . .' That was his first blood, and he was Billy Antrim then.

At New Mexico's eastern border in De Baca county, which was part of Lincoln before they divided it, the great plains abandon themselves to the desert. There's only a two-lane highway across Lincoln. Fifty years ago it would have been a lonely unmetalled track, lit by the same deceiving light which now drags distant mesas across sixty miles or so of alkali flat and makes them seem like great grey-blue monsters resting by the road. Across De Baca, Clovis country and western radio gives out to an intermittent buzz. This is a pale beige land, spotted cucumber green by saltbush. The thin highway cuts an opalescent groove through it, scattering gas stations like prostheses. And the sun; there is always the ball of the sun, grinning.

Lincoln County isn't much of a place to hide out, you'd need true friends in terrain like this. Perhaps Billy had a few whom he could trust but they say it was a friend who let him down. Pete Maxwell, brother of Paulita, the whole clan one of the most prosperous families in the west. Paulita and Billy the Kid were sweet, possibly lovers, and Pete Maxwell snitched on his friend to save the honour of his sister. Paulita was a married woman. Decades after they covered the Kid with New Mexico dirt, she said that it was Celsa Gutierrez who had taken Billy's heart, but if that was so, why would Pete have given him up? He loved the Kid.

At the Bosque Redondo Memorial – the concentration camp as was – there is me, the Ranger and an Indian woman wearing Navajo silver and carrying her child. Around the memorial is a fence of blackened cottonwood sticks.

Once, in Lincoln County, I watched a locomotive pass trailing 220 wagons behind it. At a guess I'd say it took ten minutes to trundle by and another half-hour to disappear from view. The chrome fixings along the sides caught the sun and sent mission-less searchlights into the sky. It was headed for the California coast, I think. Heat busied off that machine as it does from a funeral pyre. And it wasn't even a train hardly. It was a caravan.

I'll let you into a secret. The authentic life and death of Billy the Kid is lost to us. But it doesn't matter a great deal, historically speaking.

The fort at Fort Sumner has collapsed. In the place where it stood is a square of brilliant green Bermuda grass criss-crossed with neat cement paths. Plaques mark the places where the old fort's kitchens and parade grounds were. What good is guilt whose only outlet is information plaques and neatly clipped Bermuda grass? Rage still comes up through the dirt.

According to Western formula, the hero-villain must have an atoning death, there must be treachery involved and an element of martyrdom. Pat Garrett said that the Kid died with his boots on and his guns blazing, but then he needed a villain to be a hero. Billy wanted to go that way, it's true. He wrote to Governor Lew Wallace: 'I am not afraid to die like a man fighting but I would not like to be killed like a dog unarmed,' but when the time came he had no choice in the matter, for that is how he was when Garrett shot him. In his hand there was a small knife for cutting meat, and he was wearing socks but no boots.

Lew Wallace, you know, was a star-fucker. He played a tawdry game with Billy the Kid. He hinted at pardons and promised amnesties. Maybe he thought that by patronizing the Kid some of Billy's mystique would rub off on him, for the Kid was notorious around the southwest. Pretty soon the Governor won the political favours he was looking for, went out East, made his name writing *Ben Hur* and discovered that Billy the Kid didn't count for much among the smart set. By the time the Kid really needed an advocate, when he was sitting in jail at Lincoln convicted of the murder of Sheriff Brady (he had a hand in that, but it wasn't just him: the Sheriff died with nearly a dozen bullets in his back) Wallace had already backed out of the game. I think he got bored as much as anything.

Not that I'm on the side of the Kid. Not the Kid or McSween or Murphy's Firm or Garrett even. The legend of the Kid has only served to obfuscate a bigger and more typical tale, which is how the establishment got their way in Lincoln County.

There were four hundred people living in Lincoln town at the time of the Lincoln County War in 1878. Now there are supposed to be seventy-five, although I can't say this for sure, because I never went there.

Something Alfred Adler wrote struck me. He thought that a legend isn't a reflection of its time but an indication that the time needed a legend.

It took a century for the Bosque Redondo Reservation site to be declared a New Mexico State Monument. Billy the Kid, though, became a national historical monument the moment Garrett fired the shot that killed him. The Kid said 'I'll be with the world until she dies,' and perhaps he will. He's made it this far, after all. Those three thousand Indians at Bosque Redondo, the ones who died of Pecos River water and cutworms or from hail and drought, they are with us too, if not in our hearts, buried deeper in our consciences, where things putrefy and stink, but won't quite rot away.

To get to the grave of Billy the Kid you have to go through a museum, then a gift store. I suppose it's only two or three hundred yards from Bosque Redondo, but when I went it was a good deal busier. The museum is privately owned and set in a wooden, nineteenth-century building, painted brown. Inside is a byzantine collection of paraphernalia, including two life-sized wooden cowboys shooting crap, tins of DIY sutures and antidotes for snakebite. There are copies of documents from the Lincoln County war, pictures of the Kid and his compadres. The shambolic hoard of western memorabilia can have no pretence to shed any light on the facts of Billy the Kid's life or death, but it is a fitting souvenir of the chaotic scrabble for wealth and power in Lincoln County, of which Billy the Kid was unwittingly made a part.

A billboard in town reads. 'We've got the Kid and so much more.' I didn't see any more myself, excepting a few agricultural sheds, a couple of motels, diners and an impoverished general store. At Tito's Burritos they serve a chile-soaked beef enchilada like Billy the Kid might have eaten. And the customers are all cowboys. But it would be unwise to go in with a tearing hunger, because the service is slow, slow, slow.

I am alone out on the road from Fort Sumner finally, keeping pace with lilac cirrus scudding across the tracks of the railroad. From Fort Sumner the two-lane highway pushes out across the plain, past mesas black-edged from storm clouds and a sign advertising hogs and hounds for sale, though none is about.

And the ball of the sun is grinning.

HISTORICAL ADDENDA

Bosque Redondo Memorial and the Long Walk: Brigadier General James H. Carleton became commander of the Department of New Mexico on 18 September, 1863. The following year he sent Colonel 'Kit' Carson with a party of New Mexico Volunteers and Ute Indians to round up Navajo in the Four Corners region of northwestern New Mexico, and concentrate them in a 'reformatory camp' at Bosque Redondo, where they could be supervised and persuaded to 'assimilate'. Meanwhile, another party forced 450 Mescalero Apaches to walk to Fort Sumner from their homeland in the south. After the use of much of their ranching land by anglo and Mexican settlers, the Navajo were in part dependent on federal agency for supplies, so it was easy for Carson to threaten and then starve them into submission. Thousands were made to walk the 350 miles south to the camp at Bosque Redondo, where they were instructed to pitch tents next to the Apache, their traditional enemies. Any who were weak and slowed up the marchers were shot or left to die.

At Bosque Redondo the Indians were fenced about and left to till the land, the idea being that they should become self-supporting within a year, but, the Apache and the Navajo were traditionally keepers of livestock, not arable farmers. For them farming was unfamiliar and degrading. Besides, the land they were given was unirrigated, and the nearest water source, at the River Pecos, unreliable and highly saline. Year after year, their crops failed, and the Federal War Department had to send meagre rations to keep them alive through the winter, many of which were embezzled on the way. Crooked traders offloaded their excess stock at government expense. Wagons supposedly containing sacks of flour turned out to hold straw or pairs of women's shoes. In 1867 the Apache escaped and returned to their homeland in the Sacramento Mountains and a year later the US Army finally admitted that the concentration camp experiment at Bosque Redondo had failed. Around nine thousand Navajo were marched back up to their homeland, and a reservation put aside for them, from one-third of the land they had come to regard over hundreds of years, as theirs.

Billy the Kid: the story of the Kid cannot be understood outside the context of the Lincoln County War, for it was the war which determined the quality and length of the life he subsequently led.

Lawrence G. Murphy came to New Mexico with the Yankee army, set up as a post trader at Fort Stanton and was fired for crooked dealing. From there he fetched up in Lincoln where he opened a store and a saloon, establishing a monopoly on the supply of beef and flour to Fort Stanton. Evidently Murphy was an ambitious and egotistical man, for he once reportedly said 'You might as well try to stop the waves of the ocean with a fork as try to stop me.' Certainly he was a crook, selling his wares for inflated prices and obtaining contracts for supply of beef by sending out hoods to rustle stock from honest ranchers and by forcing farmers and cattlemen who owed him money to sell their produce to him cheap. Thomas B. Catron, mason, Republican and part of the Santa Fe Ring, an economic and political cartel, formed an alliance with Murphy, their joint objective being to eliminate a competitor called John Chisum. The Catron clan owned the law around Lincoln county and much of the rest of New Mexico territory, so they already had one up on Chisum and his men. In the meantime, Murphy's partner Fritz had died on a $10,000 assurance policy, which sum was to be administered by a young lawyer, Alexander A. McSween. McSween was most likely a man of probity, and was reluctant to release money from the policy because he thought Murphy's 'Firm' would immediately seize it from the rightful beneficiaries, Fritz's family for alleged debts owed by Fritz at the time of his death.

In 1876 an Englishman in his early twenties, John H. Tunstall, arrived in the territory, engaged McSween as his attorney and began buying land and stock, intending, no doubt, to oust the Firm from its position as monopoly supplier of beef. Tunstall set up a bank in Lincoln, too, with John Chisum as its president. One of the hands Tunstall engaged to work at his ranch was William H. Bonney, Billy the Kid.

Meanwhile, a sharp young hustler named James J. Dolan had bought out Murphy and was pressuring the Fritz family to obtain a court order to force McSween to pay out on the Fritz assurance fund. Sheriff William Brady, of Lincoln, who belonged to the Firm, got up a posse to claim McSween's and Tunstall's property against this court order, but Tunstall heard of the posse in advance and left his ranch, claiming that he would settle the matter in the courts. Tunstall, as you will have gathered, had a sufficiently strong sense of fair play that it clouded his appreciation of reality, in the traditional English manner. The posse followed Tunstall and shot him down.

Billy the Kid and some other Tunstall men, supported by much of the local Mexican-American or 'greaser' population, got a gang together to avenge Tunstall's death and teach the

Firm a lesson. They called the gang the Regulators. And thus the Lincoln County War began.

In essence Billy the Kid's life and deeds were managed and manipulated by the bigger issue of who would gain economic and political control of Lincoln County and the surrounding area. Billy was a poor, half-literate man, whose strings were pulled by much wilier men than he. This is not to say that William H. Bonney was a victim or that he was wholly another's puppet. Rather, he was simply scrabbling for a pennyworth of power on a chaotic frontier by the crudest of means. Above him, much greater stakes were being played for by a number of much more sophisticated men with capital behind them and a good deal more to lose.

Pat Garrett wrote up the Kid's story in *The Authentic Life of Billy the Kid* because Garrett was a drifter and a loser and he needed to create a villain big enough to make a hero of himself. The irony of it is, that Pat Garrett died the same night he shot down Billy the Kid because no-one will ever remember him for anything else. Years later, Mrs McSween said that he had produced some fine children, but we know nothing of them, do we?

Motels

'He prowled the pool
Of the Holiday Inn
And felt a fit of uselessness'

SAM SHEPARD

One morning I'm sitting in my motel room wrapped up in a live liposuction procedure on *Good Morning America* when a curl of thin white fumes begins to edge around the door. The door doesn't feel hot, though, so I pluck up my courage, clamp a wet face cloth around my mouth and open up. Outside in the corridor is a pall of white smoke, billowing out from one end by the staircase, and, just visible, a boy, holding something in his arms.

'What the hell's going on?' I shout, looking for anything resembling the source of the fire and hoping that he's just let off the fire extinguisher as a prank.

'Stalker's fleas,' says the boy and the smoke begins to clear sufficiently to see that the thing the boy is holding on to is not a fire extinguisher, but a brown and white mutt; and the fearsome cloud is nothing other than a large jar of Fleezee.

'You do realize this is a motel?'

'Oh yeah,' explains the boy 'we came here last year. Dad doesn't like us doing it in the yard.'

Stalker, meanwhile, gets it into its head that I am a dog lover and lunges towards my legs bringing with him a cloud of smog, and drooling in that hopeless doggy way mutts do. God I hate dogs.

'Can't you just go out in the *desert* someplace? Why does it have to be a motel?'

Stalker approaches, growls and shakes itself, sending puffballs of Fleezee into the air. If that thing comes near me, I am thinking, I will fucking pulverize it.

'Uh uh,' says the boy, shaking his head 'Stalker gets agrophobia.' Holy Mary.

Something occurs to me:

'Does it actually *have* fleas or is this just a precautionary measure?'

'Oh yeah, he definitely has fleas,' says the boy. 'That's just how it is.'

'Can't you just stay in your room? I mean, who *knows* when that stuff will get vacuumed up out here.' My voice reveals a light panic.

'We tried that,' says the boy, 'but they put a smoke alarm in.'

In the southwest, where even substantial towns are often little more than offshoots of the highway, a motel can serve as the sole locus in a placeless landscape. Motels assert themselves on the desert massif as part of the detritus, or reliquary if you will, of the automobile cult. Solidly banal, sourly utilitarian, motels nonetheless nurture whole towns in remote regions where towns would otherwise have no business being at all.

TUCUMCARI TONITE!
STOP! TOrC HAS QUALITY ACCOMMODATIONS.
YOUR JOURNEY ENDS AT GILA BEND.

Whereas hotels tend to be self-supporting, motels are symbiotes, bringing with them the Denny's and the JB's and Circle Ks and laundromats and the International Pancake Houses and the Philips 76s and the Texacos and all those nowhere diners. They force an outward aspect on their clientele. People take vacations in hotels, get married and host barmitzvahs and funeral breakfasts. In motels they only camp for a night or two. Motels are little more than sex stop-offs and temporary wombs for travellers. Their winking neon colours towns which would be swallowed up in brown desert dust without them.

In America the democratic principle diffuses down into the smallest and most mundane aspects of everyday life. Each motel guest, for example, whether business mogul, serial killer, deadbeat or movie star, is given, as it were, due process and equal weight – a randomly allotted cubicle in an undifferentiated location. There are no penthouse suites in motels, no ocean views, no poolside ambiences. Were *Sylvester Stallone* to show up at a motel in one of the desert towns between Amarillo, Texas, and Yuma, Arizona, he would be asked to fill in the registration card with his name, address and occupation, provide proof of his identity, pay in advance by credit card, cash or travellers' cheques and be handed the key to a faceless room at the rear of the building overlooking an empty lot, in a row of faceless rooms with identical aspects. He would discover that the rooms in these Motels are merely the outer packaging for TV sets. His telephone would not bill to the room, the towels would fail to stretch around his bicep, the soap would be caustic, the shower small. The air conditioning would be noisy but functional and there would be two heat-wrapped plastic cups on the dresser plus an advertisement for the local take-out pizza place. At nine the following morning a housekeeper would let herself (it always *is* herself) into the room to tidy round, and when he was done, Sly Stallone would drop his key in a box outside the office, walk to his car in the parking lot and drive away, same as everyone else.

The motel chains cannot ever substitute for mom-'n'-pop motels, because the mom-'n'-pops are iconic, part of what the west wishes to think of as itself. Strange though it is, these dingy little places, with their absurd, grandiose names are some of the few glad souvenirs of western history. I suppose that they remind us of human persistence and continuity in a terrain whose scale is incomprehensible, and whose own history is counted in geologic time. They touch us, these motels, because they have the quality of monuments. Nothing the chains can offer – free ESPN, continental breakfast and the indecent reassurance of driving six hundred miles to end up in the same place, can compete with the nostalgic melancholy of a Desert Splendour Motor Inn in the middle of nowhere with a broken-down soda machine and an infected pond for a pool.

There is something intimate about the mom-'n'-pops, partly owing to the simple fact of their age, partly on account of the way they are built. Whereas the chains are constructed to carefully monitored plans drawn up in uniform and precise manner in order to maximize economy, safety and privacy, old motels so often seem to have been built to be nothing more than doggedly expedient. Many old motels, I mean from the fifties and sixties, were constructed on a quad principle, where each room looks down into a central plaza, and all are linked by a series of open walkways. In most modern motels, the windows face away from each other onto anonymous car lots or wasteland, and the rooms are set along internal corridors. To get to your room, or to the vending and ice machines in any ageing motel you have to walk past the windows of many other rooms, encountering a kind of peep show of mesmerized, conveyor belt characters clutching cans of Bud with neon blue light flickering over their faces. Old motels function as public spaces, the enforced intimacy of which more modern chains have rejected in favour of a desolate kind of privacy.

Despite their air of faded respectability ('families welcome', 'American-owned') most mom-'n'-pop motels are unable to rid themselves of the reek of eroticism. Perhaps it's that the lost, forlorn decor of the places makes them intolerable to all but the poor, the desperate and the carelessly impassioned. In any case, age-musk reminiscent of the scent of sex seeps out of the wall-paper and hangs like a fug in the closets. Often the curtains are unlined and spin nighttime shadows out onto the central courtyard. The rubbed marks on the wall by the head of the bed, the slump of a mattress heavy with decades of body fluids, the way the Yellow Pages fall open at escort agencies, the worn mirrors stained in the cracks with the salt from tears, all these things are suggestive of sex. In the chains, by contrast, the pre-vailing odour is of budget disinfectant. The beds are sprung and perky, the sheets unstained, the curtains lined with heavy plastic. Undoubtedly men and women find it in themselves to ignore the sterility of these places, but if I were planning on all-night, all-day sex I'd start with the mom-'n'-pops.

There's a motel on the outskirts of Albuquerque called the Cactus Inn which kept me its prisoner for two weeks. I don't know why I didn't leave, but I didn't. Three times I requested a room change, in the vague expectation that the change of scene might induce me to quit, only to discover that each room was identical to every other, except in one or two most minor details. Each was huge, the size of a New York apartment, and so stocked with redundant furniture that it was difficult to move between the bed and the bathroom. Thick white electric cables strung across the walls, linking a main light to a smaller one, both of which were shaded over in off-white plastic. Under the main light there was in every room a small round white formica table set on an inverted trumpet of white plastic, and two captain's chairs in leatherette. The carpets, brown acrylic, bore pocks near the bed, where careless smokers had thrown their butts. Mysterious cupboards whose doors were painted up ran along the walls towards the door. An immense TV sat on a gargantuan formica chest with chromium handles and drawers the size of coffins. The windows were designed not to open, a tiny rancid frigidaire belted out heat and the air conditioning was seemingly geared for Alaska. The smell of solvent prowled around the final room, which, given the general ambience, might have doubled as a tropical bordello.

Spanning the entire length of each bathroom ceiling was a stain of spicy-smelling mildew. Tiny filaments of it fell onto the tiles. The bathroom fixtures were grimy white and square. It would have been impossible to settle comfortably on the toilet bowl without the buttocks of a corn-fed cow. Each time it was flushed the suction threatened to take you under and spit you out in the Auckland municipal sewerage system. Inside the bath lurked a flat perishing piece of rubber, a plugless plug chain and a specimen spider. In one of the rooms there was a pubic hair built into the rim of the vanity unit. In another, it appeared in the ice bucket.

The Cactus was never full, and what custom it did have drove in late and left early. Nonetheless, there was an atmosphere of collective goodwill among the guests, because the moment each one of us put our marks in the registration book we became comrades-in-arms, united against the malevolent *maîtresse* who presided over the hotel office. When not casually squeezing the lifeblood out of some paying guest, this perjury of a human being would be savaging the desiccated amoeba who sat at her side and bore the joint burden of being her husband and business partner. 'I don't wanna leave,' she used to say to him as soon as anyone walked into the office 'but I gotta leave cos you so goddamned useless.' The *maîtresse* had a way of implying that the misery of her marriage to the amoeba, who in fact seemed pleasant enough, was a form of torture dreamed up solely by whoever happened to be standing at the reception desk. 'Look at him,' she'd say 'how d'you expect me to stay with that, eh?' You would go into the office to pay a bill, or get a bulb replaced and emerge a broken soul.

About an hour after I first checked in she rang my room to ensure I had not been admitting 'overnight' guests and an hour later the amoeba came by to 'install a toilet roll' and do her spying. The next day, when I walked into the office to request a room change, she turned to the amoeba and barked, 'She don't trust us none.' Each time after that it was the same 'She don't trust us,' in a low growl. Once she said 'She don't trust us, but we European too,' which made no sense to me then and makes less sense now. Her husband never spoke. I comforted myself into thinking that he was on my side whereas in truth I believe he was beyond all feeling.

I had great difficulty ever leaving that place. Its grimness wove a web around me. My rooms filled up with fast-food droppings, I watched TV all day and most of the night, usually with the curtains closed, smoked Camels and drank warm Margarita mix. A derelict cleaner came every other day but never stayed more than a few minutes. While she vacuumed I would take the opportunity to buy in a fresh supply of cigs and Margarita mix. One night, after watching *The Great Gatsby* on the television, I rang Fergus, and he said 'Get Out,' so the next day I packed up and headed north. As I settled my bill, the *maîtresse* turned to her amoeba, smiled and said; 'See, I told you; she never trusted us none.'

Love Junky

'Why oh why must one grow up, why must one inherit this heavy, numbing responsibility of living an undiscovered life?'

D. H. LAWRENCE

It is the busiest weekend of the high season in Santa Fe; the streets are clotted with tour coaches and the whole city, it seems, has been held to ransom by bad-art collectors with fat pockets. Mornings you see them all spilling out of the Hilton downtown to spend the day trawling through galleries of shapeless air-brush art, snuffling around for bargains like truffle-hunting pigs. In the restaurants and cafes and bars all conversation has ceased save the dreary roll call of purchases intended, resisted and made. The City of the Holy Faith has gone theme, and the theme is pretentious, portentous, pedestrian art.

I'd been staying for a couple of weeks in the north, walking, reading the New Age texts, filling my notebook and I had come to an impasse. Every day I'd head down to the same cafe in Taos for breakfast, then to the same spot in the shade of a ponderosa pine where I'd read and doze. Familiarity, even of the most banal kind, was intoxicating. For two weeks I spoke to almost no-one and was happy to be silent and alone. I re-read D. H. Lawrence's novel *The Rainbow*, which he had written before he came to Taos, and it struck me how imprisoned in herself the heroine, Ursula was. I suppose Lawrence's greatest theme is that love is the only freedom, and even that is contingent. Then one morning, I drove into Taos, parked Caboose, took off through Kit Carson Park and wandered down to the Brodsky Bookstore, expecting to see in the window Lawrence's work, or, at least, a biography of the man, but there were only sagebrush sticks tied with ribbon and a poster of a Navajo thriller by Tony Hillerman.

A few doors up from the bookstore the coffee shop was opening up in anticipation of the day's first batch of tourists. I wandered down to the Plaza and sat in the La Fonda Hotel for a while and contemplated visiting the exhibition of Lawrence's paintings there without having any real urge to see them. The owner of the hotel, who was also the owner of the pictures, had apparently offered to return them to Britain on condition that the British send the Elgin marbles back to Athens, but the British government had politely declined to come to terms. Poor Lawrence, I thought, his work really didn't stand a chance in its supposed homeland. It's a wonder that the Americans, who are even more squeamish about sex than the British, put up with the paintings at all, but then the man who owns them is a Greek. In the end, I didn't see them. Perhaps, having got so close, I should have done, but I suspected that I might find Lawrence's art as florid and overwrought as I find much of his writing, and, besides, the isolation of Ursula still troubled me. Although it evidently obsessed him, I don't think Lawrence had much idea about love. On that ground, he and I, and the rest of the world are united.

I left Taos that day, planning to drive back down to Santa Fe and visit a sufi woman, whose name had been given to me by someone I met in Phoenix. About fifteen miles from Taos, just before Vadito on the highroad down to Santa Fe, I stopped and got out to admire the view of Wheeler Mountain, still snowy on the high peaks. The summit of Wheeler is the highest point in New Mexico, about two and a half miles above sea level and a good mile above Taos itself. I thought about the air up there, clean air, so thin it would make the heart race, so icy it would bring blood to the cheeks, so rare and pure and cold it would feel like a lover's fingers. There would be nothing but the wind to disturb the silence up on Wheeler. Just in front of me stood Vadito, still obscure through morning mist, the mobile homes and wooden huts of the village's slight population part-hidden behind ocotillo fences. No-one was about and nothing stirred. A few plastic crosses strung with beads and fabric flowers clung to the verge as a reminder to travellers that whatever they may escape by moving on, mortality remains at their side. Someone had set a temporary shrine to Our Lady of Guadalupe under a juniper bush just by a farm track and in it a nightlight burned smokey black off kerosene. A mess of dying perky sue and an unclothed doll lay beneath. Just a little out of the village there was a hut selling red and green chile peppers threaded onto string and Indian fry bread. New Mexico did not feel like America of a sudden. It felt like some other place.

At the Aztec Cafe in Santa Fe I run into Walker hiding out in a back room. Remember Walker, ex pro-surfer, ex west-coast hip-hop, ex-everything? We skirt around each other making small talk, then Walker introduces me to his friends, Austin and Marky, who are sitting at a table set out for playing card games, smoking. Austin, Marky and Walker are all in a band, and someday they plan to be generational heroes. Right now, Walker has a job as a pizza chef in a grill downtown, while Marky chops the vegetables.

'The Trip are playing Madrid a couple weeks' time. You could, like, check it out, if you're still around,' says Walker.

'Hip hop hard core funk psychedelia,' I reply, fishing around in my memory banks.

Austin throws me a look of poetic contempt. We sit in embarrassed silence for a while. Either I'm severely cramping some style, or kids don't talk so much these days.

'So have you all been rehearsing?'

'Oh, yeah,' Walker studies his latte with improper intensity. 'Uh, I've been a little busy.'

'Oh?' I feign interest. Austin looks on, silently begging his friend to get rid of the square across the table.

'Uh, yeah,' says Walker, 'I've been undergoing a huge vortex of personal change.' He hesitates, flushes, then adds in uncertain tone:

'This city is, like, a place of intense lessons?'

'Austin's an artist,' pipes up Marky, attempting to divert the conversation 'He's way cool.'

'I'm giving it up, anyway' replies Austin staring at his glass.

'Austin just got back from San Francisco.'

'And, like, it sucks,' says Austin, draining the last of his tea, 'It's like, empty.'

'Austin's mom lives in San Francisco,' interposes Walker.

'In this like, commune thing, it's just, like, so depressing, fucking boomers in their fucking caftans with their fucking, like, freak rock and their, like, fucking dope. The whole scene made me wanna off myself.' Then he adds, 'but I'll probably go to LA next week anyway, 'cause there's nothing to do around here and I think my dad lives in Pasadena so I can, like, get a bed there.'

'Yeah,' adds Walker, a little behind or ahead or out of kilter with the conversation. 'It's like, the violence thing, in LA? I mean, the whole world is getting more polarized and there's so much more violence, so there's gonna be more, like, consciousness. Consciousness is way the future. It's like, love, you know, you have to love yourself first?'

'She should meet Tobi,' says Austin, snickering.

'*Tobi*,' Walker joins in. 'Like, Tobi told Austin he was Beelzebub, and then she said he was Zeus? And she's got these weird ideas, like, she channels god?'

'And she's got this daughter,' adds Marky, smirking knowingly.

Walker pushes his plate away, wipes his fingers on the edge of the table and twirls his earrings slowly in their lobes. Austin and Marky get up to leave and, suddenly, Walker and I are left alone together. Under Walker's left eye a tic begins to pump like a jumping bean.

'What I was saying about, you know, this city? You're gonna find this difficult to believe.'

'I doubt that, Walker.'

'When I was about two? my folks were driving through Santa Fe and there was this blizzard, and they had to stop the car? And I was just sitting in this car, like I was two, right? And I just had this amazing past-life experience where I was this air stewardess who was, like, in this air crash? And, it was like, I kinda got this feeling that Santa Fe was really powerful so I sorta decided to come back here. So it's like I'm living out the metaphor of this past-life experience.'

'Walker, are you telling me you were a two year-old air stewardess?'

Walker looks uncomfortable for a moment.

'Uh, I don't think so. It was more like a past life?'

Well, that makes sense.

'I dropped out of UCLA and decided to become a professional surfer and then I was doing acid, like, five hundred trips in a coupla years and I was losing, my friends were all losing to drugs, or dying or what not, and I was, like, disconnected. It's like none of us loved each other or nothin', we were all, like, screwing around, and getting AIDS and stuff. But I'd go down to the beach every day and it was god-like, you know, it was just something, being on the surf, like seeing the interconnectedness of things. It was just like another drug, right? So I said, waaaiit, you're in trouble, man, and I came out to Santa Fe to work on myself.'

Walker is looking inward. He has crumbed the remains of his muffin and is passing the seconds sliding his thumb and index finger up and down his latte glass, eyes screwed up in an expression of roving boredom.

And we lived on communes and stuff, before my mum and my dad split up and then my dad sent me to the Nizhoni School for Global Consciousness? and man, I made all kinds of inner discoveries. I don't care what goes on out there any more.' He waves to indicate the world. 'My life is becoming what I dreamed it should be as a little child – a continuous synchronistic event.'

'Right,' I say, pitching him a comradely sort of look.

In a way, Walker's life makes sense to me. He represents a new kind of dispossessed: one of the hoards of wealthy, loveless lost boys. Walker is a double cliché – a GenX cliché and a New Age cliché. I wonder if this troubles him.

'OK,' I venture, 'So what *do* you believe in? Money?' Obviously no, Walker had never needed money enough to believe in it. 'Sex?' He shakes his head in vague amusement. 'Politics?' 'Uh, we did politics and all that at Nizhoni, but I forgot most of it.'

'Love?'

'You know,' he says, in a bedraggled tone 'if you are privileged and you have access to your higher self and all, you have a responsibility to use it to its fullest. I guess you have to have self. You have to have self before you can even think about the rest.'

I smile, from confusion as much as anything else.

'Anyway, you should meet Tobi,' he concludes, rising to leave.

Tobi lives above her store, Wild Things, on Montezuma, only a stone's throw from the cafe. The store is laid out on the ground floor of what must once have been a modestly impressive clapboard house. She's given it an oriental flavour by the application of brightly-coloured lacquered paint. Wild Things with its stock of miscellaneous debris from dead old ladies' wardrobes and suburban garage sales, seems to exist solely as part of the upkeep on Tobi's persona. Tobi even has a door policy: 'No squares.' A clientele of lacklustre boys and skinny girls patronizes the place compares ascendant signs among the scattered ruins of nylon separates, deals mushrooms in the changing room.

There is no mistaking Tobi. She is the loudest creature in the store, and the most perspirant, the gaudiest and the most louche, the oldest and the most downright tacky. Tobi is the sort of person who wears underwear as overwear.

Today Wild Things is peopled with students on their summer breaks. Tobi has taken upon herself responsibility for the welfare of a skinny young puppy over by the shirts section:

'All that purple up here, and here,' she observes, pointing above his head, presumably to his aura. 'You're obstinate, you are in the service of Lucifer and you have a choking fear.' A small crowd gathers round.

'Cool,' says the boy, whereupon Tobi hitches up her black lace skirt, lowers herself to the floor and howls like a dog.

'Waaoool, waaaoool.' The boy backs away minutely before recovering himself.

A mongrel wanders in off the patio, sniffs at the prostrate flesh on the floor and lopes off.

'See, this is what you have to do for a choking fear. Waaaooool, rowf, clears the throat chakra. Rowf rowf rowf.'

'Cool.'

Sensing she has made her point, Tobi lifts her bulk off the floor, pops a recalcitrant breast back into its lacy bag, and looks me up and down.

'You have a problem with your chakras?'

'Uh, maybe, but I'm looking for some shorts?'

'Oh,' says Tobi, removing my hands from a pair of Levi cut-offs. 'We'll find you some over here,' and leads me away to a far corner of the store where all is quiet and dark and dusty.

'See, I channel God,' she mentions, digging around in a dust-bin bag full of garments.

'I've heard.' She seems pleased. 'What's he, she, it like, then, God?'

'Oh, pretty much like the pictures.'

Tobi turns around with a pair of yellow bellbottoms about size 20 in her hands.

'Here,' she says 'try these.' So I put them on over my shorts, and not surprisingly, they make me look like an anorexic clown.

'Hmm,' says Tobi, studying the dismal spectacle in front of her, and instructing me to hold the trousers *up* properly so that she can give them the once over.

'Are you a writer?'

'Sort of,' I reply, non-plussed clutching the waistband of the bellbottoms.

'Hmm,' reflects Tobi, 'I channelled a book from the Archangel Gabriel once, but I didn't have the time to write it down. How old do you think I am?'

Wild Things is becoming distinctly more weird, like a scene from *Performance*. I do a swift calculation – think forty-two: say

'Thirty-five?'

'Forty-eight. I was at *Woodstock*. look at me. Do I look forty-eight? I did the summer of love, I know where my bliss is.'

'Know why?' My yellow bellbottoms have sunk to my ankles.

'It's because I honour the red, yellow, orange chakras, it's because I am a priestess of sensuality, it's because I am the Goddess.'

'I don't think the trousers . . .' I murmur, planning my escape route.

Tobi's hands drop back to her crotch. The eyes open and the corners of the mouth turn down.

'I feel sorry for you,' she says 'you really need to do some work on your higher self.'

'All because I don't want the trousers?'

'I guess you could go to Lama, I dunno. They're weak on the red and yellow chakras but they'd probably be OK for *you*.'

'Oh, uh, that's too bad.' I have taken the trousers off now, and am grasping the nearest thing around my body in lieu of a shield. Tobi throws me a look of 100% disdain.

'D'you wanna buy that caftan?'

I shake my head. A wrinkled column of red velvet that once hung around a Haight Street hippy falls from my fingers to the floor. 'Get your fucking hands off it, then. I have laundry bills.'

Picture a baby in a womb. That baby is at perfect peace, aware only of its own flesh and the warm dark fluid of the womb. Its needs are met, it has no sorrows, no guilt, it is ignorant of passion. The baby is extinguished in its surroundings. It passes its days in a state of bliss, up to the moment of the first pang of labour. How puzzling and enraging it must be for that baby when it is forced to confront the world outside. How it must resent the blur of colour and noise and hunger and pain that it must now endure. Imagine if you offer that baby a return to formlessness, to a life untouched by change and untroubled by experience. What would it choose I wonder.

I have been travelling on my own for a spring and a summer, and for most of that time, I have resisted the spiritual experience of solitude, even though I have been alone. Whenever I have found myself alone I have invented a persona, a sort of golem as company. The consistency of that persona has been of paramount importance to me. A number of times on my journey I would lose confidence in my production, generally when my physical situation changed or I made some small, hitherto unknown, discovery about myself. And then I would know it was time to invent another golem, better adapted to the changed environment. I think we are all character chameleons. What is interesting to me are the circumstances that make us change our colours.

I check back into the King's Rest Motel, where they tell me Gita has left and gone to live with her mother. That evening, I absorb myself in my notebooks and *Wheel of Fortune*, then at around midnight, I swallow two unisom and fall into a dazed unconsciousness. I wake the next morning feeling unrefreshed. A hangover from the sleeping pills spews back the night's dreams, a dizzy patchwork of perpetual motion. Skipping breakfast, I wander down towards the plaza, trailed by the uneasy feeling that something is hard on my tail. At Montezuma Street it catches up with me: Lama. By lunchtime, I am checked out of the King's Rest and headed north once more.

Beyond Arroyo Hondo the road follows a tear in the plain where the Rio Grande runs, rises and dips and rises again past a sign to Lama Mountain. Six miles from Questa, I turn onto a track and drive east towards the Sangre de Christo mountains. After a short while the track narrows, becomes deeply rutted and pocked with holes inhabited by slime. Several times Caboose stalls, but we lurch on, tracing a crazy path back and forth across the bunch grass stripe in the centre of the track. A mile on we rise steeply and begin to wriggle up the side of Lama Mountain. Junipers give out to piñon pine then to ponderosa and the sky changes from the breathless grey it was when I left Santa Fe to azure blue, on which sail the rags of clouds. Eventually a sign appears welcoming visitors to the Lama Foundation. 'Please drive with care,' it reads, as if it would be possible to drive any other way. From the car park at the base of the Lama Foundation the air is cool and thin, wheezing insubstantial breaths through the pines down the mountainside west to NM522 and the river beyond.

I park Caboose between two bohomobiles, take my camera and tape recorder from the back seat and, locking the door, set off up a stone path which appears to lead to the Foundation buildings. About half-way up, squatting at the side of the path, pausing for breath I am gripped by the sudden compulsion to go back to the car and leave it unlocked. I set off again but the voice in my head insists so I give in to it, turn and wind my way back down, take a pair of boots and a pocket knife from the front seat and lock them into the boot, leave the rest unlocked and begin the climb up again.

The path flattens off giving out eventually to a complex of buildings set about with poles from each of which there are strung rows of silk Tibetan prayer flags. A few innocuous blonde wood huts resembling camp dormitories lie sown through a clearing in the forest, in the haphazard way that buildings are generally arranged when there is enough space to allow it, and sometimes when there is not; there is no-one about. Further up the hill at the end of a wooden trail I discover a large kitchen, open to the outside, unoccupied, but with pots boiling on the stove. In five minutes a lumpy woman appears from a path ahead, carrying a bunch of herbs.

'I was looking for Gary,' I volunteer, but she signals me to be quiet, gesticulating towards the room above the kitchen.

'Wait outside,' she whispers, pointing to a wooden bench set behind some juniper bushes. I float up the path, past the bench and through to the tree line, passing a cold frame filled with lettuces, a row of tents and a man in the lotus position who will not speak to me. For a while I amuse myself by watching a piñon jay feed its young in a nest which has come adrift of its branch and is stuck at an angle under a blossom-covered shrub. From where I am sitting, I can see across the sagebrush plain below to the first pale hills, and beyond those stretching across the horizon, forests of cobalt, malachite and ultramarine. For a time I sit and stare at the canvas of stripes, moving my head from side to side to change the perspective, and the scene ceases to be a scene at all, but becomes a composition of colours and shapes abstracted out of nature altogether, like the phials of different coloured sand sold on the beach as seaside souvenirs.

After about two hours, a huddle of people emerge from the room over the kitchen, laughing and talking, and the fat chef begins to lay out large bowls of food onto a table behind a juniper windbreak. While waiting for their lunch, the people hug; they hug each other, they caress the wooden stilts supporting the building, they cling to the juniper windbreak. One or two simply hug themselves. From among the crowd I locate Gary. I wave and he comes over to welcome me and asks if I'd like a hug. Yeah, I think I would like a hug, I say, anticipating with pleasure the first physical contact for many months, but it disappoints me. This has nothing to do with Gary's technique, which is without fault, but to the absence of a motivation. It is a hug that leaves me thinking, why bother?

'Did you bring your tent?' Gary asks, untangling me from his torso. 'You'll get to know everyone very well very quickly. Don't worry.' I am not conscious of worrying, but I suppose I must have a nervous-looking face.

At lunch I make a point of reintroducing myself to the fat cook, who, as it turns out, is not the cook. At least, everyone at Lama is a cook, and a launderer and a gardener by turns. Cecily is given the cooking rota once every seven days, and she always makes the same thing – borscht and home-baked bread. Damned good bread and damned good borscht.

'I'm just glad to pieces you could eat my cooking,' says Cecily and leans over to give me a hug.

I feel like a gatecrasher at a family wedding, surrounded by groups and sub-groups and within them cliques long established. Opposite me sits a serene woman with short grey hair, who passes the odd comment to another woman sitting at her side, but is otherwise locked in a peaceful, voiceless kind of camaraderie. She does not volunteer conversation with me as if to emphasize the point that, as the outsider, I am expected to make all the moves.

'How long have you been here?'

'Oh, a week or thereabouts, same as the others,' she replies nonchalantly.

We carry on in silence for a while, listening to the buzz of more distant conversations.

'What did you come here for?' I venture finally, somewhat cowed.

'Same as you, same as all of us. Peace, spiritual renewal, love.'

And with that, she proceeds with perfect calm to catalogue the story of her life. It all started in Dade County, Florida, after the sudden death of her sister. She turned her back on her husband and their restaurant business and never returned to either. Sloughing off the old life she filed for bankruptcy and quit Florida in an RV with her son and an older sister. Nine months on her sister and her son returned to resume their lives in Florida, and Christos was left on the side of a freeway with a tent and a couple of hundred dollars.

Since then she had been living with a Mexican woman down on the border, washing and fixing meals for her board and keep.

We get up to fetch some fruit and she says:

'You know. The whole world is in crisis. Capitalism's finished. It just doesn't work.'

'So what will you do?'

Christos, I realize, is a woman whose life story has been told over so often that it has come to resemble small-talk.

'I'll wait, and then, when it's all over, I'll let my intuition guide me. What will you do?'

What *will* I do? It's strange to run across so much millennial angst in a country still resonant with new beginnings.

At two a bell sounds and we process up a flight of wooden stairs to the room above the kitchen for daily 'heart time and consensus'. We sit in a circle barefoot with heads bowed. I slump cross-legged and look for clues from the others, picking at my toe nails and chastising myself for my spiritual inadequacy. Nerves. After five minutes or so, a man in a T-shirt bearing the imperative 'Get Naked!' opens the meeting and everyone looks up and smiles oversized smiles, which makes me wonder if we all use the same muscles because everytime I try to emulate them, it hurts. Most of these people intend to stay through the summer, some will teach workshops to short-stay visitors, some will tend the garden, and a few, like the two white boys with dreds, will do nothing but Buddhist chanting. Unless the 'consensus' kicks them out, that is. All decisions at Lama are made at 'consensus' and the apparent purpose of this one is to decide who should be allowed to stay through the summer season and who has failed to meld and must leave.

'OK,' proceeds Get Naked, 'Who'd like to say something about Jane?' In the circle, Jane blushes. There is a pause in which fully to appreciate Jane's predicament, then Christos comes up with:

'In the few days we've been together, I feel Jane has become a daughter to me.' Jane acknowledges this with a nod.

'Mmmm, we're so very close.'

'My heart tells me that we met before in a past life.'

Get Naked! claps his hands to his knees in appreciation.

'Aren't we all just looking for a home?' asks a southern man, irrelevantly, 'and aren't we all scared this isn't going to be it?'

To which Get Naked says, 'Thank you so much for sharing that Christos, and thank *you* too George.'

'Praise be,' agrees a man in army fatigues.

Get Naked announces that it is time for the consensus, so please to close our eyes and delve into our innermost selves. We join hands and close our eyes and so I imagine we look into our hearts. After a long pause Get Naked whispers 'yesss' and the woman next to him whispers 'yesss' and when it comes round to my turn I whisper 'yesss' and so it goes on. The group resumes its mammoth smiling and I wonder if it's just me who hasn't the least idea what all the yessses are intended to add up to.

Trouble starts during the 'heart time' when an earnest man in a cravat says:

'I'm really having problems with the 'tunings'. I mean, some people are just not getting up in time. Either we all have to get up by seven, or there's just no point. Robin didn't come in till nine, yesterday.'

'Uh.' Get Naked looks anxiously about, holds his hands up to intervene. 'Could you rephrase that Gerry?'

'Oh,' says Gerry, a little taken aback 'Sure. Uh, what I mean is, you know, we all have to work together.'

'Right?' replies Get Naked

'Yeah, I mean, it's not just Robin. Kay never makes it on time. Never.'

'Uh, Gerry,' smiles Get Naked, 'thank you for sharing those thoughts. I think we're going to need just a little adjournment for, uh, contemplation. We don't judge anyone at Lama, Gerry.'

Jeez, maybe that's because you don't *know* anyone, I'm thinking . . . or does that make it easier? When we return from the adjournment Get Naked announces that Gerry has something to say so Gerry stands up and says:

'What I just said came from a place of selfishness and dishonesty. I have disrespected this heart time. I have not been dealing with my anger vibrations and I'd like everyone to help me with that. Especially Kay and especially Robin.'

Kay and Robin stand, move through the circle and give Gerry a damned good hugging.

'Blessed be,' says Get Naked and everyone agrees that the heart time has been a hard day's work.

It is suddenly not difficult to see the shadow of puritanism in New Age thinking. Although their ethics are quite different, both puritanism and the New Age fixate on the relationship between god and the self. In New Age thinking, that god is 'the divine within,' so New Agers, even more than puritans, value soul-searching above all other ritual as a route to transcendence and sacredness. Turned in upon themselves, the outside world can seem uninteresting and profane, even irrelevant to New Agers. Faith is no longer a matter of trust, something to which one must abandon oneself, but an exercise in introspection, whose outer expression is sincerity. Hence the New Age preoccupation with 'authentic experience', and with sincerely-expressed emotion, for to New Agers these are both a protest against post-modern life and a visible manifestation of the sacredness within. The tear and the hug are the sacraments of New Age ritual.

Perhaps larger still than the influence of puritanism on the New Age is the influence of medieval gnosticism, which was brought to the attention of the twentieth-century public by Georgii Ivanovich Gurdjieff, who was also influenced by contemporary psychoanalysis. Gurdjieff thought there was a difference between a person's 'essential being' or higher self and their personality. The higher self was a kind of force according to Gurdjieff, without identity, but also without ego, beyond pain and love; quite like the Buddhist state of nirvana, except in so far as one is personalized while the other describes a state of being. Human beings, he said, were unfinished things, under the sway of external stimuli. Gurdjieff thought that enlightenment consisted in waking up the inner self from its imprisonment in personality. One of Gurdjieff's greatest apologists was the heiress Mabel Luhan Dodge, who set up an artists' retreat in northern New Mexico. It was Dodge who tried to foist Gurdjieff's ideas onto D. H. Lawrence during his stay outside Taos, but Lawrence did not bite.

The New Age idea, borrowed from the gnostics, that reality is a self-made construct has fitted happily into an individualistic culture in which there have been persistent crises of faith extending all the way from religion and politics through love and trust to identity itself. If a person can convince themselves that reality is based entirely on the creations of their mind, then faith is simply a matter of self-belief.

After heart time is done Joel offers to take me around the Lama campus; we wander a few steps into a low cave-like building housing the Foundation's library of books on personal growth. After the library we fetch up in a central atrium with a picture window giving out over the mountain slope onto the crazed windblown plain with its fringe of blue-teethed hills. In the centre of the atrium are the two young white boys in dreds, one bearded, both raggedly dressed and drumming. Joel takes my hand and we follow the path of a drying stream up beyond some sheds, through the recycling heap, and the Tibetan flag workshop and still higher until we reach a pine bosque, where we stop for breath. A warm, placid wind runs silent through the juniper, picking up its bitter oil. Joel looks at me, I look away. Joel looks at me, reaches for a branch, pulls it down towards him and begins to shake with silent tears.

'They wrecked me, they ate me up,' he wails.

'Who wrecked you?'

'My parents,' sobs Joel 'my own parents.'

'Oh.' Deep waters. I move closer to him and put a hand on his shoulder. My words leave me, followed briskly by my feelings. I am left searching for a response.

'I'm not sure pain ever goes away, it hides every now and then and that's as much as you can ask of it. At some point you just have to carry on. I mean, what else is there?'

He looks up, fiery-eyed, seemingly violated. Then he palms his hands over his eyes in order to shut out the light. I wonder what it is that I have said. Then I recall that to offend an open display of vulnerability, as I've just done, is to flout the rules of New Age therapeutics.

'You don't understand,' sobs Joel, 'I'm clearing the parents.'

'Uh, look Joel, I have to be getting back, I think.'

'Do you need a big hug real bad, like now?' No *way* do I need a hug from a middle-aged parent clearer, but he gives me one anyhow.

'Blessed be,' he says, pulling away and planting his lips over the crease between my brows. 'You'll find so much love here.' At that moment I have a dishonourable urge to lay into him with my fists. For Joel, and many New Agers like him, an intense emotional response seems proof of an authentic response, and is thus good. Tears and hugs and interminable therapeutics are just the rituals of membership, New Age identity badges. In any case, that's the last time I see Joel. Someone tells me later that he wandered off into the forest to find his wild man.

In the later part of the afternoon, I pitch my little $12 WalMart tent alongside a row of others in a grove of ponderosa pine, setting it to face west so I can watch the sun set. The woman next door, Cinnamon Rose, wanders by to offer assistance, tells me I am about to experience the most loving environment I will ever happen upon. I don't mention that I've survived an *epidemic* of most loving environments. There is a hollowness in her voice, as though life has juiced her, and left the pulp behind. I wonder vaguely if her body might wash up on some psychiatrist's couch in five years' time, drowned in mercurial dreams.

Crawling into my tent, unpacking a can of root beer and a few books. Sun comes in warm through the canvas and cooks up a resinous smell. Next I know someone is leaning over stroking my face. It is Cinnamon Rose, who has woken me to ask if I'd like to go sufi dancing. If not, would I like to come and hug some ponderosa pines? Perhaps I should say yes, but, remembering that 'there are no shoulds in New Age thinking' (a piece of advice gleaned from my God Insight Box), I decline politely and fall instead to my books, sitting cross-legged outside in the last of the sun. When the light grows dim, I read by kerosene lamp. I am dipping into Blavatsky's theosophical writings and through her work the New Age reveals its history. There isn't a unique New Age Movement, of course, no single explanation as to why the beliefs current among the large and disparate group who regard themselves as New Agers have found such widespread acceptance in America. New Age is the consumer culture's answer to spirituality. It takes what serves it and leaves the rest. Nonetheless, one of the most persistent New Age leitmotifs is the hope of recovering syncretic truths that once were clear and are now lost, and this was Blavatsky's dream also. It is no co-incidence, either, that Theosophical ideas enjoyed their greatest popularity at the turn of the last century and New Age ideas are so much in vogue right now, for at the heart of both are fantasies of decay and utopian dreams of new beginnings.

Helena Petrovna Blavatsky always claimed she had travelled alone through Tibet in search of spiritual guidance and found a group of teachers from all the great religions, whom she called the Ascended Masters. Whether or not Blavatsky physically removed herself to Tibet, which was more or less closed to travellers at the end of the nineteenth century, is irrelevant for she possessed that quality of all pretenders; an incapacity to distinguish between humble fact and fantasy. What is for certain is that she sailed to New York City, announced her privileged access to this Supreme Court of spiritual life, and began to act as a conduit between its masters and ordinary folk. Beyond the illusory dream-world of reality, said Blavatsky, there was another dimension of existence inhabited by spiritual or angelic beings, where the real business of the cosmos was conducted. The battles played out by mere mortals were tender irrelevancies to these beings, who were beyond all ethics and metaphysics. According to Blavatsky, the Ascended Masters' plan was to raise the world into this dimension, which they were prevented from doing by the Dark Ones, who still feature strongly in New Age rhetoric, generally as sinister aliens. The appeal of Blavatsky's ideas was that they provided a source of spiritual authority incorporating all the authorities of the great religions, but also, crucially, during the moral upheaval of the *fin de siècle*, that they did not of themselves require a particular set of moral behaviours.

Reading Blavatsky reminds me to go back to my notes from the time in Taos. I can only imagine that I had forgotten who or what I had decided to be for a while then, for I seemed to have spent a great deal of time thinking, feeling and doing almost nothing. Personality shifts that way; it's not something you have, it's something you surf. One day you are greedy, say, and quick to make decisions, and you may remain that way for days or months or years, but sure enough, at some point you will find yourself dithering and ascetic and you will be shocked to discover that you no longer fulfil your own expectations as you once did.

At about nine the forest is suddenly, inexplicably filled with the sparks of fireflies. Their dipping, unreliable illuminations are the last detail of my day, for I remember nothing else.

The next morning, like Kay and Robin, I don't make it in time for the tuning. At breakfast I sit next to Gary. In the Sixties Gary went on the anti-Vietnam protests, but he got drafted, signed up and was shipped off. In 'Nam – I suppose this was '70 or '71 – he picked up a drug habit, but he never did any fighting; he worked as a driver. When his time was up they demobbed the carapace of a man, and put it out on the streets with no job, no money and no junk. The carapace spent the next fifteen years of its life poleaxed with booze and dope. At some point Gary got married but he says that he doesn't remember much about the marriage or the woman. She left him, anyway, and he eventually fetched up with a guru, ditched the booze and the shit and got into personal growth.

It's odd that a generation so convinced of its political significance should turn its back on politics so quickly; by the seventies the demonstrations, banners and save-the-world slogans seemed to have lost out to the greater lure of personal transformation. The hippy idealism that had kept the marchers on the streets span off in another direction, leaving behind its commitment to a political future. It wasn't long before the cult of personal transformation and the pseudo-intimacy it inspired had assumed the language of the barricaded campuses and drawn about it a community of the committed. So seductive has this mediated intimacy become that all other claims to spiritual and political authority among New Agers are now written off as the imbecilic warbling of betrayer-politicians and sleaze-bag preachers. Uncluttered by the demands of the outside world, many New Agers' aspirations go no further than the assurance of a seamless, pain-free life. In teepee retreats and encounter groups throughout the 1970s and 1980s, and now into the final decade of the century, the American Dream no longer pulled like the dream of a suite in Motel Nirvana. Liberal-minded baby boomers all over America ditched the disintegrating fictions of nationhood and picked up an alternative axiom, which runs along these lines: all being is spiritually and morally interconnected, and thus the individual, being a manifestation of the cosmic whole, is him or herself the ultimate arbiter of reality and therefore morals. And so a whole generation of white middle-class men and women consciously turned their backs on political life and did not trouble to teach it to their children.

I sound so bitter, but I'm not bitter. I think I'm just sad.

I have decided to visit D. H. Lawrence's sarcophagus, or more accurately, I suppose, the place where his ashes are kept, the Lawrence ranch, about fifteen miles from Lama. The keeper of the ranch, Al L. Bearce, is a man whose body parts seem to be only lightly glued together from the grease of a workman's overall he hasn't taken off in years, but his heart still pumps the raw red stuff. At the door of his cottage hangs a hummingbird feeder and a piebald cat twists up and down the steps beneath it; I have in mind that this might be the sort of rural idyll that would make a fine literary setting for an impassioned *affaire de coeur*, but Al Bearce tells me that Lawrence wrote little here, and set no love scene in these mountains so far as he could recall. Judging from the aged visitors' book, the priest of love doesn't get many visits. Whoever wrote 'nice place, but what are all the rodent turds doing?' probably didn't have a deep, intuitive sense of Lawrentian values. Al is an autodidact, living a life remote enough to be untouched by the awkward contradiction of others' opinions. He has his, and they are fixed.

On Lawrence's tomb:

'It was Frieda brought D. H. here. Wouldn't have chosen this place. He liked the warm. Come the winter we get snowed in here.'

On Santa Fe:

'Full of snobs, pseudo-artists and politicians. Never go there no more, never miss it.'

On Lawrence's paintings at Taos:

'Get nothing more from them than the notion that Lawrence wasn't much of a painter.'

We chat at the door of his cottage for a while, about Nottingham mostly. I try to impress upon him how far the high pine-crested mountains and desert plains are from the sullen, pinched, semi-industrial landscape of Lawrence's home, and how alien and enchanted they must have felt. I have heard it said that people who live in a series of different landscapes or in a series of different cultures are in search of their soul's home. Lawrence wandered constantly, from 1919 when he left England up until the time of his death in 1930. He gave a number of explanations for his wanderlust, one of which was the pursuit of what he took to be our elemental nature. I'm not sure I believe in elemental natures. To me, each person makes a series of conscious or unconscious choices which formulate their personality. If there is an elemental nature guiding the choices it's not possible to know it. So far as I see it a new environment is not so much a fresh and transcendent geography for the soul as an instrument with which to change the personality. I have proved this to myself by standing on the plain and turning to face the four compass points. At each turn, nature makes a new relationship to both itself and the viewer. Even if that newness seems only to be a different pattern of rock and sky, the scape is irrefutably altered and the brain forced to compensate. One is on the plain still, but at one's feet and eye-line are five quite separate worlds. Each transmutes the personality, however slightly. The same process happens at home, although we scarcely notice it. Tramp a familiar neighbourhood drunk, tired or with a hangover even, and it can seem that with every step you are entering not only a different world but a different character.

Lawrence's ashes came in by train to Lamy, which is en route to my eventual destination, Madrid, New Mexico. The priest of love died in Vence on 2 March 1930, but Frieda wanted his ashes buried in New Mexico. My guess is that Frieda loved the place more than D. H. and wished to lay her mark upon it, which she did by offering up her husband's remains. In any case she had Lawrence's ashes shipped over from France to the United States and sent by train to Lamy, the waystation nearest the Lawrence ranch at San Cristobal. On the day appointed for their arrival, Frieda and a party of friends motored down to Lamy and sat drinking in the Saloon Bar, waiting for the blue smoke and tickertape rattle which would announce the arrival of the locomotive. The train was late and Frieda's party were early so, by the time Lawrence's urn arrived they had put some distance between the first drink and the last. Frieda signed for the urn but rather than rush back straight away the party decided to have one final drink back at the saloon. Some time later they left and headed for home, which was then a journey of half a day by car. It was only when they arrived back at San Cristobal that Frieda realized they were without her husband's last remains. A messenger was despatched to Lamy, and the Lawrence urn discovered lying under a table at the Lamy saloon bar where his wife had left it. Love is a fragile thing.

I think it was Dostoevsky who said that there are two kinds of love: active love and the love of dreams. Anyone who has experienced either will know this. Dream love gives of itself, but it lacks the strength or the grace to receive. Dream love has no real object, is rather a longing to be caressed by the pull of destiny, an attempt at reconciling isolation. Dream love is love reflected back on itself. Active love, on the other hand, as Dostoevsky said, is work and pain, work and pain.

Madrid, my destination on this stretch of the journey, is one of New Mexico's hippy centres, along with Chloride and a few other obscure little ex-ghost, ex-mining towns. Half a mile out of town the old Madrid mine-shaft is still visible and alongside it there remains a series of old clapboard cottages, partly obscured by shale. The air smells of coaltar. Many of the hippies live in RVs and caravans on a hillside facing these cottages. The town itself, in common with most western towns, is fashioned around the road, so it has no centre, only a middle. Scattered along that road is a carnage of hippy stores and mining museums and cafes and old adobe houses, whose owners lived in Madrid when the place was utterly obscure and unvisited. Despite a persistent reek of shit and rotten food Madrid maintains a sort of dimmed presence not quite amounting to dignity. At one end of the middle of the town is a blue-painted hall, opposite the main bar, and this is where Walker's band, Mobillus Trip, is playing. A few twentysomethings have already driven in from Santa Fe and are hanging about in the cool air, smoking weed. Behind the bar building two people kiss pressed up against a wall, while inside yet others are drinking themselves happy. It occurs to me suddenly, and for no obvious reason, that there isn't anything of substance to have faith in anymore; no gods, no institutions, no family. All that remains to be had is faith in the self, which is an unlovely kind of fundamentalism.

Inside the blue building a DJ starts a warm-up. The kids behind the bar disentangle themselves and move in. Although there is still a little light remaining in the sky, it is quite dark inside, and humid with bodies. I stand in the corner, sucking on a bottle of beer, and after a few minutes a guy in a tie-dyed shirt approaches me and asks if I'd like to buy an E, and I say to myself yeah, why not? So the guy hands over a pill in a ziplock bag and I spend the next seven hours feeling more me than me.

I wake up in the sagebrush just outside town as the dawn is breaking, thinking, where the hell is faith?

Driving

'. . . I wish I could care what you do or where you
go but I can't . . . My dear, I don't give a damn.'

A thousand miles a week; me, the land, the road and four wheels.

Take the road: an unseemly scar through an immensity of
terrain. You'd think the road would be swallowed up, but the
contrary is true. Where the road runs it is king, the plain and
the rock beside it merely subjects. The road is the selvage, the
holding edge, the place from where the land seeps out either
side. Asked where the land ends, you will say it ends at the point
where the road slips beyond the earth's curve. Even the colours
of the road assert its dominance: stark black, brilliant yellow,
against brown-grey city, against red dust plain, against pale
green bunch grass, against muddled chaparral, against sallow
prairie.

In the west whole towns are constructed around the road, and
without it they would simply not be. The west's architecture of
ranches, fast-food joints, rest areas, resort towns, motels exist
in service to the road. Indeed, western cities and western towns
are *defined* by the frequency, size and variation of their asphalt
stripes. If it has two interstates, several arterial freeways and
a complex grid reaching into suburbs you know you're in a
metropolis. A two-lane highway with no median, where there
are no gas stations or help points in view and you know that
you're in the remote desert.

The archetypal western road; one lane each side, straight
as a knife blade, slicing up the far far distance, the sky arched
over it all like a food cover. Perhaps a chromium-clad truck

189

thundering in one direction. A placid, whining wind sending tumbleweeds tripping across the median. Ravens on the shoulder, dust dancing about the plain. Otherwise completely, utterly empty. Light stirs the pavement into a watery tarpaulin, then into a trench of quivering mercury, finally into a line of electric air. The debris of movement lies upon it: tyre castings, garbage, roadkill. And yet, paradoxically, the road is a stripe of stillness in a fluxing landscape.

Take the land: a great grand swathe, beamy at the sides, and ample both in front and behind. All around the desert plain, the livid blue sky, patterned in places with clouds, red and navy coloured mesas rising on the horizon, yucca bushes and sage. An open country, a *Lebensraum* for giants, a terrain so spacious that it almost demands movement. Be still, be swallowed up. Sometimes, when the road runs through a gorge or between cliffs, and the terrain is suddenly obscured from view, you emerge the other side to find that nothing is changed except that you have moved on. There is the sage still, and the same bald sky. In America, people navigate by the unchanged points of the geographic compass – east, west, north, south. You drive east along one highway, say, then north along another, so the terrain is always the immutable fixed point. One mountain range remains south of another, a plain to the east of a town is always to its east. In Britain, by contrast, we tend to regard ourselves as the still point. We drive left and then take a right. A hill is positioned according to our particular point of view; to the left of another hill, to right of the river.

The landscape of the southwest does change, of course, however constant it may appear. In spring the rivers become plump with snow melt; only a month or so later they have wasted away to alluvial arroyos. The wind picks up sand and soil from the plain and dumps it up against the mesas or into the bottoms of canyons. In the dry season the desert expands, during rain it shrinks. Lightning strikes shake the skies, crack open rocks and electrify trees and cacti. The rain that comes with the summer storms floods riparian areas and chaparrals and transforms the plains from dusky rock faces into muddy green seas.

Driving

Take four wheels: out on those southwestern roads, four wheels are the best friend a person could hope for. The more you travel the more the space inside your vehicle comes to resemble home. It provides the necessities – shelter and shade, and the comforts – a place to keep root beer cool (under the passenger seat), music, air conditioning, light. Before long, you have come to regard it as an amenable mechanical companion. It has few needs – a drop of water, some gas, an oil change every three thousand miles or so – and providing these becomes a part of the ritual of the friendship. You begin to rely on the vehicle's rhythms; you develop an affection for its little quirks. The mysterious ticks become the means by which you document your journey. After a few thousand miles your own identity and that of the vehicle have blurred somewhat. Is that your arm on the wheel, or an extension of the wheel itself? Does your foot pump the accelerator, or the accelerator pump your foot? By the time your journey is up you are already an automaton.

White Light, Greenbacks and Redskins

'The land is an Indian thing.'
JACK KEROUAC

At the Aztec cafe in Santa Fe one morning of the week following, I heard two advertising executives discussing their presentation for a catalogue of home furnishings:

Advertising Executive #1: 'This stuff has to say Santa Fe, New Mexico. What is there about this city that zings?'

Advertising Executive #2: 'Georgia O'Keefe, Giants of American Art?'

'I kinda think minority has a buzz right now.'

'You mean Indians, right?'

'Sure, that stuff is hot.'

Advertising Executive #2 puts his pen in his mouth and thinks hard for a minute or two.

'How's 'bout Naturally Navajo?'

A few days after my arrival in Santa Fe I received a fax from Fergus, with a photocopy of an article he had spotted in the *European* newspaper. Thinking that I might feel removed from my roots, Fergus routinely rifles through the *European* and faxes over snippets of news from home. I haven't the heart to tell him that his jejune little stories of rioting French farmers and Norwegian whaling expeditions head straight for the trash can. Evidently, Europe is to Fergus little more than an ill-managed, oversized medieval farm. The fax included a piece about a Parisian ex-stagehand who had quit Paris, renamed himself Cheval Debout and gone to live in a leather teepee in the forests of Le Var, where he was earning a living chopping down trees for the local landowner. Cheval Debout had gathered around him a little community of Parisian Indians, who also lived in leather teepees and also chopped down trees. Their hero was Johnny Halliday. When the interviewer asked him why he had decided to become an Indian Cheval Debout replied, 'Everybody wants to be an Indian now.'

These two trivial incidents had an enormous impact on me, for they brought with them the heavy realization that I had spent two full seasons in 'Indian Country' (which is how the southwest is often marketed) without taking anything but the most cursory interest in Indians. Sure, I'd *read* about them in histories of the west. To me Indians had become a part of America's past. But the more I thought about it, the more obvious it became that they were not all gone and done with. Was the failure mine? How was it that the Indian presence in the southwest had been rendered as nothing more than a piece of history? I wandered into a corner bookstore and headed for the Native American section: *Bury My Heart at Wounded Knee*, the story of Geronimo and a couple of books filled with portraits of cute little Hiawathas in beads. The New Age section, on the other hand, was replete with Native American titles. I found *Dancing Healers: A Voyage of Self-Discovery with the Lakota Sioux, Magicians of the Universe: A Native American Path to Enlightenment*, and innumerable others in the same vein, along with some well-thumbed Carlos Castenada. Under politics there was nothing, under economics nothing also. I left empty-handed. Jeez, I didn't even know what to call these people. Indigens? Indians? Aboriginals? Native Americans? There was no consensus in the literature. So I rang Fergus from a phone outside Healthy Dave's Vegetarian Eatery and asked his advice. Fergus replied that there was a tradition of free speech in America, so as far as he was concerned I could call them what I liked.

'C'mon, Ferg, I'm in a payphone,' I said, trying to wheedle him into co-operating. It's so damned difficult to get him to take anything seriously.

'The orthodoxy is always changing,' he said, responding to my tone. 'I know it's not redskins.' Then, relenting a little, he added, 'I have a friend who's part Arapahoe or Navajo or something, I could ask him.'

That really raised my hackles.

'What d'you mean Arapahoe *or* Navajo. Don't you know the difference, for chrissakes?'

'OK, what's the difference?' Fergus was sounding impatient.

'Well, how should I know, I'm not a damned *American* for chrissakes.'

'And how should I know, I'm not a fucking Indian.'

He had a point. Despite being British, I don't know the difference between Picts and Celts. I asked him to head to one of the big New York City bookstores and find me some decent books about Native American culture and send them express to the King's Rest. A couple of days later a package arrived containing a dense but solid Native American history, two volumes of cute little Hiawathas in beads and a book by a man with the unlikely name of Jerry Mander, entitled *In the Absence of the Sacred*. For three days I sat on my bed in room 12 and read. By the fourth day I understood enough to realize that the whole Indian business (I don't know what to call it – question, issue?) was a long drawn-out story of despoliation and pollution, of the environmental kind, but also of a culture, an entire way of living. The clean-up job, has been so cursory and underimagined that a sort of scum is left, trapping the life below and suffocating it.

And so I decided to retrace my route around the southwest, beginning in Santa Fe, heading north to Taos and from there up into Four Corners where Colorado, Utah, New Mexico and Arizona meet, turning south into Arizona through the Navajo and Hopi reservations and eventually winding my way back up north and east into Santa Fe. On this journey I would try to gain some measure of the Indian question. Recalling Cheval Debout's line, 'Everybody wants to be an Indian now,' I decided to concentrate my efforts on the New Age attitude to Indians, in part because I imagined it might be more positive and less brutal than most. In any case, I came to the conclusion that if I used my eyes and ears and gathered what I could, whatever I learned would be better than knowing nothing.

I began scouting through the newspapers for Indian stories, and found plenty, most dismal accounts of arcane bureaucratic infighting between federal agencies, the Bureau of Indian Affairs and the Indian Tribal Councils. Others documented in detail the progress of the so-called 'mystery disease' which had killed a dozen Navajo folk in the Four Corners region. Some press accounts even referred to it as the 'Navajo disease,' though non-Navajo people had also contracted it. In any case, neither disease nor bureaucracy interested me much, and I made up my mind to begin the trip before the weekend, in order to be back in time to catch my flight back to London and give me sufficient flexibility to be able to stop off for a few days here and there if I chose. As luck would have it, I came across an article in the Santa Fe *New Mexican* a couple of days later, written by Rick Romancito, himself a Zuni/Taos Pueblo Indian. The piece was effectively a diatribe against what the writer saw as the co-opting of Indian culture by New Agers on the hunt for spiritual rejuvenation. Now this is the meat, I thought.

Since Rick lived in Taos, we agreed to have lunch together the following day, which is when my second journey began. I set off from Santa Fe early and made Taos in an hour and a half, which left me with an hour to kill, so I found a bar and ordered up a couple of bloody Marys, with the result that I was hopelessly late, of course, and hopelessly hopeless. Rick ordered a half-pounder very rare. I vaguely remember thinking 'Wow, Indians eat raw meat.'

While we were waiting for the food to arrive Rick told me how his mother had been working in the kitchen of her home in Taos Pueblo, a famously picturesque Indian village a few miles north of Taos, when a group of Dutch tourists walked in and started taking pictures of her oven. When she asked them to leave, they said they had permission. Permission from *whom?* This is *my* home, she said. We got *permits* replied the tourists. The problem was worse elsewhere. Tesuque Pueblo had demanded to be removed from tourist maps, after a group of touring New Agers was found lying butt-naked in an Indian burial ground awaiting the spirits of the dead.

'Yeah,' I said, my voice curdled with booze, 'But isn't it all pretty harmless?'

'No.' Rick sounded pissed off, 'It's not harmless. By appropriating what they think is Indian mysticism New Agers diminish its importance in the eyes of people who can actually get things done for Indians. Our political agenda and the New Age agenda have totally different paths,' he said, 'We don't want their help.'

There was a silence while he ate, then he added, angrily this time, 'They do more harm than good. They just take what they like with no appreciation for the whole. They've just made a decision to be ignorant.'

I was lying out in the sage that night trying to decide exactly where I should head next – the Navajo reservation, Apache, Ute, the Hopi lands – when it came to me that the best place to begin was the beginning, at Mesa Verde, where the Anasazi had lived. I went back to the motel and dug out Fergus' dense but solid Native American history and read until the the sun came up, washing the room in orange light and leaving a ragged impression of the moon like an old stain in the sky.

At the top of Mesa Verde in Colorado is a sandstone city. Some parts of the city have disintegrated with age, but, nonetheless, there it is, with its towers and multi-storey houses and grain stores and underground ceremonial kivas lying protected under sandstone cliffs. The Anasazi are something of an enigma to anthropologists; around 1400 they seem to have quit Mesa Verde, leaving no written records. Like the Hohokam, they disappeared. From their buildings, pictographs and petroglyphs a way of life can be discerned, but what fascinates tourists is, I think, not the Anasazi way of life or the reliquary of their achievements but this unresolved narrative of their 'mysterious' disappearance.

The site is open to individuals and parties, but in some of the more delicate parts of the city groups only are allowed accompanied by a ranger. I joined a tour party of Americans from Wisconsin at the top of the mesa for a tour of Balcony House one of the most spectacular and fragile buildings on Mesa Verde, built into the cliff face itself. At the beginning of the tour, the ranger gathered us around and said,

'Now I want you all to imagine being characters in the Robin Hood story because it's about the same time that these Anasazi

Indians were roaming around. Some of you guys can be archers, others can be cooks.'

As we walked through Balcony House, the ranger would stop us every now and then and say 'See that wall? Well, that used to be a kitchen and you cooks would have done your cooking there' or 'The Anasazi bathed in that sink hole right here, so Maid Marians, this is where you'd have made yourself ready for a date with the handsome Robin.'

Now, I've passed through Sherwood Forest many times on my way from London to the north. It's a flat swatch of rain-soaked oaks and beech trees, redolent of the time long long since gone when England was deep in forest. Mesa Verde, on the other hand, is a cliff thrust up from a semi-arid, salty plain. On the plateau at the top stunted piñon pines submit to an endless wind. Below, on the plain, the Anasazi planted corn and squash. Fourteenth century England was a Christian country, in common with most of the rest of Europe. Brigand Hood, if he existed and believed in anything at all, would have been a Christian. By contrast the Anasazi were almost certainly believers in a hierophanic universe, as the Hopi are today. They believed in an unseen reality of mysterious and sacred archetypal forms which existed in a timeless, mythological space, and were made manifest in nature. To the Anasazi, as to the Hopi, the high mesas were places where this spirit world communicated to the mundane world below. Mesa Verde was halfway to heaven.

By comparing the Anasazi to the Robin Hood myth, the ranger had without ill-intention promulgated a series of misconceptions so fundamental that it was difficult to see how the Wisconsinites would ever be persuaded that Anasazi culture was anything else but a politically correct swashbuckling soap opera. At the end of the tour, I turned to the ranger and asked if she always used this Robiin Hood routine and she said yes she did;

'It's a little unorthodox, I know, but it gets folks involved. Otherwise it all seems a bit remote. People really take to it. No-one knows why they disappeared, you know.'

Back in my motel room in Cortez, I lay on the bed with a can of root beer contemplating one of those generic prints of an

Indian warrior which can be found in almost any budget motel across the southwest. Fergus' history book lay unopened next to me, along with a number of leaflets from Mesa Verde. I was not much interested in obsidian arrow heads and whether pinole was made with or without chile, nor was I hooked by the poor magic of seers and keepers of ancient truths, and mysteries and disappearances. I wanted to know how it might feel to live in an enchanted world; to understand why it rains, why one sleeps, or dies, to be confident, beyond the banality of fact, of the greater *meaning* of every last detail of everyday existence. That would be something.

They seem so remote to me, the Anasazi, so self-contained. It might be said, with only a little irony, that their greatest achievement was to disappear centuries before Manifest Destiny would have rendered it necessary to exterminate them. As it is, they do not suck up federal funds, they are silent on the issue of water rights, they make no claims on our guilty consciences, intimate that they might be anything we do not want them to be. And they have left us with a mystery, for which we, who have none of our own, are duly grateful.

I left Cortez just after dawn. The light was still low and soft with sun. In places the sun had not yet reached, night air hovered like death's breath. A few Navajo men sat wide-kneed at the side of the road waiting for day labour.

'Why is it that the whites moved through the west leaving behind them a trail of place names that disrespect the land?' a Navajo man at a gas station said. I asked him to explain. 'I don't have to explain, look at a map.' There they were: Devil's Bridge, Hell's Backbone, Purgatory, Nothing.

The Navajo Nation, or Dinetah, stretches across a lunar scape of pink and orange sandstone hills, frilled about with heaps of matt grey rock and set on a yellow plain, like a plate of scallops. Driving across, it would seem to be almost infinite. When the Dinetah was legally established after the failure of the Navajo and Apache internment camp at Fort Sumner, back in 1868, the tribe was handed an acreage representing 0.1 per cent of its claim and one third of the land it had previously occupied. Today some of that confiscated land has been returned and the tribe has purchased a considerable area from the federal government, but the Navajo Nation is still nothing like the size it was before the time of legal boundaries. Officially a sovereign state within the Union, its remote, arid terrain is some of the harshest in the lower forty-eight. There are few population centres of any size. Many Navajo travel into Gallup, Page, Flagstaff and other towns on the periphery for their shopping. An air of transience pervades the little villages on the reservation, most of which consist in a few mobile homes, the occasional satellite TV dish and a gas station. In the more remote areas there are still hogans, the round mud and daub dwellings of more traditional Navajo with their accompanying beehive-shaped ovens. Every public space – whether it be the parking spot outside a trading post, a feed store or a gas station forecourt – seems frail and little used. Once I saw a sign advertising 'fat sheep for sale,' but there were none about. A statement of defiance, dug into the sand against a lonely backdrop. The Navajo Nation is not so different from much of the rest of the desert southwest, which is almost all thinly-lived, sparse and feral. And the life is not so different either, for where the land might suggest mobility and freedom to screenwriters and tourist organisations, the truth is that it constrains and confines those who settle on it. There are few life-styles that can accommodate such isolation, or such rawness; there are few life-styles that can tolerate such poverty.

In any case, on Navajo land the sense of transience is deceptive, because the Navajo way of life – they call it the way of the beautiful rainbow – is ancient and persistent. Traditionally, the Navajo are herdsmen and women. I say women advisedly, for Navajo women are very often the principal property owners in the traditional Navajo clan. In common with any herding culture, the Navajo way is semi-nomadic; clans move with the seasons, from one grazing range to another. The Navajo say that when their people are separated from their sheep they die of *ch'eena* or broken hearts. Nomadic cultures are rarely acquisitive; a nomad can put to use only as much as he or she can carry. Nomadism implies a systematic way of life that runs in contradiction to the relentless Western thrust of growth and goods and it may be because of its strangeness to our settled materialist lives that we tend to regard it as a lesser achievement; as a deracinated culture, an uncommitted culture, a culture both malleable and fickle. The reality is, of course, otherwise. Homelessness, of both the physical and spiritual kind, is one of the defining characteristics of *Western* life in the late twentieth century. This is a political issue. Until we are willing to address the fact of our own deracination, anomie, fickleness, the historical loss of a few acres of bald salt-washed plain will seem to be of little consequence. But to the Navajo, it was the beginning of the death of the beautiful rainbow.

When he heard of my intention to drive back through the southwest with different eyes, Fergus at once suggested I return to Sakina's place, on Pinon Jay Drive in West Sedona. I confess that I had almost forgotten about Sakina, but Fergus' idea seemed like a sufficiently good one to risk making the journey so I headed south from the Dinetah into Sedona on a Thursday at the beginning of September and found Sakina sitting out in her porch in the shade of a Marlboro umbrella, just as I had first found her. She hadn't made it to California and didn't quite know why her plans had changed, except that Spirit had obviously willed her to stay.

'What do you know about Indians?' I asked.

First, she said, they are actually the descendants of the lost tribe of Atlantis. If I needed evidence of this, I had only to look at a map of Mexico; the letter group 'atl' appears all over Indian land. Ixhuatlán, Atlixo, Atlatlah, Miahuatlan.

'Also,' she added, picking at her nostril with one hand and brushing away a pestering mosquito with the other, 'Also, I think that the problems Indians have with alcohol and gambling are there because most of the Indians these days aren't really Indians.'

'Oh?' I said, intrigued.

'No,' she replied 'the alcoholics and the gamblers are reincarnations of nineteenth-century white men, paying back bad karma.'

'How do you know?' I asked.

'Real Indians are spiritually pure,' she said. 'I'm giving a ride to a couple of 'em at the weekend, dear. If you're still here, you can meet them.'

She suggested that if I really wanted to know about Indians, she would put *Dances with Wolves* on the video, so I said yes, I really did want to know about Indians. She could recite the words by heart, she said, 'What a magical, magical movie.'

On Friday night Sakina drove 150 miles to Second Mesa on the Hopi reservation and on Saturday morning she returned with a Hopi woman called Rowanna, Rowanna's son, Coco and about five members of Rowanna's family. Coco had been chosen to put on a display of Hopi dancing in a high-class shopping mall in Sedona, and Rowanna was hoping that she would be able to sell some kachina dolls. It was the woman's bad luck, Sakina told me, to have got hitched to a reincarnation of a nineteenth-century white man who beat her up for a year or two, stole her welfare cheques and left her pregnant. To keep herself and her son, Rowanna began carving wooden kachina dolls for the tourist market and somehow she met Sakina, who lent her a few hundred dollars. Rowanna could not repay the debt in cash so she repaid it in company.

It was exceptionally hot that Saturday. By two in the afternoon, the temperature had risen to 102. Whatever tourists there were didn't venture out from their hotels. Poor Coco danced the Eagle Dance in full costume to an audience of three. That evening he returned with blisters on his feet and a sweat rash from neck to waist. Rowanna was upset for her son and also because she had failed to sell a single Kachina doll, despite hanging around all day at the shopping mall. She and Coco were exhausted, she said, so we all sprawled inside Sakina's house on cushions, drinking iced tea and trying to escape from the heat. Rowanna's relatives remained utterly silent. In retrospect it occurred to me that Rowanna's relatives might not have spoken English, or that they had chosen not to speak it. About nine, just as the temperature was becoming bearable, Sakina appeared and announced quite unexpectedly that she had been preparing a medicine wheel in honour of the guests. A few minutes passed in silence, before Rowanna said

'Oh good.'

The ceremony of the wheel was originally practised by the northern plains Indians, but it has found its way to the southwest as part of a wave of Native American traditions adopted by various tribes to plug holes that remained after their own traditions were lost. The wheel itself can consist in stones or pretty much anything arranged in a circle with four spokes representing the compass points. East is the direction of yellow, north is black, south red and west blue. The wheel's centre symbolises the axis of the cosmos.

So the eight of us sat cross-legged and a little dazed around Sakina's medicine wheel, Rowanna and I holding hands and breathing in sage smoke. At the wheel's centre sat Sakina dressed in her Lakota Sioux outfit with Wellington boots, grasping an Indian talking stick and chanting. Beside her there were crystals and the skull of a small herbivore. Rowana said it was her 'magic rabbit.'

'Hail Great Spirit,' said Sakina, after a while, reaching into the sky. 'We give you thanks for the stars.'

Rowanna nodded. Rowanna's relatives remained silent and implacable.

'Thank you Father Sky,' continued Sakina raising her magic rabbit.

Rowanna nodded.

'Thank you Mother Earth,' she said, grinding a piece of it with her Wellington boot. Rowanna's relatives dozed quietly. Coco said he needed a pee. Sakina, oblivious, continued by scattering cornflour and bits of sage about, mumbling what sounded like prayers to the compass points. One of Rowanna's relatives began to choke.

'It is now time to speak,' said Sakina, leaning over and prodding Rowanna with her talking stick. So the relatives sat in silence, while Rowanna, flustered and exhausted, searched hard in her head, but could find nothing to say. Coco said he needed a pee.

'Your turn,' Sakina homing in on me with her stick.

'Uh, what do I say?' I asked.

'Whatever is in your heart,' replied Sakina. Her teeth shone through the dark like bones.

What was in my heart? For a few seconds I sat and thought. Zip. There was something in my head though; Leonard Cohen. Leonard Cohen was in my head.

> Oh pleez don't pass me by (no)
> For I am blind, but you, you can see
> Yes, I've been blinded, oh, totally
> Oh pleez don't pass me by

Something like that.

'I'm blind, but you can see,' I said.

'Hmm,' replied Sakina, turning on her feet and picking up the magic rabbit. From deep in her chest there bubbled up a bizarre demonic wheeze. 'I am going to do some intense praying for you.'

A reflective peace settled over the group. Rowanna dozed, Coco forgot his bladder and took to tracing a pattern of beetle tracks in the dirt. The relatives remained silent and petrified. All the while, Sakina's benediction drifted along outside the scene, loosely attached but nonetheless separate, like a kind of hyperreal journey through a collective slumber.

Afterwards, Sakina made herbal tea and settled herself in an old chair on the porch looking out over the yard.

'That went so well, dear,' she said. I smiled embarrassed and fixed my eyes on two mosquitoes dipping in the light.

'Sakina,' I began to ask, to fill a gap as much as anything, 'Was that prayer you said in the Hopi language?'

'No dear,' she replied, taking in her tea. 'It's ancient Anasazi.'

'I thought . . . ?'

'I know it from a past life as an Anasazi oracle.' Sip. 'I spoke it to a man who channels an Anasazi elder' sip 'and he said 'Exact, amazing, let me translate it for you,' but I didn't have it translated because he wanted twenty-five dollars' sip 'and, besides, I know intuitively what it means.'

I slept in the open under the porch that night. The heat woke me at around ten. Hearing I was awake, Sakina appeared with a cup of coffee and asked me if I would like to visit the spot where she gave herself up to Spirit. Absolutely, I said, so we drove to Boynton Canyon in Caboose and parked at the canyon mouth by an immense red hoodoo called Kachina Woman. The Yavapai Apache say that the canyon is the birthplace of their tribe. According to their story, there was a great flood in which everyone perished, except one girl. The girl, Kamalapukwia, was saved by crawling into a hollow log with some food and a bird. Her soul wanted to leave and join the dead in the spirit world, but the sound of the birdsong was so beautiful that it was captivated. A number of days passed and the log came to rest at the top of Boynton Canyon. Kamalapukwia crawled out. Feeling lonely, she prayed to the sun and the rain for a child and immediately found herself pregnant. This child had a child in turn, and together, Kamalapukwia and her grandson, Sakarakaamche, established the Yavapai Apache tribe. The story has it that Kamalapukwia's spirit still lives in Boyton Canyon.

'And I'll tell you something,' said Sakina, 'I was Kamalapukwia in a past life, although I haven't told Ted Smith.'

'Who's Ted Smith?' I asked.

'He's the Yavapai chief,' replied Sakina.

Not so long ago the canyon bottom was given over to grazing. There was a gate at the mouth, up by Kachina Woman, to keep the cattle in and the Yavapai would come and go through that gate to pay their respects to Kamalapukwia and the other the canyon spirits. Quite recently, though, the mouth and much of the interior of the canyon was developed into a tennis resort called Enchantment. Where the gate once was there is now an electronic barrier with a control pod and a uniformed guard. A hiking path flanked by razor wire winds along one side of the resort, and disappears off into the depths of the canyon. When the Yavapai come for their rituals these days, they walk along the hiking path.

'They won't let you in,' said Sakina, 'unless you say you are going to the bar,' so we climbed up to a conservatory overlooking the resort and ordered some iced tea. We were alone, except for a bored-looking couple drinking fancy cocktails in one corner.

'You wouldn't believe the rumours about this place,' said Sakina. 'They say that the tennis courts are built on Indian graves.'

Below us, golf buggies whined around the paved paths, between immaculate lawns of Bermuda grass kept lurid by eternal water sprinklers. Two young white couples in matching tennis outfits played competitive doubles on the hard courts. To one side of the bar was an unobstructed view of Kachina Woman, the place of Sakina's spiritual revelation. Sakina chirped away with some story about how the Spirit had come to her as a raincloud while I looked out through the picture window onto the burnt red rock at the opposite side of the canyon and remained silent and thought about nothing much. The bill for two glasses of iced tea came promptly, in a lined leatherette pouch. At the cash register we were handed two complimentary mint chocolates. We strolled back to the car park past a sign reminding diners to sport 'proper attire and reservations'.

'Connie reckons this place is a front for the World Government,' whispered Sakina once we were safely inside Caboose. 'Says she's seen black helicopters with aliens just over there where the landing strip is.'

As we were ushered through the exit barrier, she added 'I don't know, I think it's kinda neat.'

Back at Pinon Jay Drive, Sakina handed me her copy of a pamphlet I had seen on sale in all the New Age bookstores in Sedona on my last visit but never troubled to pick up. The author had drawn a rough map of Boynton Canyon, marking the spot where there was reputed to be a subterranean crystal cavern containing the evolutionary light codes of the planet. 'When the living crystal holographic computers become completely activated, all light and consciousness on the globe will be integrated at Boynton,' read the pamphlet.

No-one I asked seemed to know quite when Enchantment had begun to be built or how it was constructed. They spoke in generalities, as though reading from a ready prepared text. Even the local historian was confused about the progress of events. I rang the resort's publicity officer who said she hadn't been working there all that long, and she didn't have the information I requested. Rumour, and there was plenty of that about, had it that the development had proceeded in spite of the fact that the bulldozers had uncovered an Indian burial ground at the mouth of the canyon. Sakina said human bones had been found dumped on the development's landfill site, along with other debris. There were whispers that the Yavapai had set a curse on the development. Investors pulled out, a couple of times it floundered. Talk was that the developers had delivered corpses to the Hopi who re-buried them on their reservation. Eventually, the developers agreed to allow a track to be run through their land to the canyon bottom and as a mark of respect they promised not to dig around the burial site but to lay their tennis courts over it instead.

I looked Enchantment up in my New Age pamphlet. It said: 'the Enchantment resort will have an opportunity to play a key role in awakening the earth bond of many people who are in a position to directly affect banking and industry. A visit to Enchantment may help to re-awaken the spiritual nature of people who are in a position of power, who will be able to do things which will help heal our planet, and bring mankind together.' I wondered whether it would fall to the tennis couples or the cocktail drinkers to help heal the planet and bring mankind together.

The extraordinary aspect of the Enchantment story is not the narrative itself, which is a regular tale of avarice triumphant, but the way it had been silenced into whispered rumours and low-level gossip. Nothing documented, all hearsay. Mention Enchantment to any resident in Sedona and they would search their minds for something to say before telling you how good the disco was on a Friday night. For a day and a half I sat in the public library and records offices in Sedona wading through official papers and planning regulations but I came up with only one item of any interest, from *Sedona Red Rock News*, written after Enchantment had opened. 'The fears of both objecting groups [hikers and Indians] have proved unfounded,' said the writer. 'Since the present owners of Enchantment have, as they promised to do, provided convenient trails to the canyon,' as though the desecration of a sacred site by razor wire, seven-course dinners with proper attire, tennis courts, adobe-textured casitas, heliports and the moan of golf buggies were somehow wholly cancelled out by the presence of a public pathway.

On our way back to Pinon Jay Drive, Sakina mentioned that Grandmother Eagle had told her Enchantment existed because Spirit willed it. I didn't ask who Grandmother Eagle was but when we arrived at the house I went down to the nearest phone box at the Circle K and called Ted Smith, Chief of the Yavapai Apache tribe. Six times I rang. He never returned my calls. One day he answered the phone in person.

'I rang before,' I said, 'and left some messages.'

'Uh huh.'

'What I wanted to know was whether any bodies were found at Enchantment?'

A pause.

'I imagine so. I wouldn't know.'

I asked if I could pay him a visit, but he said that he was very busy, for a long long time to come.

I finished Jerry Mander's book sitting in a rest area just outside Sedona. One paragraph I copied out into my notebook. It was a quote from Dr Merill E. Gates, president of Amherst College back in the late nineteenth century, who wrote: 'To bring [the Indian] out of savagery into citizenship . . . we need to awaken in him wants. In his dull savagery, he must be touched by the wings of the divine angel of discontent . . . Discontent with the teepee and the Indian camp . . . is needed to get the Indians out of the blanket and into trousers – and trousers with a pocket in them, and with a pocket that aches to be filled with dollars!'

While New Agers content themselves with drums and happy noble savages, corporate America and the liberal and conservative lobbies, for their different reasons, would rather make real

Americans from Indians and give 'em a crack at the American dream. To this end traditional Indian economic and political systems have been dismantled, whether by brute exploitation or, more subtly, by the subversion of Indian values, often in the guise of progress or concerned paternalism. This has not always been conscious, of course, but nonetheless it has happened. The Indians have shown their resilience by adapting in places and, taking what's offered – disposal of nuclear waste, gambling – which the liberal lobby finds uncomfortable, and resisting on other issues, sometimes with violence, thereby upsetting America's conservatives.

In 1921 Standard Oil discovered crude oil on Navajo land, but was legally required to obtain drilling licences from the Navajo before it could exploit its find. Since the Navajo land was communally held Standard Oil needed the entire tribe's permission to begin drilling which was impossible to obtain within the context of the Navajo's traditional, decentralized governance. Navajo tribal decisions were made slowly; often nothing was explicitly concluded, but the ambience of a decision infused among the tribe and became noticeable as a subtle change of behaviour. Where could Standard Oil begin? Evidently, it began with the Bureau of Indian Affairs, for the Bureau summoned a band of Navajo males to act as a Tribal Business Council and provide leases for Standard Oil's projected wells. When the council refused permission, the Bureau reconstituted it. The new council refused permission. The Bureau reconstituted another. Eventually, of course, Standard Oil got what they wanted and the Navajos got a taste of western democratic government, from which they have never quite recovered; Tribal Business Councils have been endlessly trailed by accusations of unrepresentativeness and corruption. In any case, there are now four coal strip mines, five coal-fired power plants, thirty-eight uranium mines and six uranium mills on the Navajo Reservation. They say that the plume of smoke from the Four Corners Power Plant on Navajo land can be seen half way to the moon. The sky is often hazy over the Dinetah on account of it.

In 1934, under the guise of democratizing (and bureaucratizing) Native Americans continent-wide, the US Congress passed the Indians Reorganization (Wheeler-Howard) Act, promising federal aid programmes to tribes who would give up their traditional political organization in favour of Tribal Councils – to be elected according to the Bureau's 'democratic' rules. This was intended to be a liberal reform. One hundred and seventy-two tribes signed – they needed federal funds badly – and in return forever relinquished political structures which were various, complex and ancient for a particular institutional view of democracy that had been in place for little more than a century and was not, in any case, well adapted to Indian culture.

One night, driving just before dawn along the remote road that passes by Black Mesa, I saw what appeared to be a spherical green light a little way above the horizon line. The light oscillated like a flare and yet its position did not change. Imagining the light to be a radio transmitter, I carried on driving towards it, without much more thought, but as I drew closer I realized that there was not one light, but a string of lights suspended between two points like circus illuminations. Around each light was a smoky cloud of illuminated air, and behind each cloud there were glimpses of a huge fragmented tubular object. This object, whatever it was, unsettled me. As I drew up beside it, I could see that the lights were strung between two metallic towers and that below them stretched an immense white conduit tube which opened out over a riveted metal holding tank. Smoky fumes rose from a series of pipes curling up over the tank and into the dark. The whole weird machine appeared to be enclosed in wire fencing; it looked like some captive chrysalis about to burst and shrug off its skin. A sign illuminated in the sickly flare of an overhead bulb read 'Peabody Coal. Keep Out.' About five miles on, I turned and looked back east, into the rising sun, and saw the mesa itself, one of the most sacred sites for the Hopi, lying part-skinned and eviscerated on the desert plain. Later, I checked Peabody in Mander's book and read there that one estimate had valued the coal removed by surface mining from Black Mesa up to 1980 at $311 million while the royalty to the Navajos in the same time period was $5.9 million.

I don't wish to present 'the Indian issue' (if it can be called that) in conventional western tropes, the struggle of good against evil, greed against moral purity, I am simply trying to give a sense of its complexity. Not everyone wants in on a slice of the American Dream but those who do should have the opportunity at least to grab an equal portion.

The day after my visit to Enchantment I headed south into Phoenix, checked into the Motel 6 on Camelback, took out an old copy of the *Arizona Light* from the trunk of the car and on a beige motel phone rang Meria Heller, medicine wheel ceremonialist, healer, spiritual guide:

'Are you Indian?' I asked.

'Jewish,' replied Heller in a thick Brooklyn brogue. She didn't sound too pleased that I'd asked. 'I call my medicine wheel ceremony a universal wheel ceremony.'

'Does that mean it's non-denominational?'

'Exactly.' Sounding decidedly impatient. 'As seen in the media. Look, why don't you come? Tonight, six thirty. You'll love it. My yard has an unparalleled desert setting.'

Heller was right about the setting. The tawny coral mountain reefs of the McDowell range stood anchored in the distance like wrecked ships beneath the sea-blue sky. In the foreground stretched Paradise Valley, a sandy landlocked beach peopled by sunbathing saguaro. Heller's house was one of a row of more or less identical dream suburban homes, each with an enormous yard, clipped front lawn, swimming pool, Italian water garden and unparalleled desert setting.

I arrived late. In Heller's backyard a dozen fortysomethings, men equipped with drums, women with pound cake, had gathered nervously around a tiny, muscular man with an eagle feather necklace, big gold jewellery and a haircut copied from an Argentinian football magazine. This was apparently 'an Indian'. Heller herself, a nervous, urban mosquito, hummed in and out of the crowd, while her business manager followed swiftly behind to pick up a $15 apiece 'donation'. I milled around by a jug of grape Kool-Aid awaiting whatever creatures might come down to water. I'd been standing there just a few minutes when a wiry man of great age with a beaded drum in his hand and a bandanna around his head approached the Kool-Aid jug.

'One cup,' he said.

I looked at him, and smiled wanly, but he simply repeated himself and pointed to the jug without making eye contact. It was not a time for tact.

'I'm not the waitress,' I said. He bit his lip and pretended to have something stuck in his eye.

'English?' he finally volunteered, looking out over the crowd to the mountains beyond.

I smiled, a little less wanly, but pretty thinly nonetheless.

'Fine man, Churchill,' he said.

My conversational skills had been honed so finely during the months of casual encounters that I could by this time, in all modesty, claim to be something of an expert on the royal family, William Shakespeare, soccer hooligans, roast beef and Yorkshire pudding, Margaret Thatcher and the BBC. Churchill, on the other hand, had completely passed me by. I had no ready-prepared small talk on the topic of Churchill whatsoever.

'Thirty-seven per cent of all Americans recognize the phrase "Never in the field of human conflict was so much owed by so many to so few."' I had no idea whether this was true, but it seemed plausible. In America it is naturally assumed that if one does not know something, one dreams up a pleasing statistical factoid in its place. It doesn't matter what the factoid is, only that it be able to cover what might otherwise develop into an embarrassing silence.

'I was in England when that guy was president,' continued the man, then dropped the subject and began instead to explain that the 'real Indian', apparently a friend of Heller's, had been imported in from Florida for the express purpose of attending the universal medicine wheel (as seen in the media). So far as I could tell the suggestion was that we should be stupefied by the honour of his presence.

Heller's universal wheel was a circle of stone and desert debris about fifteen feet in diameter, spread out on the crust at the end of her yard. Inside lay heaped crystals, sparkling things and feathers. At the very centre a bowl of yellow powder the colour of a duster sat on a small piece of coarse cloth. The desert around was as silent and animated as a dream. Beyond Paradise Valley, the mountains watched, as if in wait.

At about eight the real Indian mentioned that he thought it was about time for the ceremony to begin and so, auspiciously enough, it began. A foot away from where I stood a tiny pink scorpion dug itself from the crust and scuttled away. The sun was setting and the floor of the night sky was in the process of becoming, swelling from the soil, lifting up the blooms of prickly pears. I remember thinking, if a cloud passes over Orion's belt, it will be a sign that there is a Great Spirit. If it doesn't, then we really are on our own.

'I'd like us all to visualize a healing white light,' Heller said. We closed our eyes and I imagined myself under the fluorescent strip in the shower back at the Motel 6.

'Do you see a white light?' The assembled nodded, eyes tight shut, sitting cross-legged around the wheel.

And then the Indian began to drum, a soft thud stirring the air around him like bricks falling from a hod onto sand, the leather on his drum tangy as ripe wheat after rain. Heller clicked a tape into her boogie box and began to sing:

'We are the world, we are the children.'

'Alright,' said the man beside me, swaying and taking my hand.

'We are the ones who make a brighter day . . .'

At the third verse, 'We are the world' died back into the desert and we passed around a talking stick. A woman said she would like to read a poem that had been channelled to her by an angel, in a dream. It was about love, I think. Silence. A mild, unvoiced panic set in and lingered for a few minutes until a woman broke it by giving thanks to the Spirit. The benediction rose on a thermal and fell earthward, silenced by loneliness and regret. I gazed up into the star-pocked sky and imagined myself on the moon.

'Let's sing another song,' smiled Heller, flipping on her sacred boogie box.

'Imagine there's no hea-ven . . .' warbled the crowd, 'I wonder if you ca-a-a-a-n . . .'

And then it was the Indian's turn. In oral cultures, such as most Indian tribes are, sound carries history, intention, the nuance of that most intangible thing, common consciousness. He opened his throat and a full guttural sound crossed the laterite and spun towards the mountains. Indian songs are calls to the spirit of things.

The rest of us, sated, sat back and felt the noyz.

'Did everyone pay?' asked the assistant.

Afterwards, pound cake having been devoured and fruit punch drained and chocolate fudge brownies melted into empty mouths, the crowd shuffled off to its four-wheel drives and roared back down Shea Boulevard into town.

I forgot to watch for the cloud passing over Orion's belt.

Back at the motel I remembered something Dostoevsky wrote in *Notes from the Underground*, about modern living having nothing to offer beyond a greater variety of stimulation. To many New Agers, Indians represent a way of life unpolluted by materialism and the tyranny of trivial choice, a life of psychological purity. Some New Age types even imagine that vision quests, sweat lodges, drumming and dancing ceremonies are rituals specifically *designed* to be psychotherapeutic. I never once saw, heard, or read any indication that New Agers have grasped the possibility that Native American spirituality, or any other set of ritual behaviours, including their own, furnishes a community in a particular environment with metaphors for shared communal meanings. Every Navajo act is imbued with a spiritual context in part because the land the Navajo inhabit is harsh and unreliable. In order to survive, Navajos must be finely tuned both to their environment and to each other. The narratives of our prosperous, materialist society are no longer spiritual; they do not describe mythological archetypes but psychological truths, elements not of a greater transcendent reality, but of the human condition, the here and now. The search for transcendence goes on in our culture, but no amount of birthing drums or suburban medicine wheel ceremonies can ever hope to capture Indian mysticism, being empty of Indian context. By appropriating those pieces of Indian spiritual life they can readily assimilate, New Agers not only deceive themselves that their experience is part of a greater whole, but they do damage to Indian issues. As Rick said back in Taos, if the public perceive Indian rituals as the rather absurd indulgences of New Age affluents, it becomes all the more difficult for Indians to persuade them of another view, or even to claim their attention.

In western culture the idea of the spirit world manifest in nature was defeated by the triumph of christianity over paganism. Since the Enlightenment what has passed for spirituality has in fact been only progress, progress, progress and the inevitable linear march of days and years. These days time's arrow hardly pricks us as it passes. We live too quickly to pick up the soft, slow pulse of the natural world. Our archetypes are reduced to logos, our community to the communality of the shopping mall. To transcend the dreary tide of materialism we must look first to our own culture. Our rituals of birth, death and marriage, for example, have fallen so foul of consumerism that they are are become little more than excuses for consumption. How about starting there?

One evening I drove up to Pojoaque Pueblo and played the slots. The Feds have given Indians special privileges in setting up gambling enterprises to enable them to create a stable economic environment on their reservations. As a consequence, there are now gambling dens on many Indian reservations, and the business is growing. Most of the gamblers at Pojoaque were poor folk playing quarter slots. The dollar slots were almost empty. In an aspirational materialist culture like America's it is so often those who benefit least from consumerism who are most in its thrall. The wealthy can afford to be more relaxed. Even though Indian gaming constitutes a mere three per cent of the entire gambling industry in the USA, both liberal and conservative whites living in New Mexico have found it hard to wish the Indians well. Liberals don't like the idea of gambling spreading, conservatives don't see why Indians should be given any breaks. On 30 April 1993, Donald Trump, the billionaire real estate investor and businessman, filed suit against the US Federal Government, claiming that the Indian Gaming Regulatory Act, by providing favourable licenses for gaming on Indian Reservations, was unconstitutional.

Outside the Palace of Governors in Santa Fe on a Saturday in September, licensed Indian women sat under the shade of the boardwalk with their jewellery and beadwork spread over Navajo blankets. Few seemed overly concerned to make a sale, some were knitting, others fanned themselves in the heat. On 29 November 1990, Congress passed law PL 101–644, the Indian Arts and Crafts Act, requiring Native American artists to be registered as a member of a tribe recognized by the Bureau of Indian Affairs before being able to advertise their work as Indian. Although its intentions are honourable, the notion underlying PL 101–644 is that a painting produced by someone of European stock represents a universal art, while those of Indians are expressions of particular ethnicity. By the same rules that now apply to Indians would Andy Warhol's work be Slovak or American? Would it be worth more or less if Slovak? Who in hell cares? Strolling across the plaza that day in September, I decided on an impulse to buy a pair of Navajo earrings, so I headed over to see what was on offer. As I approached the women lined up along the boardwalk my shadow fell across them and crept up the adobe wall of the Palace of Governors. The symbolic weight of that shadow was too much for me; I felt quite paralysed with guilt. The following weekend I went into one of the stores on Guadalupe Street, run by a white couple over from Santa Cruz, bought a stash of silver and put it all on plastic. Guilt is the slayer of good intentions.

Just before Rick Romancito left me he said 'You know, we Indians regard ourselves as the plumbers and electricians of the universe. All we're doing is trying to keep things from falling apart.'

Prozac Dreaming

'The fish is the last one to know that it lives in water.'
Chinese aphorism

What happened to the woman whose face stared back from a TV screen in the King's Rest Motel at the beginning of the spring? Not much, and a great deal. She quit the southwest, went back to her own country and supposing that nothing momentous had happened, either to the place she had left or to herself, she carried on with her life as before. Nearly a year later, she was standing in Camden market waiting for the change for two grapefruit, when it came to her that she had been quite wrong. In fact, so much had changed that she could only imagine the process had started years before, without her ever noticing.

The more she reflected on the time she had spent out west the more it became clear to her that there was an undeniable parallel between the outward journey and the procession of her inner world. For two seasons she had wandered about, dispossessed, rooting out women and men who were in search of themselves and yet it had not crossed her mind to scrutinize her own sullen attempts to shrug off the mess of her unpredictable moods and lugubrious fears. She grew angry with herself for her failure to reflect.

For most of her early twenties she had dipped in and out of therapies of one sort or another, according to the fashion of the time, but it seemed to her they were simply an attempt to compensate her for the irretrievable loss of childhood magic. The *inner* child she felt to be a mere invention, a sort of Peter Pan of the soul. In any case, whoever she was or might have been, that poor inner child rapidly became a little stool pigeon for a series of psychoanalytic fixations. The Freudians would talk of reconciling her to her infant lusts, the Jungians would make her a prisoner of her dreams, and the psychosynthesists (whom she knew as the photosynthesists) demanded she perform bloodless acts of retrospective violence, by hurling soft furnishings at walls and thereby apparently braining her childhood competitors and satisfying the cuckoo within.

In company of her inner child she imagined herself on sun-drenched beaches, in caves, on the open road and in the womb. She relived moments of past confusion, sometimes she wept, but most often she was puzzled. In order to try to find answers to questions she had never posed, she turned variously to Quakerism, to Catholicism, Buddhism, Sufism. She did the Tao of most things and the Zen of everything else, but nothing relieved the tenuousness of her life. Later she realized with some guilt that the endless demands and discontents of this inner child had begun to bore her, so she extinguished it and walled it up in her body and it was never mourned, nor needed to be.

At night she took sleeping pills, which did not make her sleep, and during the day she took uppers, which did not make her feel awake. Often she would catch herself hallucinating on the journey into work. She lost her spatial sense, she saw everything in two dimensions and as though it were at a far distance. Each day seemed to pass as in a dream or a psychedelic trip, and this enlivened the boredom of the office routine. The morning would begin in a blue funk hangover from the effects of mogadon or temazepam and grind towards afternoon in a pleasing swirl of pink and orange paper clips. By the end of the week she could scarcely recall her own name. No-one seemed to notice. Her superiors would buzz in and out from time to time to deposit the week's memoranda on the mildewed stack, like blowflies leaving eggs on rotten meat. She never really cared to find out what they wanted, and they never troubled to tell her. During the first brief hour of sentience, from nine to ten, she would open letters and peel off the stamps for charity, then from ten o'clock onwards she'd play around with India ink and rubber stamps marked 'Repl'd' and 'Confdl', flip post-it notes and fall asleep in the company toilets. Letters would leave the office neatly stamped but entirely blank, agreements would be made to be forgotten. She would initial a few forms at random, colour in the company logo and despatch miscellaneous office stationery to distant warehouses. Every few months or so the memoranda men would request the pleasure of her company over a cheese 'n' pickle sandwich lunch and remind her of her rosy prospects. Meanwhile, the salary cheques would dissolve into books and booze and records, which were her solace through the wakeful nights.

Once a year some worthy remedial institute or other would send her a personality test in plain brown wrappers to fill out and post back. The questions they posed were generally bizarre – she was puzzled as to how to answer. Did the recipient enjoy torturing animals? On how many occasions had Satan spoken personally to her? The self-consciousness of existence wore her out. She tired of meaninglessness and she tired of the search for meaning. Her personality seemed so contingent she could no longer reach it. Occasionally, she wondered if it still existed. During this time, her office overlooked the Thames, and she would while away hours in erotic suicidal reveries. How would the water caress her? Would she panic, or would the moment of death be a kind of sensual climacteric? How long would it take before she submitted finally to the river bed? One time, in the coffee and biscuit break between a divisional marketing meeting and a staff assessment meeting, she conducted an experiment in electroshock therapy by pushing her fingers into a light socket. The voltage blew her with some force into a bank of suspension files, but did nothing for her depression. She graduated from psychotherapists to psychiatrists. The psychiatrists would pre-scribe tricyclics for her moods or, later on, prozac, and reassure her that she'd soon feel her old self. She'd take the drugs for a time, though she had no idea if she *wanted* to feel her old self, or even how she would know if she did. After a few weeks, she'd quit the drugs and life would continue on as before. The psychiatrists, interpreting this as a streak of masochism, would refer her to a therapist. The therapists would begin by assuring her that every psychological state from suicidal desperation to existential unease was most definitely curable these days. They suggested that she learn to recognize her true essence, and part company with all the people in her head. An unreflective life was hardly worthy of the description, they'd say. An unfeeling life was worse still. The point of it all was to reflect 'n' feel, reflect 'n' feel. She saw the wisdom of the idea, but therapeutics provided her only with psychological explanations; they did nothing to sustain her spirit. After a while the therapists would write notes back to the psychiatrists along these lines: 'subject appears to be a fantasist and occasional compulsive liar with severe insecurity complex; often unable to distinguish between reality and her own fictions. Mildly disassociative, at times violent. I recommend a course of tricyclics or you might try prozac.' And the show would go on.

Lovers came and went. After a brief period of infatuation they would scurry off protesting against her various qualities: her remoteness, her wilful sexuality, the way she became detached from herself, her indomitable insomnia. Friends fell away, although she was not sorry that they had; she had never understood quite how to present herself to them. Their company made her anxious, their attentions perplexed her, she was crass with them. She sensed that the few who remained were nonetheless fearful of her. In an attempt to understand her 'state' – the word she used to describe her life (on the grounds that it seemed to have ossified quite inexplicably, while the world about it ballooned and fluxed) she read books on depression in the library, but their placid little incitements to wholesomeness and self-love made her ever more perplexed.

In 1990 she felt that she should mark the beginning of the last decade of the century with something of significance, so that when she looked back she might be able to say 'In the first year of the final decade of the twentieth century this is what I did.' She thought of producing a baby, dismissed the thought, considered criminality, contemplated suicide. Finally, she settled on a course of study from which she learned that it is not possible for human beings to live without meaning, but that meaning cannot be rationalized or described, it has to be sensed. She recognized the anxiety that sprang from living at the century's end. How often it felt as though human beings were teetering on the edge of global panic and disintegration! She recalled the wholesale manner in which the culture of the eighties had dispensed with all the lingering fragments of communality. It was difficult to imagine how any guide could lead the collective soul beyond the sense of its own ending. The key, she began to see, was transcendence, the momentary experience beyond rationality or irrationality. In the power of transcendence was to be found strength and hope and the renewal of collective purpose. For there was nothing numinous in her life, nor in the lives of the people around her. The city and its inhabitants felt dimmed and spiritually broken.

That year she took MDMA in its pure form for the first time. As the drug took root and began to send out tendrils she sat in a garden and watched the light change. For seven hours she watched the light. She saw each constituent of the light, whether it was yellow, or cream or blue. She noticed the way the colour of light changed around the objects it lit. She saw how it would illuminate a single leaf with a thousand different colours and how each gobbet of shade delineating the veins and folds of the leaf was of a unique depth and quality. She saw nothing that was not there, no hallucinations, yet everything she did see was of such complex beauty that she could scarcely bring herself to believe it was a part of the commonplace world. It had seemed that her mind had been inhabited by a roomful of people, some well known, others strangers, whose conversations distracted and diverted. MDMA opened a door from this room onto a panorama of spacious plains and mountains. Although the sweep before her was empty of people, she knew that others had been given the same view from the rooms they occupied. She felt that what she was seeing was some sinless, primordial state which persisted behind and in parallel to the everyday, like the lining of a dress; and that, even though it was seldom if ever seen, each one of us had glimpsed it during moments of unexplained wonderment, in a word overheard, a smell, an episode of *déjà vu*. She did not understand why this was meaningful, nor did she wish to know; it contented her to sense simply that it was and that there was a path to it which she might now rediscover.

Late in that year, her father died, quite unexpectedly. She never saw his body; it was flown back from Spain in the cargo hold of a 747. The Spanish undertakers had abandoned him to a Hammer Horror coffin – a camp, black, papal affair – which would not do at all for a man who had always professed a dislike of Catholicism and who was to be buried in an Anglican church in the middle of rural Sussex. His corpse was transferred into a more discreet casket, fashioned from light oak. After the funeral she left her mother to her grief and ran away to the southern Sahel, imagining that the desert would mirror her desolation. She hoped that she might discover the shape of her shadow lurking there. In any case, her familiar world had left her and so she was quitting it. Perhaps she believed the solecism that symmetry is synonymous with order. But she didn't accomplish what she had set out to achieve because what she had set out to achieve – a complete understanding of herself – was not achievable. Four months later she returned to her old job, to the dregs of an English summer and to an overwhelming feeling of panic. She was referred to a psychiatrist who told her that depression was not an illness but a way of seeing the world. He told her that she could make something from it, but she neither understood what he said, nor gave much of her attention to it. After all that had happened, she still presumed that she was in search of peace.

And then I went to America.

For the first few days after I arrived I continued popping prozac, which left me, as it always had, charged and wakeful. One evening at the end of May – I forget just where – I was sitting eating a Taco Bell burito grande and watching TV in my motel room, as usual, when it suddenly became clear to me that I had become a grifter. The small comforts, the routine, the root beers stacked neatly in Caboose, the calls home, they were all part of the same grift. Life, as I was choosing to live it, was becoming a little cosier each day. As a devotee of the grand gesture, I had no option but to throw the whole of my remaining supply of prozac down the toilet, secretly thinking as I did so, hell, there'll be a doctor somewhere who'll give me some more. The whole of that night I lay on my bed, somewhere between consciousness and sleep, and by the morning I had invented a companion, Fergus, from a mixture of the characteristics of certain friends and others imagined. I knew that if depression hit, I should be unlikely to be able to talk myself out of it, but, as a failsafe, Fergus might. Fergus, I decided, would not put up with ill-temper, panic or cowardice. And that was how I put an end to the grift.

During that spring and summer it became clear to me that the world was not the disintegrating, disorganized place I had supposed it to be, that rather it was at times random and unpredictable. The randomness and unpredictability was in itself a part of the pattern. After years spent struggling to control and reinvent it I no longer required my experience to be accommodating and consistent. If an experience, a feeling or a even a meeting didn't make sense to me on reflection, then I shelved it. The relentless search for peace which, under the guise of self-sufficiency and of solitude, had taken up so much of my life no longer held its previous appeal. Every so often I wondered in an inarticulate fashion where on the road I had given it up what had pushed me to it.

For some time after I first threw out the prozac I went into a long upswing, which was followed by a long depression. After that, the swings were smaller in both directions. On an upswing I would abandon myself to alienation, living like a tramp, on cigarettes and booze and root beer, without ever feeling drunk or hungry. Usually I'd remember to check into some motel; on occasion I slept in the car parked on the side of a road wherever I happened to be as night fell. I'd wake at dawn, start up the engine and keep on driving. My sense of time became distorted; I'd find myself watching TV through the night or striding out on midnight walks thinking it was the middle of the afternoon and wondering why the streets were empty. I would spend many hours in late-night diners, often the sole customer, drinking tepid diner coffee, smoking, reading sometimes, other times just watching. Walking around towns built for cars made me realize how much emptiness there was and how few people there were around to fill it up. Southwestern cities are not the same as New York or LA where nightlife breeds as fast as roaches. It was a desolate, abandoned emptiness, the lonely turf of anomie.

I'd like to say I sloped around with the city's lowlife on those nights. I'd like to say I saw TVs tottering stiffly along on hard stiletto heels, I'd like to say I slumped drunkenly among the long lines of human trash scoring tricks and junk, I'd like to say I witnessed drive-by shootings and cop beating and gang warfare, I'd like to say that I was right in the middle of it all when the city unzipped itself, but I wasn't. Occasionally I'd pass a sullen woman in stockings or a wiry, bare-chested boy in tight jeans hanging around on the corner of a street. Mostly, I saw cars and trucks moving along the freeways leaving trails of red and yellow lights behind them surrounded by a citywide web of bloodless boulevards and shopping malls and untrod pavements.

I've read somewhere that each time a goldfish circumnavigates its bowl it confronts a new environment because its memory can't store a past of more than thirty seconds. It felt like that, sometimes, during those days of upswing; my world conflated and transformed with such rapidity that I gave up the struggle to impose order and substance upon it. With each upswing I would lose the self-consciousness that had dogged me as an adult; I would no longer be an overbearing encumbrance to myself. It felt almost as though I had glimpsed nirvana.

But the upswings never lasted long. Depression, generally followed after a plateau of a week or so, the change of mood would often come as a relief. As every depressive knows, depression does not necessarily describe a condition of unhappiness but the bafflement of one's assumptions about the world. I experienced a paranoia of the senses. Patterns, shapes and certain colour ranges would develop meanings quite outside their usual associations. Triangles, circles and any pattern obviously appropriated from nature seemed to me to become inexplicably sinister whereas squares, lines, the blue range, and abstracts remained unchanged. Just as time sped by in periods of upswing, during the depressions it slowed and became distorted. This affected my spatial sense. I would drive for an hour without the backdrop moving. The desert would appear to be some huge and stifling cover, and the mesas, buttes and mountains merely points the cover had not yet swallowed up. Quite often I would fetch up in some town in the southwest without quite knowing how I had come to be there, or why. I would check into a motel, or sit down in some diner, fetch my map and try to place myself from the last town I was sure I had visited. My notes from those times are a confusion of apathy and fear. It would be midnight some days before I realized that I hadn't eaten, other times I'd stuff myself full of taco chips and all the crap you can buy at gas stations. Some days I'd just lie on my bed and watch the feint progress of the moon and dream of escape.

And then there was the second grift. When my spirits were low, and the barrenness of the desert seemed to match them, I would take comfort in logos, all the multiplicitous commercial iconography of America. McDonald's yellow arches, the red and white scrawl of Coca Cola, smiling Colonel Sanders served as markers, they provided me with a sense of cultural, temporal and physical place. Deceiving though it was, the labels, brands and trade marks gave me a feeling of belonging, they became a source of meaning in themselves. I'd see the tips of a lazy M over the horizon and would be reassured and comforted.

Many countries are protective of their iconography, but not America, whose commercial icons have together become a sort of cultural pornography about as descriptive of the country, in the end, as the split-beaver shot is of sex, but none the less compelling. In common with other kinds of porn, Pornamerica provides its consumers with some – albeit self-defeating – release from the prospect of isolation. Even as 'first world' travel books and magazines berate the global spread of KFCs and Coca-Cola and prophesy the death of cultural difference, their readership of cultural voyeurs keeps them in business.

Cultural voyeurism is itself a kind of essentialist pornography, and we in the West are eager consumers of it. We sally forth, with the intention of buying up all experience, then retreat in the face of difference, like sullen hermit crabs. We are deflated by the popularity of Bart Simpson among the Thais, and yet we are also secretly thrilled by the potency of our cultural exports. We invest in 'third world' folk art, but never trouble ourselves greatly with their politics, excepting to send in our boys when the local population accidentally elects some devil-in-a-turban. The disease of essentialism is so prevalent that Pornamerica, which is nothing but the concoction of the advertising and pro-motions industries, has come not only to represent the culture of the United States to Americans and foreigners alike, but also the idea of contemporaneity itself. This is as reductive and disre-garding of American culture as it is of any other. Nonetheless we become daily more and more accepting of the notion that the essence of humanity lies in the consumption, aspirational or realized, of American iconography. Pornamerica is beginning to be our unifying spirit.

When the Coca Cola company can print billboard posters with the legend 'We taught the world to sing,' then our spiritual aliena-tion is in part complete.

Back in the early spring, I drove across the Texas Panhandle towards the New Mexico desert imagining vaguely that I was entering a land so empty of associations it would absorb what-ever meaning I discovered in it. I would shape it to my own requirement, or so I thought. For as long as I could remember I had been attracted to the empty parts of the world, to thin landscapes and thin cityscapes, newtowns and ghost towns, industrial wastelands and transplanted capitals, to desert and wil-derness. They appeared to be empty of unresolved or contradic-tory associations. I could not rid myself of the idea that in such a terrain I would stumble upon my most essential self; that a sky whose only blemishes were ravens circling up like bonfire ash before the current might prove to be my liberation.

The longer I remained in the desert, though, the more I began to understand its complexities and limitations. For although it was true that the limitless sky and naked plain seemed at first to promise freedom and release, it quickly became impossible to ignore the fragility of the desert, its fullness and its claustrophobic quality. Over the months I could feel how the sky reduced the frame of everything under it. The sun and arid air made me aware always of the boundaries of my body. I recognized how exquisitely balanced the desert was, and how replete with unpredictable occurrences and seeming randomness. After a thunderstorm, the plain would change colour overnight, and the following day the verdure would be solemnly razed by rain or sandstorms. Far from being a void, the desert was often a battleground. The more intimately I knew it, the more surprising it became. There were moments of transcendent joy; when a ray of sun first escaped over the horizon at dawn, or a roadrunner tumbled across the highway. And yet, whenever those moments arrived I was never able to surrender to them, filled as I was with the desperate expectation that I was about to learn something profound about *myself*.

The New Agers I met were suspicious, as I was, of the profanity of rationalism, and they were a little afraid also of the pace and alienation of the times. Technology too had invaded and terrorized their spirits.

The world, to them, seemed to be in the process of decline. They felt overwhelmed by loss – the loss of intimacy, the loss of community, the loss of symbolism, the loss of belief. Disillusioned by conventional religion, which called into question their right and duty to think as individuals, horrified by the rise of Christian fundamentalism, they had decided to make their own way towards meaningfulness. In the desert they saw a painless place, a void, from which they might begin to reconstruct their confidence in belief, and regain everything they felt they'd lost. In the wilderness they dreamed of finding intimacy, community, love, and a simple moral world. They set about to turn their lives into havens for the satisfaction of positive emotions. They ran from pain and 'negativity', but they lived lives of terrible self-consciousness as a result, lives of over-reflection, of constant doubts about the authenticity of their experience. All their hugs were thus contingent and their loving neurotic.

And they were bound to fail, for they had no understanding that the transcendent moment will not sustain scrutiny. Their lives had become solo performances to be applauded by onlookers who were themselves also pursued by the same gaze. They hugged each other but without abandon. They chanted and banged and paid attention to their tunefulness. Fear prowled about them, self-consciousness and literalism ate them up. They concerned themselves with living in the moment merely because they were fearful of the future, and often of the past. They had no stomach for pain or suffering of any kind, but this in itself could not prevent it. The New Age beliefs that sustained them were so radically at odds with their own experience that they had constantly to reinvent their experience. Deaths became reincarnations, betrayals alien abductions, losses the conspiracies of the World Governments. Fat-pursed entrepreneurs ripped them off, but they ripped themselves off too. The self-deception they routinely demanded of themselves showed up as a kind of nervousness behind the New Age mask of positivity. Denying what they saw as negative emotions made it impossible for them genuinely to experience positive ones. While I met few New Agers who seemed, on the surface, down at heart, I met none who were particularly joyful either. The desert was merely a metaphor for their own listless dreams of self-annihilation.

Back in London it became clear to me that the New Agers and I had a good deal in common. Prozac was my nirvana. It projected me into a world without fear of pain and in that way it helped me cope with the peculiar business of life. But that was all it did. When the prozac hit the toilet bowl I was conscious of opening myself to the extremes of depressive perception, extremes that were unaccountable and without clear purpose but exciting too. I no longer felt compelled to unravel myself or anyone else. And because the changes in my mood and perception came about at unexpected times in unpredictable ways I realized that I too was unexpected and unpredictable.

Although I suffered and was often confused, I knew that the suffering was never permanent, not because happiness would inevitably follow, but because there would always be random intervening moments of transcendence and through such moments life would be infused with a kind of formless meaning.

Therapeutics, I am now convinced, are a diversion from these moments, and if we spend our energies constructing a formula for nirvana, we will miss them. The trick, it seems to me, is not to be able to see into oneself, but to see beyond oneself, to the transcendent landscape distant from the crowded room. For that is where life's joy is born and flourishes. And what is Nirvana, in the end, but a painless, pointless sleep?